FUNDAMENTAL CHANGE IN LAW AND SOCIETY: HART AND SARTRE ON REVOLUTION

STUDIES IN THE SOCIAL SCIENCES

edited by C.A.O. van Nieuwenhuijze

6

FUNDAMENTAL CHANGE
IN
LAW AND SOCIETY

HART AND SARTRE ON REVOLUTION

by

WILLIAM LEON McBRIDE

1970
MOUTON
THE HAGUE · PARIS

LIBRARY OF CONGRESS CATALOG CARD NUMBER: 77-118280

Printed in The Netherlands by Mouton & Co., Printers, The Hague.

To my parents

ACKNOWLEDGEMENTS

I owe special debts of gratitude to Professor A. P. d'Entrèves of Turin, whose warm inspiration encouraged me to begin, and without whose CONSIDERABLE help this effort of mine would have been very much the poorer, and to Professor Richard Bernstein, now of Haverford College, who gave me a great deal of his time when he himself had very little time to spare.

In addition, I extend my sincerest thanks to Professor Rulon Wells of Yale, with whom I have discussed a number of the relevant issues; to Professor George Schrader, Chairman of the Yale Philosophy Department, who made some valuable suggestions concerning Sartre's ethics; to Professor Wilfrid Desan of Georgetown University, with whom I have had several helpful discussions about the subject-matter of Section Three; to Signior Gavozzi of Turin, who wrote detailed comments on my treatment of Kelsen; to Professor Robert Ehman, now at Vanderbilt University, who read several parts of the original manuscript; and to all the other members of the Yale Philosophy Department who, at one time or another, have stimulated my thinking along various lines that I have followed out in this study.

A fellowship from the Social Science Research Council made it possible for me to devote my full time during the academic year 1963-64 to studies that led to the writing of this book, the major part of which was originally prepared as a dissertation, presented to the Faculty of the Graduate School of Yale University in candidacy for the degree of Doctor of Philosophy in 1964.

Substantial portions of Section One have previously been published in the form of two journal articles, and it is with the kind permission of the editors of the respective publications that they are reproduced here. The first is *The Monist*, the July 1965 issue of which contains my article, "The Acceptance of a Legal System", much of which is to be found primarily in the present Chapter Eight, "Acceptance". Some portions primarily of Chapters Two, Five, and Six – "Kelsen", "Analysis", and "Analogy" – were first published in my March 1968 *New York University Law Review* article, "The Essential Role of Models and Analogies in the Philosophy of Law".

CONTENTS

INTRODUCTION

> The self-styled poverty of philosophy, committed with all its concepts to the given state of affairs, distrusts the possibilities of a new experience. – Herbert Marcuse[1]
>
> There can therefore be no legitimate resistance of the people to the legislative chief of the state; for juridical status, legitimacy, is possible only through subjection to the general legislative Will of the people. Accordingly, there is no right of sedition (*seditio*), much less a right of revolution (*rebellio*) . . . – Immanuel Kant[2]

Fundamental change in law and society – political and social revolution – is one of the more obtrusive phenomena of our age. The first of the two passages cited above challenges philosophy's credentials for the investigation of such change, and the second denies it philosophical justification. Marcuse holds that at least one method of contemporary philosophizing, that of linguistic analysis, is, by its very nature, opposed to considerations even of the possibility of fundamental social change; Marcuse writes from the perspective of a severe critic of contemporary society, strongly influenced by Hegel and Marx, who advocates such a change. Kant presents the by now classical argument against revolution in the sense of a fundamental change in a legal system:[3] legitimate authority, he holds, is the source of all 'right', and therefore there never exists a justification, under any circumstances, for overthrowing such authority. I disagree with both of the views expressed in the passages cited, and I intend this book to be, among other things, a clarification of the misunderstandings that have given rise to them.

1 *One-Dimensional Man* (Boston, Beacon Press, 1964), p. 178.

2 *The Metaphysical Elements of Justice* (tr. by John Ladd) (Indianapolis-New York-Kansas City, Bobbs-Merrill, 1965), p. 86. I do not mean to imply that this passage necessarily presents a fair picture of Kant's entire legal and political philosophy; I am using the passage here only as an illustration of a certain philosophical position.

3 Kant is known to have approved, on the other hand, of certain non-political, non-legal revolutions.

The phrase, 'fundamental change', is my own. A great deal has been written about 'revolution', much of it not by philosophers. The word 'revolution' has acquired many emotional overtones, which are hard to set aside, and which render a dispassionate consideration of the concept quite difficult. But there is a further, more important reason for not focusing exclusively on the word 'revolution' in this book, and that is that the primary sense of this word has come to be associated exclusively with a certain kind of POLITICAL revolution, that is, with the overthrow of one government and the replacement of it by another. Now, it is quite possible to give an empirical description of several such revolutions that have actually occurred, and in addition to find elements that are common to all the revolutions described. Such an enterprise would most likely be undertaken by an historian or a political scientist, though in the discovery of common elements one already begins to discern a type of enterprise that is characteristic of philosophy. In any event, it is furthest from my intentions to argue at this point about where political science may properly be said to end and political philosophy to begin; what is important is that, within the framework of the very popular sort of description and analysis of political revolutions that I have mentioned, some of the most interesting philosophical problems cannot be raised. For sufficient reflection will reveal that there are several quite different perspectives from which to consider the notion of 'revolution', just as there are several quite different levels on which it is possible to conceive of the State, and furthermore that, on any of the more common, narrower interpretations of the meaning of POLITICAL 'revolution', it will be impossible to come fully to grips with the extra-political problems which even the commonplace examples of revolutions suggest. That is the principal reason why I prefer the comparatively neutral phrase, 'fundamental change'.

What might be the bases of a philosophical interest in fundamental change in law and society? As individuals, of course, philosophers are by no means removed from the interests of their non-professional contemporaries. Thus, for example, Jean-Paul Sartre approached Daniel Cohn-Bendit, the student leader in the May 1968 events in Paris, with almost the same openness and eagerness to learn about the students' motivations and projects as any ordinary, alert Frenchman would have evinced.[4] No one today, whatever his profession, can avoid having some concern about the meanings and directions of the fundamental changes

[4] Daniel Cohn-Bendit *et al.*, *The French Student Revolt* (tr. by B. R. Brewster) (New York, Hill & Wang, 1968), pp. 73-83 (Cohn-Bendit's interview with Sartre).

that are taking place all around us. But there is nothing about THIS situation that is peculiar to the philosopher.

It is true, however, that philosophers have often served in a special way as witnesses to their times; as Hegel said, quite rightly, "Philosophy . . . is its own time apprehended in thoughts."[5] (Though philosophy may also be MORE than just this.) If fundamental change dominates our times, then perhaps philosophers have a special obligation to describe it, discuss it, place it in some sort of theoretical framework. This would make current philosophical interest in revolution contingent on the peculiarly revolutionary character of our own era.

But there may be a yet closer tie between philosophy and fundamental change. It is, precisely, Herbert Marcuse, with those view of the method of linguistic analysis I am later going to demonstrate my disagreement, who best makes the claim that traditional philosophy has been potentially revolutionary by its very nature. This may seem paradoxical in light of the roster of great philosophers (e.g., Plato, Kant, and Hegel) who were politically somewhat, or even extremely, conservative, but the case is in fact a very plausible one. Marcuse argues that the great past philosophies always played the role of criticizing the given (social) reality by holding forth some conception of a radically better, possible reality. In some philosophies, the latter conception was essentially religious or mystical, rather than being concerned with the empirical possibility of a radically better state of affairs in THIS world, but, in any case, the CRITICAL function of philosophy was common to both types. Philosophy, then, as opposed to ideology (the theoretical *apologia* for the *status quo*), IS revolutionary questioning. It thus has a close, though not a necessary, connection with activities in support of fundamental change. Philosophy is always potentially subversive.

If one accepts this conception of philosophy, then it is obvious that the philosophical interest in problems of fundamental change in law and society should be very great. Such problems may be usefully, though not absolutely, divided into two general areas: problems of explanation and problems of justification. Though the latter (questions of the so-called 'right to revolution') often arise first in the minds of concerned individuals, I believe that they can be better understood if they are regarded, as I shall regard them here, as arising out of problems of EXPLANATION, that is, the effort to render revolution, which at first glance may appear to be a counter-rational surd, intelligible within some thought frame-

[5] G. W. F. Hegel, *Hegel's Philosophy of Right* (tr. by T. M. Knox) (Oxford, At the Clarendon Press, 1942), p. 11.

work. I shall now proceed to outline a few of the major questions in these areas that will serve to guide the development of each of the two parallel sections of this book.

Let us use as our starting point the general notion of an 'explanation' of 'fundamental change in law and society'. What would constitute a satisfactory, adequate explanation? We might look first to the meaning of the words in this complex concept. But what is the best method for systematically going about the analysis of the meanings of the words? Are those meanings so static that it is possible to become clear on and to report them without interjecting some element of interpretation and thus in some way altering them? If the words are used, as most words are, with at least slightly different meanings by different groups of people (e.g., by political philosophers and by the mythical 'common man'), is there some privileged usage, whether ordinary or technical, that should serve as our standard in the business of analysis? At this point, we might even ask what is a more radical question, namely whether it is at all possible or desirable to go about analyzing concepts in a genuinely SYSTEMATIC way.

It might be retorted, in answer to this last question, that the concept of fundamental change in law and society can be explained only if it is given a fully systematic treatment, to wit, a treatment which places it in the framework of a fully developed theory of social philosophy. Such a theory, it might further be argued, would be FULLY developed only if it were not only internally consistent, but also in complete conformity with all the phenomena for which it was supposed to account. But let us reflect once again, very carefully, on this concept of fundamental change in law and society: does it seem at all plausible, when we contemplate whatever empirical examples of such change may first come to our minds, to say that there must be a single 'true' theoretical account of fundamental change? Is there some unique method of arriving at an understanding of social phenomena which alone can explain them comprehensively, sequentially, and in their internality?

At this point, we are reminded of a standard fact about explanation in general. As applied to the concept at hand, it is that, if we are to explain fundamental change in law and society at all, we must of course explain it in terms of something other than fundamental change in law and society itself. But there is a universe of phenomena other than fundamental change in law and society, and we have our choice: what kinds of other phenomena are most likely to explain satisfactorily our phenomenon of fundamental legal and social change? We might try to draw on comparisons with other kinds of change – biological change, for example. But might we not then find ourselves constantly forced later on to warn that legal systems and social institutions are really NOT organisms, and that fundamental changes in them are therefore really NOT deaths and births? Or we might, on the other hand, attempt to find, by abstraction from the appearances of fundamental social changes, some deeper reality that underlies them and functions as the agent in them. But what sort of entity would this reality be, and what evidence (other than some private 'intuition') would we have, if this reality was assuredly not to be found among the phenomena themselves, that we had discovered the 'true' underlying reality? In the case of either of the suggested alternatives, we would seem dangerously close to lapsing back into a reliance on myth in our search for an explanation of fundamental change in law and society.

All of these problems and many more present themselves before any attempt to explain our original concept can fairly be gotten under way. Could we not disregard these methodological questions and, relying on common sense and perhaps a certain dose of instinct, proceed to talk about the concept as about something with which we are all more or less familiar? Surely at some point we must, with a certain degree of arbitrariness, call a halt to the raising of such questions; but we disregard them at our peril, and we can be sure that, to the extent to which we have disregarded them, they will continue to engender misunderstandings in all our subsequent discussions. But let us suppose now that we WERE to set aside our questions of method and to proceed, very judiciously, to an examination of human social behavior as a first step towards a full explanation of how fundamental change in law and society takes place. Once again, a very large number of problems would have to be faced. How would we begin to give a systematic explanation of human social activity? Probably by attempting first to find regular, repeatable patterns in it. Next, we might want to show how the regular, repeatable patterns of human social behavior differ from those found in the rest of nature: how, we might want to ask, are the rules which govern human behavior distinguishable from simpler regularities? And in fact how are different kinds of human social rules – for different kinds there certainly seem to be – distinguishable from one another? And finally – and this is indeed a crucial problem for any would-be explainer –, how is the view that human social activity is rule-governed to be squared with the fact that human beings can change the rules, i.e., can bring about fundamental changes in law and society?

This fact, the fact which we have been seeking all along to explain, might indeed tempt one to essay a new approach to the more general explanation of human social activity. The new approach would make much of the FREEDOM of such activity and would emphasize its functions of creation and fulfillment. But this approach, too, is by no means without its inherent problems. It would certainly supply us with the element of genuine novelty that we need to explain fundamental change, but how would it account for whatever it is that fundamental change in law and society may be said to be from and to? Would the supreme product of such activity, which would have to be some sort of ABSOLUTE change, be in any way a meaningful concept, and if so, would it not differ radically from the fundamental changes with which we are concerned? In short, are we not forced by problems of conceptualization to acknowledge that any explanation that would treat the activity which brings about fundamental change in law and society as a sort of *creatio ex nihilo*, a totally free decision and execution of the decision in a void, must be fatally flawed, and does this not throw us back once again to some explanation in terms of regularities in or about 'human nature'? But does not this regression, in turn, confront us once more with the crucial dilemma that the 'rules' approach appeared to pose for the explanation of fundamental change?

The suspicion might arise that there was an element of truth in each of the major alternative ways, suggested above, of explaining the human activity that brings about fundamental changes in law and society, and that some *via media* might be found which could combine both approaches. The possibility of fundamentally altering the rules that govern behavior, for example, might be seen to depend on the possibility and perhaps even on the necessity of, in some sense, making free choices; the possibility of making even genuinely CREATIVE choices, on the other hand, might be seen to depend on the fact that any choice made by human beings must always, in some sense or other, be rule-governed. But the rules that govern choices to bring about fundamental changes in law and society cannot be the rules of legal systems or of social institutions; what COULD they be? And the states of affairs that the bringing about of such changes is intended to produce must be conceived of in some more meaningful way than as the mere existence of new systems of legal and social rules (for rules have no reality that is independent of the human beings who act in accordance with them); what IS that more meaningful way?

At this point, we might discover that we had begun to pass from problems of explanation to problems of justification; for is it not the case that the previous questions can be answered only in terms of choices made in accordance with good reasons, and of systems of rules which, if followed, could be expected to produce better states of affairs? If so, then we shall have to face the fact that the justification of fundamental changes in law and society poses essentially ETHICAL problems, and not 'merely' legal and social ones.

This last discovery brings us, finally, to a difficulty which I have deliberately avoided mentioning up to the present, but which must now be expressed: ought I really to have given myself a warrant to combine at the outset two quite different concepts, 'fundamental change in law' and 'fundamental change in society', into a single one, and to treat the matter as if there were not in fact two separate sets of problems involved? My justification for having done so is that I claim, by this device, to be able to raise a whole new cluster of problems in a particularly pointed way. For one of the relationships that the concept of fundamental change puts most acutely into question is that of law, or legal rules, to other social phenomena, or social rules.

I refer back, first of all, to my initial explanation of why I have elected to stress the term 'fundamental change' over 'revolution'. EVERYONE thinks he knows what a revolution is: such events are frequently mentioned on newscasts. Fundamental changes are a slightly different matter: what is it, we may more readily be led to ask, that can be called a REALLY FUNDAMENTAL change? Suppose that all that appeared to change, in a given case, was the identity of the rulers? Suppose, that is, that, either by a natural calamity or through a deliberate *coup* or in some other way, the old 'gang' was thrown out and a new one took its place, but that otherwise the institutions of government and society, including especially the laws, remained exactly the same as before: would we want to label this a fundamental change? For most purposes, we would probably not. Nevertheless, we must acknowledge that theorists have advanced a number of radically different proposals for identifying fundamental changes, and that many genuine issues lie concealed below the level of merely verbal disagreements.

The only possible way out of this mare's nest, it seems to me, would be to reconsider the relationship between law and other social phenomena; and this, of course, is what I have been agitating for from the start. Law, after all, is only one type of social institution, albeit an extremely important type in today's world. Perhaps it would have been unprofitable to begin by raising the question as to what truly constitutes fundamental change in law and society from a legal perspective: perhaps we might better ask ourselves what a fundamental change in society would be. But such a question appears, at first glance, to be a rather peculiar one. At least the legal philosopher has some readily available, clear-cut data to work with, namely legal systems, with some of the basic principles of which we are all more or less familiar; this is what contributes to the initial plausibility of some of his proposals. But a 'fundamental change IN SOCIETY' – what could that possibly MEAN? One of the best ways of trying to answer this question, paradoxically enough, is to focus on the possibility of abolishing all of a society's legal institutions. For is it not the case that the very existence of law, merely by virtue of the fact that it governs human behavior according to some determinate pattern or patterns rather than others, PREVENTS the thoroughgoing achievement of that state of affairs which coincides unreservedly with the highest aspirations of the members of a given social collective? And if so, would not the most totally fundamental social change possible be one in which the institution of law itself was abolished? But, on the other hand, is such an abolition conceivable? If so, what would it mean? Is what we call law or at least something like what we call law not an essential, abiding element throughout all conceivable fundamental changes in society, past, present, and future?

I have now presented a general outline, in a sketchy, preliminary fashion, of some of the basic philosophical problems with which I shall be dealing. Against Marcuse, I am forced to maintain that there are perhaps several different philosophical methods, and certainly not just a single privileged one, which, properly used, can lead to an exploration of 'the possibilities of a new experience' and thus to an explanation of fundamental change. Against Kant, I uphold the right to revolution. But such dogmatic claims as these solve no problems at all: I further maintain that, in the case of the concept of fundamental change in law and society as in the cases of many other concepts, problems first arise in the process of rendering our concepts more precise, and that it is GENERALLY as a result of a failure to render them sufficiently precise that the most dramatic, dogmatic philosophical disagreements eventually come to be expressed. Thus this present study, while it takes as its central concern the concept of fundamental change in law and society, purports also to offer a number of recommendations for dealing with other, related concepts in legal, social, and political philosophy, and indeed – at least by implication – in other areas of philosophy as well. The concept of fundamental change is, by virtue of some of the problems that it raises in a particularly acute way, peculiarly well suited for suggesting such further recommendations and reflections.

Most of this book will be devoted to the thought of two contemporary philosophers who approach the subject of fundamental change, insofar as that concept has a bearing on issues in social philosophy, in radically different ways. Neither of them, as a matter of fact, treats of revolution from a traditional, narrowly political perspective. H. L. A. Hart is primarily a philosopher of law, and what he has to say about fundamental change is somewhat incidental to, and merely a part of, his general analysis of 'the concept of law'. One important school of legal philosophy which has had an influence on Hart maintains, as we shall soon see, that the State is nothing but the personification of a legal system; but Hart does not hold dogmatically to any such view, and he sees that law itself is only a part of a broad range of social phenomena. J.-P. Sartre used to be regarded mainly as an existentialist interpreter of the human individual, but he now claims to be a systematic social philosopher and to be writing within the framework of what he considers the dominant thought of our era, that of Karl Marx. (It is this 'later' Sartre, not the Sartre of *L'être et le néant*, with whom I shall be concerned in this study.) As a neo-Marxist, Sartre is particularly interested in fundamental change in society, but it must never be forgotten that, while he painstakingly lays the abstract theoretical groundwork for comprehending this phenomenon, he can remain true to the spirit of Marx[6] only if he can preserve some distinction between 'revolutions' and 'THE Revolution', or between other fundamental changes in society and the allegedly definitive one which would, among other things, abolish the legal and political 'superstructures'.

The contrast and interplay between these two very different approaches will, it is to be hoped, contribute to a somewhat deeper understanding of the meaning of 'fundamental change', and indeed also of 'revolution', along the lines that I have drawn. My choice of Hart and Sartre as the vehicles for bringing out the desired contrast is by no means arbitrary. Just as fundamental change in law and society is one of the more obtrusive phenomena of our age, so Hart and Sartre are among the best representatives of two major contemporary movements in philosophy. Hart is an 'analyst', Sartre a 'dialectician'. Hart comes

[6] It is quite another question, a very complex one, to ask to what extent Sartre has remained true to the LETTER of Marx. I shall try to avoid this issue as much as possible and to treat Sartre's theory on its own merits, rather than as a more or less accurate or inaccurate representation of Marx's thought.

from a philosophical tradition in which it is customary to dampen the premature ardor of would-be system-builders with healthy doses of sceptical *douches écossaises*,[7] whereas Sartre's is the tradition of the system-builders, who, taking philosophy as their starting-point, propose to continue constructing according to their original plans until they have succeeded in explaining the entire world. Both traditions are long, and, to any but a rabid partisan, both are honorable. But every era in philosophy is faced anew with a serious problem, the problem of finding some means of bringing the two traditions together without simply reducing the one to the other. At the present time, this problem is rendered particularly acute if the follower of the system-building tradition should profess, as happens to be the case with Sartre, that he is a disciple of Karl Marx; for philosophy, and especially political philosophy, is far from remaining 'untouched by the loud noise of world history'. But if, in addition, the central theme around which one chooses to focus the contrast between the two traditions should be that of revolution – then, indeed, passions are likely universally to be aroused, and mutual misunderstanding to be the only issue. It will be my purpose, in this book, to try somewhat to dampen the passions *à l'écossaise*, and to reduce misunderstanding with a *soupçon* of system.

[7] My first acquaintance with Hart's major work came about through a discussion with a young student of his who had seen *The Concept of Law* in manuscript form, before it was published, and who exemplified this sceptical tradition to the point of caricature. Hart's book, he said, had to be understood as the product of a nearly homogeneous culture (90% White Anglo-Saxon Protestant), in which, as a consequence, there existed none of the revolutionary questioning of established ways of doing things that was common in AMERICAN jurisprudence and philosophy! It was in part my disbelief (justified, as it turned out) in this one-dimensional portrait of H. L. A. Hart that helped stimulate my interest in his treatment of fundamental change, once his book had become available. The Hart who, for example, has played such a prominent role in debates concerning suggested reforms of British laws governing homosexual behavior, and has taken such an interest in Israeli *kibbutzim* experiments, is NOT the totally sceptical, conformist, rather uninteresting individual suggested by the student's report.

I

AN ANALYSIS OF THE CONCEPT OF FUNDAMENTAL CHANGE IN LAW

1

INTRODUCTION

The analyzing of certain problems and puzzles about the world and its most peculiar phenomena, notably man, is the activity in which philosophers have always engaged. But 'analysis' as a particular kind of philosophic method has achieved popularity and attracted some of philosophy's ablest minds, especially in the Anglo-Saxon cultural sphere, only in very recent times.

The division of philosophy into rival 'camps' [1] or schools is to a certain extent both justifiable and in practice necessary: concept-formation, the construction of useful labels for phenomena, is the human consciousness' way of grappling with the rest of reality – as the analytic movement, abetted by Kantian and earlier insights, has shown in detail. BUT, just as there is nothing immutable about our present linguistic structures, and just as legal and social structures, which are the subject-matter of this present analysis, can and do change in fundamental ways, so too it is a mistake to regard such terms as 'Anglo-Saxon cultural sphere' or 'analytic philosophy' as being descriptive of hard-and-fast, self-enclosed structures, incapable of contamination from other spheres or schools, as self-sufficient as the Aristotelian prime mover or polis.[2] With this essential preliminary *caveat*, then, I may proceed to label H. L. A. Hart, former Regius Professor of Jurisprudence in the University of Oxford, Past President of the Aristotelian Society, as a notable representative of the British analytic movement.

[1] Seneca's bold declaration of philosophical tolerance, "Ad castra aliena transeo", illustrates the age and extent of the grip of this military metaphor on the thinking of philosophers.

[2] History itself has shown the inadequacy of the doctrine of αὐταρκεία in political thought; an excellent case can be made against its analogy in philosophical theology, either from within Aristotle's own system, or else independently, as in Paul Weiss's *Modes of Being* (Carbondale, Southern Illinois University Press, 1958, esp. p. 361). These matters are not unrelated to the central questions of the present section, as will be seen especially in Chapters 5 and 6.

Hart's recent book, *The Concept of Law*, has been enthusiastically hailed by respectable reviewers as being 'modern British philosophy's' DEFINITIVE 'systematic treatment of problems about law' [3] and as demonstrating "that progress in philosophy is possible".[4] Be this as it may, I take Hart's book to be at least a moderately important and good illustration of how contemporary analytic philosophy can deal with central issues in the philosophy of law. Furthermore, Hart's many references in *The Concept* and elsewhere to other distinguished representatives of the analytic movement make it plausible to assume that he has been influenced by their ideas and that, consequently, a consideration centered around HART's treatment might conceivably provide a better understanding of the potential merits, difficulties, and limitations of the movement as a whole.

The central theme of the present essay is fundamental change in law and society; the choice of the comparatively neutral phrase, 'fundamental change', is, as I have already explained, my own, not Hart's. But this is not a serious objection to my dealing with the concept in Hart, especially in view of the warning that I have just given about the danger of rigidifying our concepts.[5] Hart considers what I have called fundamental change in law most directly in a short section of his book entitled "The Pathology of a Legal System". However, as I shall show in some detail later, what he says here can be understood only in terms of several other key ideas and theories which he treats elsewhere, and which themselves relate to a number of other basic philosophical issues.

Hart is not 'just another analytic philosopher': unlike most of his colleagues in the analytic movement, Hart takes law and jurisprudence to be his primary concerns. This implies not only some difference in his point of view, but also a difference in the recent theories which have had major influences upon his thinking. For, historically speaking, recent developments in the philosophy of law have not always exactly

[3] L. Jonathan Cohen, review of *The Concept of Law, Mind* 71, 283 (July 1962), p. 395.

[4] Herbert Morris, review of *The Concept of Law, Harvard Law Review* 75, 7 (May 1962), p. 1461.

[5] A similar warning is contained in Ludwig Wittgenstein's now famous dictum, "Philosophy is a battle against the bewitchment of our intelligence by means of language." (*Philosophical Investigations*, tr. by G. E. M. Anscombe (New York, The Macmillan Company, 5th printing, 1961), #109, p. 47e.) It is relevant also to recall Gilbert Ryle's point that an 'idea' or 'concept' summarizes a whole train of thought, and that, therefore, "Statements about ideas are general statements about families of propositions." (*Philosophical Arguments*, Inaugural Lecture (Oxford, At the Clarendon Press, 1945), p. 8.)

paralleled developments in other areas of philosophy. At least three twentieth-century movements in jurisprudence, American legal realism, Scandinavian legal realism, and the normative positivism of Kelsen's school, have had important effects not traceable to the philosophy of analysis upon Hart's legal theories; for understanding Hart's analysis of the concept of fundamental change in law, I consider some reference to the latter two movements, especially Kelsen's, to be almost indispensable.

The above considerations point to the rationale behind the ordering of chapters in this first section. I shall deal first with Kelsen's 'pure theory of law', emphasizing the importance of the role played by 'revolution' in his conceptual scheme; in the last part of this chapter, I shall summarize some revealing disagreements, stemming from Kelsen's theory, among Continental doctors of legal philosophy. The next chapter will concern the highly empiricist 'Scandinavian school', chiefly Karl Olivecrona and Alf Ross, and its reaction to Kelsen. It will then be possible, in Chapter Four, to turn to Hart himself and to recount the central themes in his analysis of fundamental changes in legal systems, the more detailed exploration and criticism of which will occupy the remaining chapters of this section. Chapters Five and Six will concern aspects of Hart's philosophical methodology, the former the method of analysis itself, the latter his use of analogies and models. Discussion of the dominant analogy between legal systems and games in Chapter Six will lead to an examination of Hart's notion of rules in Chapter Seven. The next chapter will begin with an analysis of what Hart means by 'acceptance' of his 'rule of recognition' and will continue on into the area of legal and moral obligation. Finally, what Hart says about 'the minimum content of natural law' in this connection will lead to an investigation, in Chapter Nine, of the relation between Hart's philosophy of law, as seen primarily through his analysis of fundamental change, and sociology. But in making this move we shall have been taken beyond the confines of the philosophy of law itself, and then a new perspective and a new methodology will be in order.

2

KELSEN

Hans Kelsen's claim to first place in influence among twentieth-century legal philosophers on the Continent is almost undisputed. 'Legal positivism', the very vague term so often associated with his name,[1] has come to seem, to many, the only viable approach to the study of law which is truly scientific. Hart, too, while he explicitly takes issue with Kelsen, as will be seen, on several major issues, acknowledges a tremendous debt to the Viennese theorist.[2]

My intention here is not to summarize Kelsen's whole doctrine (just as I shall not attempt to summarize all of Hart's philosophy, either), but rather to emphasize his general approach to those issues, centering around the concept of fundamental change in law, with which I am principally concerned. Kelsen has the great merit of making perspicuously clear the character of his methodological preferences and prejudices. His 'general' or 'pure' theory of law aspires to be a SCIENCE (*Rechtswissenschaft*), according to his understanding of the term, 'science'. The general theory, then, (1) must be rigorous, systematic, and unified, (2) must exclude from its scope 'ideals' and 'ideologies', (3) must be empirical and descriptive, (4) must have as its subject-matter something quite distinct from any other science, and (5) must be applicable to all instances of truly legal orders, regardless of whether or not one happens to approve of a given such instance. I shall now, briefly and in reverse order, develop these themes that I have singled out.

[1] In an interesting note in *The Concept of Law* (Oxford, At the Clarendon Press, 1961, p. 253), Hart distinguishes five contentions often associated by writers with the expression, 'positivism', and states that Kelsen agrees to only three of these. (These contentions are to be distinguished from the five Kelsenian themes listed in the following paragraph.)

[2] This is clear throughout *The Concept of Law*, and is also made explicit in Hart's review of a book by Kelsen, *The Communist Theory of Law* (in *Harvard Law Review* 69, 4 (Feb. 1956), pp. 772-778). Here, Hart expresses regret that a man to whom he personally owes so much, namely Kelsen, should have permitted himself to write a work of such mediocre quality.

Hart, as my analysis will show, might agree in principle to all five of these characteristics as ideals for the study of jurisprudence; but he would do so only with certain important reservations and qualifications. The last-mentioned theme is the one to which Hart seems to subscribe most wholeheartedly of all: it is the basis of his position in his celebrated debate with Lon Fuller over the issue of natural law versus legal positivism.[3] Kelsen, in his defence of the ideal of developing a general theory applicable even to the legal orders of which a given philosopher may disapprove (such as the Bolshevist, Nazi, and Fascist orders, the three that he mentions), cites 'economy of thought' as his justification, and declares that 'common usage' must be our starting-point in attempting to define any concept, such as that of law.[4] But in fact these reasons, briefly stated as they are by Kelsen, are not convincing. Any appeal to 'common usage' as definitive rather begs the question;[5] what if, to cite two counter-examples, it were common usage among one group of people to say that the law of God must be obeyed rather than that of men, or among another to maintain that law, properly speaking, is a bourgeois aberration which revolutionary legality has succeeded in abolishing? As for 'economy of thought', everyone favors it, but would it not be even more economical, FROM A CERTAIN POINT OF VIEW, to regard all positive legal systems as greater or lesser approximations to the one eternal and absolutely perfect system, which has not yet been discovered in its entirety?[6] Hart is on far sounder ground than his predecessor when he advances a PRAGMATIC argument for preferring to employ a positivist concept of law, which he regards as the broader of the two kinds, rather than the sort of natural law definition which would reject bad laws as not being laws at all:

> If we are to make a reasoned choice between these concepts, it must be because one is superior to the other in the way in which it will assist our theoretical inquiries, or advance and clarify our moral deliberations, or both.[7]

[3] In *Harvard Law Review* 71, 4 (Feb. 1958), pp. 593-672.

[4] Hans Kelsen, *General Theory of Law and State*, tr. by Anders Wedberg (Cambridge, Mass., Harvard University Press, 1945), pp. 4-5.

[5] Hart sees this very well. In discussing the point, most likely with Kelsen in mind, he says, "Plainly we cannot grapple adequately with this issue if we see it as one concerning the proprieties of linguistic usage." (*The Concept of Law*, p. 204.)

[6] This was intended as something of a caricature, but in fact it does not differ too greatly from some ontological versions of natural law theory.

[7] *The Concept of Law*, pp. 204-205. Hart's justification differs from Kelsen's in that the former depends neither on accepting common usage as normative nor on adhering to a single methodological ideal, 'economy of thought', to the exclusion of all the others.

The second Kelsenian theme to be mentioned is the view that the subject-matter of *Rechtswissenschaft* must be clearly distinguished from the subject-matters of all other disciplines. For Kelsen, the peculiar subject-matter of legal science is legal norms. It is on this basis that he makes every effort to demonstrate that the pure normative theory has no need to make any reference to ideals, to morals, to sociology, or to any less formidable candidates for consideration. Now, again, no one wishes to deny the value, for the investigator in any field of knowledge, of the possibility of somehow delimiting the range of phenomena that he is called to investigate. Of course, law is not the SAME as morals or sociology; if it were, there would be no issues concerning their mutual relationships. What may be criticized in Kelsen is the dogmatic over-zealousness with which he pursues the unrealistic and imaginary ideal of completely separating his science from all others. That there is, as numerous critics have since seen, a profound paradox running through Kelsen's doctrine here can be illustrated by comparing the first sentence of the *General Theory* with a remark made in a much later section: "Law is an order of human behavior."[8] "... Normative jurisprudence describes its particular object. But its object is norms and not patterns of actual behavior."[9] The reconciliation of these two statements presupposes an excessively external view of the relation between actual behavior and its norms, as well as between sociology and legal science. That Hart is not guilty of such an extreme sort of formalism will be made clear later.

Kelsen's last-cited point above brings us to the next characteristic that I have noted. For, in this passage, he is attempting to isolate his normative theory from any taint of the 'sociological jurisprudence' of the American realists and others, and at the same time to deny that the difference between the two theories can be characterized by calling his own 'non-empirical' or 'prescriptive' and the other 'empirical' or 'descriptive'. The normative theory is "like any other empirical science", he retorts; it DESCRIBES NORMS.[10] This at least paradoxical assertion points to yet another tension in Kelsen's doctrine, a tension which is, un-

[8] *General Theory of Law and State*, p. 3.

[9] *Ibid.*, p. 163.

[10] Kelsen does, however, insist that there is a distinction between 'Kausalwissenschaft' and 'Normwissenschaft'. In a later formulation, he sharpens this distinction and attempts, in a footnote, to answer the objection of Harald Ofstad that he has not made clear what he means when he says that "the formulations of legal science are at the same time ought-formulations and descriptive ones". *Reine Rechtslehre* (Wien, Verlag F. Deuticke, 1960), p. 74.

doubtedly, at least partly rooted in the very concept of law itself. Kelsen contends that 'normative jurisprudence' makes general statements about actual, empirical (but normative) legal systems. This contention can be refuted only by showing that actual legal systems DO NOT, in fact, conform in all important ways to Kelsen's theory about them. Legal experts such as Hart and Roberto Ago point out that it is at least physically possible for a municipal legal system to exist without possessing any actual law(s) corresponding to one of the most essential elements of Kelsen's theory, the basic (*Grund-*) norm.[11] Ago is especially insistent in maintaining that international law, which Kelsen has chosen to regard not only as a legal order but indeed as the highest order which DETERMINES 'the reason of validity of the National Legal Order',[12] has no such single basic norm.[13] If the experts fail to find empirical evidence to support one of Kelsen's basic contentions, then surely the claim that the normative theory is also empirical and descriptive has been drastically weakened.

The fourth characteristic of the 'general theory' that requires comment is Kelsen's exclusion of 'ideals' and 'ideologies' from its scope. Kelsen takes a very narrow view of the range of reason, and displays considerable naiveté in simply assuming a complete dichotomy between thought and will. Thus he can say that "the law ... is a function not of thinking but of willing"[14] and that "justice is an irrational ideal ... not subject to cognition".[15] The latter doctrine leads him to the view that there is a tragic and inevitable conflict between scientific Truth and emotional, non-cognitive Justice.[16] To the philosopher, these simplistic positions suggests numerous difficulties, but it was Kelsen himself who, according to Lon Fuller, once raised the most obvious objection of all when he casually admitted "that his whole system might well rest on an emotional

[11] Hart accuses Kelsen of obscuring or possibly even denying, by the language that he uses in discussing his *Grundnorm* (especially the notion of having to 'presuppose its *validity*'), the empirical nature of inquiries about the existence of a legal system. He cites with approval Ago's article. *The Concept of Law*, p. 245.

[12] *General Theory of Law and State*, p. 366.

[13] Roberto Ago, "Positive Law and International Law" (tr. by Judith Hammond), *American Journal of International Law* 51, 4 (Oct. 1957), p. 725 and *passim*. Kelsen's candidate for the basic norm of international law, *pacta sunt servanda*, is either incorrect or meaningless.

[14] Kelsen, *The Communist Theory of Law* (London, Stevens & Sons Ltd., 1955), p. 12.

[15] *General Theory of Law and State*, p. 13.

[16] *Ibid.*, p. xvi.

preference for the idea of order over that of justice".[17] In other words, certain ideals of scientific method, at least, were operative in the very way in which Kelsen chose to analyze the concept of law; but this would not be a damning criticism except to someone who, like Kelsen, saw no possibility whatever of rationally comparing conflicting ideals. It may well be the case that a scientific investigation of certain legal phenomena will be abetted by the temporary setting aside of considerations about their morality and purpose; the justification for this, once again, will be a pragmatic one. But this valid point, which Hart stresses, is something quite different from Kelsen's *toto caelo* separation of goals, ideals, and norms from the scientific knowledge of them.

Finally, I have mentioned the strong insistence on rigor, system, and unity which dominates Kelsen's *reine Rechtswissenschaft*. As ideals for organizing any science or indeed the whole or human knowledge, these qualities are unimpeachable, but of course there is always the danger that they will be used to distort the actual phenomena. That Kelsen is at times guilty of such distortion, even to the point of being comical, is demonstrated very well by Hart's simple logical point that at least an elementary legal order is conceivable which would consist of a set, rather than a strict SYSTEM, of legal rules.[18] Kelsen, it is quite obvious, is guided, or perhaps misled, by the hypothetico-deductive logical model in his vision of a normative system.[19] Why should jurisprudence not be able sometimes to profit more from the application of, let us say, an inductive method to law? It is only if one first ASSUMES, as Kelsen does, that every valid legal system must be traceable back across a hierarchy of normative levels to a single highest source, an 'ultimate postulate', the basic norm, by which all the rest has been determined,[20] that one may refuse to employ any method other than the axiomatic one. But it is precisely in connection with this grand vision of the logical legal system that the concept of fundamental change, or revolution, plays its key role in Kelsen's legal philosophy, and it is to this that we may now turn.

"It is just the phenomenon of revolution", Kelsen says, "which clearly

[17] "Positivism and Fidelity to Law – A Reply to Professor Hart", *Harvard Law Review* 71, 4 (Feb. 1958), p. 632.

[18] *The Concept of Law*, pp. 230-231.

[19] Kelsen is of course not so naive as to maintain that all the norms of a legal system are strict logical deductions from the basic norm. Nevertheless, the role played by the basic norm is such as to make rather obvious the influence of the hypothetico-deductive method of formal logic in the elaboration of his own system.

[20] *General Theory of Law and State*, p. 124.

shows the significance of the basic norm."[21] For the purposes of Kelsenian jurisprudence, the state is considered as simply being the personification of a particular legal system, and the basic norm is identified with what Kelsen, using a philosophically confusing terminology, calls the 'material sense' of a given state's constitution. By this he seems to mean those fundamental provisions of a state's constitution, be it written or unwritten, which are most difficult to alter by legal means;[22] but his language elsewhere seems to suggest a more content-less interpretation of the basic norm, which would reduce the basic norm in every state to the postulate "that one ought to behave as the individual, or the individuals, who laid down the first constitution have ordained".[23] What is a revolution, though, if not a challenge to, and a denial of, this basic postulate? (This point may be illustrated from the fact that unsuccessful revolutionaries are always regarded by the law in force as being traitors, whereas successful revolutionaries, who in terms of the old constitution were guilty of the strictest illegality, are the heroes and indeed the 'Founding Fathers' of the new one.) For Kelsen, a revolution that succeeds is clearly definable, from the point of view of normative jurisprudence, as the most radical and fundamental change imaginable, namely the substitution of one basic norm for another. But now it must be remembered, from what I have already said about the systematic unity of Kelsen's scheme, that an entire legal order depends on the basic norm for its validity – or, to use another formulation, that the basic norm is the source of the validity of all the lower-level norms. A revolutionary change, in annulling the old basic norm, must therefore annul the entire old order with it. It is true, Kelsen concedes, that as a matter of fact states after revolutions continue, if only as a matter of practical necessity, to use much of the same lower-level legal apparatus, for instance many of the same criminal laws, as before. But, though the content of such laws may remain the same through the revolutionary change, their normative form, their *raison de valoir*, has been just as radically altered as the rest of the system:

> The reason for their validity is the new, not the old, constitution, and between the two continuity holds neither from the point of view of the one nor from that of the other. Thus, it is never the constitution merely but always the entire legal order that is changed by a revolution.[24]

[21] *Ibid.*, p. 118.
[22] *Ibid.*, p. 124.
[23] *Ibid.*, p. 115.
[24] *Ibid.*, p. 118.

Here, then, in the legal philosophy of Hans Kelsen, we come upon the first, and in some ways the most extreme, definition of a concept of fundamental change to be found in this study. That it is more accurate to call it a definition, rather than an analysis, may be seen from reflection upon the fact that it makes complete sense only within the framework of Kelsen's hypothetico-deductive model of a legal system.[25] Kelsen himself notes that he offers this account only 'from a juristic point of view', that is, from the point of view of his science of normative jurisprudence. If we recall the difficulties that we have already found in connection with some of the basic premises of Kelsen's enterprise, we shall be unlikely to assume that the above doctrine of total discontinuity between pre- and post-revolutionary orders is the last word possible on the subject of fundamental change, even from the limited perspective of legal philosophy.

And indeed it is not the last word, not even from Kelsen himself. Radical discontinuity implies unintelligibility: philosophical rationalism, at any rate, abhors vacuums. While we have already had occasion to see how little of a rationalist Kelsen is in ethics, in philosophical psychology, and in social philosophy, one can never doubt the sincerity of his attempts, whether successful or not, to apply reason to the field of jurisprudence. Kelsen's proposed solution to the problem of unintelligibility posed by the occurrence of fundamental changes in municipal legal orders is elegantly simple: it is to regard international law as the reason for validity, and therefore as the 'source', of all national law. He says that no jurist, for example, would want to doubt that the pre-revolutionary Tsarist state and the present Soviet state are, legally speaking, the same Russia. What makes them the same is that they are sovereign (though national sovereignty must now be looked upon as subordinate to the sovereignty of the international legal order) over roughly the same geographical territory.[26] From the standpoint of international law, according to Kelsen, a new national legal order, the result of some revolutionary or other fundamental change in a given state, "begins to be valid as soon as it has become – on the whole – efficacious".[27]

Kelsen's international law solution to the peculiar problem of fundamental change that he has created for himself is open to several different

[25] Cf. my discussion of Kelsen, which elaborates somewhat on themes suggested here, in "The Essential Role of Models and Analogies in the Philosophy of Law", 43, *New York University Law Review* 1 (March 1968), esp. p. 70.

[26] *Ibid.*, pp. 368-369.

[27] *Ibid.*, p. 220.

kinds of challenges, some of which, at least, he attempts to anticipate. For example, do not the empirical data of history clearly militate against the thesis that international law is the source of validity of national law? Kelsen is not sure that they do, but at any rate he now falls back on the claim that the superior sovereignty of international law is not meant to be an historical or political [28] thesis, but simply a logical and epistemological postulate of a national legal order. But then would it not make just as much sense to defend the alternative hypothesis that the nation-state is supreme and that the validity of international law depends upon its being RECOGNIZED as valid in each individual, national legal order? On the very last page of his book, Kelsen finds himself forced by his view that ethical and ideological preferences are irrational to admit that indeed, from the point of view of the science of law, the choice between the internationalist (which he also calls 'monistic' and 'objectivistic') hypothesis which he favors, and the rival ('pluralistic', 'subjectivistic') hypothesis of national sovereignty, is 'irrelevant'.[29] Not only does this admission contravene Kelsen's earlier claim that his normative jurisprudence is 'empirical', but it also forces us to the conclusion that, in the last analysis, Kelsen is unable satisfactorily to resolve the problem of fundamental change as he has posed it.

Another very important objection to this aspect of Kelsen's theory stems from his equation of a new legal order's 'validity from the point of view of international law' with its being 'efficacious' within a given territory. There will be no need to mention the mixed reception accorded to this position by certain of the world's foreign offices and departments of state; the philosophical opposition will suffice. A whole literature exists on the subject of how legal positivism, inspired by Kelsen's reduction of the term 'valid', with its overtones of VALUE, to the jurisprudential equivalent of the logical expression 'valid within a given system', has been brought to the point where 'validity' no longer retains any separate meaning at all.[30] But we need not pursue this question any further at present, for much of our later discussion, especially in the treatment of Alf Ross and in the chapter on 'acceptance', will center around this

[28] But H. W. R. Wade, "The Basis of Legal Sovereignty", *The Cambridge Law Journal* (Nov. 1955), pp. 172-197, makes an excellent lawyer's case for the view that, though the concepts of legal and political sovereignty can be distinguished, as Kelsen maintains, nevertheless sovereignty is ultimately a '*political* fact', not a legal one.

[29] *General Theory of Law and State*, p. 388.

[30] This reductionism is explicitly acknowledged by many who favor it. Cf., for example, Mario Cattaneo, *Il concetto di rivoluzione nella scienza del diritto* (Milano-Varese, Istituto Editoriale Cisalpino, 1960), p. 122.

problem and Hart's compromise attempt, by emphasizing the distinction between the internal and external aspects of rules, to dissolve it. I may summarize the objections to the solution proposed (though only as one alternative hypothesis) by Kelsen himself to the problems posed by his concept of fundamental change in law, by pointing out that it seems incomplete,[31] *ad hoc*, and artificial, and that its artificiality may well be due in part to the one-sided model used by Kelsen in constructing his theory. This is said without prejudice to Kelsen's general stand in favor of increased emphasis on internationalism, which I, like many of his critics, share. But, as one of the critics remarks, tersely, "To regard the legal authority of States as delegated by international law is, vis-à-vis the evidence, a falsification." [32]

In the remainder of this chapter, I wish briefly to sketch an interesting controversy that took place in Austrian and German legal philosophy during the decade between 1920, before Kelsen's own ideas had fully matured, and 1930.[33] Its central theme is, precisely, the place that revolution should occupy in the science of law, and it serves to illustrate, in a particularly pointed way, the kinds of difficulties into which the Kelsenian approach to fundamental change is likely to lead. Its chief theoretical inspiration is derived, quite obviously, from Kelsen and his 'Vienna circle', since three of the four monographs which I shall cite appear in a journal which he founded and edited, references to him are frequent, and all the writers share at least some of his ideals concerning the nature of *Rechtswissenschaft*. The controversy is also tinged with a certain poignancy, which cannot, unfortunately, be reproduced here, but which is indicated in the course of the dispute by several references to the German experience of collapse and fundamental change which took place in 1918. I do not pretend that this series of articles has had any influence upon Hart's thinking; as alternative reactions to the problem of fundamental change as Kelsen poses it, however, they are most revealing both for jurisprudence and for philosophy as a whole.[34]

[31] If a world state actually existed, for instance, Kelsen's theory would not cover the case of a revolution against this state.
[32] Guy Héraud, "Sur deux conceptions de la compétence", *Archives de Philosophie du Droit* 1959, p. 37. Tr. mine; I have used the phrase 'legal authority' as a rough translation of 'compétence'.
[33] His *Allgemeine Staatslehre*, of which the English edition of the *General Theory* is a revision, was published in 1925; his *Théorie Générale du Droit International Publique* appeared in 1928.
[34] I am indebted to M. Cattaneo, *op. cit.*, for having made me aware of the existence of these articles.

Fritz Sander,[35] the first theorist to be considered, and in his solution the closest to Kelsen, states that the greatest single problem confronting the 'pure theory' of law is that of revolution: legal science has thus far allowed itself to regard revolution as a surd and 'eine Cäsur', an element of complete discontinuity about which it can say nothing. He calls this a 'Katastrophentheorie', which he compares both to a certain outmoded geological theory of natural progress through periodic upheavals, and to a Catholic theory of fundamental social change through an occasional 'Stoß von Außen', a special act of God's will. He cites the writings of A. Merkl, with whom I shall be dealing later, as exemplifying a philosophical occasionalism in jurisprudence, inasmuch as Merkl's theory is unable to explain why a new legal system should always come into existence at the same time as a fundamental political change takes place. Sander believes that a more unified and systematic legal science, involving no complete discontinuities, would be more in conformity both with nature and with human reason: he calls on Darwin, Leibniz, and especially Kant as his witnesses. Just as Kant's treatment of substance allows for plurality within categorical unity, so, according to Sander, does the view of LEVELS of universality in legal science permit both difference and unity: "Thus, whether continuity reigns between two (empirical) constitutions may be determined, not by comparison of these two constitutions, but only by looking for a higher level."[36] Sander believes that he has discovered the highest level of the world system of law in a peculiar kind of law, which, he maintains, is no less law than many other kinds, namely in *Völkerrecht*, international law.

Sander's solution to the problem of legal discontinuity in fundamental change, the appeal to an international *jus gentium* as a higher level which legitimizes new national legal orders when they come into existence, finds no approval with our other theorists of this period. Ernst Beling, in his pamphlet, *Revolution und Recht*,[37] dismisses Sander with the brief remark that there have been times when, and places where, no POSITIVE[38] international law has existed. Beling's own solution, apart

[35] "Das Faktum der Revolution und die Kontinuität der Rechtsordnung", *Zeitschrift für öffentliches Recht* 1 (1919/20), pp. 132-164.

[36] *Ibid.*, p. 153; tr. mine.

[37] E. Beling, *Revolution und Recht* (Augsburg, Dr. Benno Filser Verlag, 1923 (?)).

[38] 'Positive', the word from which the term 'legal positivism' takes its meaning, seems to signify 'set down', 'actually formulated'. Ago, *op. cit.*, gives an excellent historical account of the derivation of this term from medieval legal theory, in which 'lex positiva' meant simply one kind of law, and of the importance of Hegel's translation of 'positivum' as 'gesetzt'. The close remembance between 'gesetzt' and the German word for a legal ordinance, 'Gesetz', is highly suggestive.

from his discussions of such questions as the dualistic (law-annulling and law-creating) nature of revolution and the non-self-validating character of legal philosophy (since appeal may always be made, above even the highest level of legal idealism, to a yet higher value-theory), is basically political and social: "The state", he says, "is a social entity". Kelsen was wrong to divorce jurisprudence entirely from sociology, just as he was wrong in failing to make the capital distinction between the legal system (*Rechtsordnung*) on the one hand, and the state as the subject, or possessor, of a legal system (*Rechtsordnungssubjekt*) on the other. Kelsen's philosophical occasionalism, says Beling, is due to this failure; in fact, the state IS NOT its legal system, and thus may continue to exist throughout the course of a fundamental change in the latter. Beling also makes the obvious charge of formalism against Kelsen:

> The error of 'normative jurisprudence' as it emerges from Kelsen's formulation, lies just in the fact that it places the formal, normative character of the law out of reach of every relational connection with the real world.[39]

Adolf Merkl, in his article,[40] is most concerned with replying to Sander, while defending Kelsen's identification of a state with its legal system. He claims that Sander has been seduced by the merely verbal similarity of 'Völkerrecht' and 'Staatsrecht', which are in fact very different; only a slightly greater seduction, he says, would be needed to maintain the view that *Naturrecht* was likewise a kind of higher law. The theory that there exists a world-wide 'law of the peoples', unlimited by territorial boundaries, is for Merkl too naive and too obviously false to require refutation, but even Sander's slightly more cautious formulation, which states that international law is what legitimizes, or recognizes, new legal orders when they do come into existence, is contrary to the empirical facts. History, for instance, shows the development of international law AS LAW, that is, in any form resembling legal ordinances as distinct from mere customary practice, to have been rather late. Merkl does not deny the 'unity of the legal world-image' (*Weltbild*), in the nearly vacuous sense that law is a universal phenomenon, but he sees no value in Sander's model of a 'hierarchy of norms established by the mechanism of delegation'.[41] There simply is, as a matter of fact, more discontinuity in the world of law than Sander would like to allow: "Continuity must

[39] Beling, *op. cit.*, p. 28. Tr. mine.
[40] "Das Problem der Rechtskontinuität und die Forderung des einheitlichen rechtlichen Weltbildes", *Zeitschrift für öffentliches Recht* 5 (1926), pp. 497-527.
[41] *Ibid.*, p. 502. Tr. mine.

not be dictated, but can only be grounded."[42] Merkl himself maintains that every unconstitutional change in a state's constitution, of which revolution is the paradigm case, is, from a legal point of view, 'transcendent', and indeed that every illegal act is a revolutionary act, in the broadest sense of the latter term. As opposed to Beling, he reaffirms the doctrine that a state is nothing more than its legal order, that a change in the constitution is a change of *Rechtssubjekt*, and that the obvious fact that post-war Germany is a quite different state from pre-war Germany furnishes one more proof for his thesis.

Max Laserson,[43] the last of our German and Austrian theorists, represents the most radical departure from Kelsen. Laserson criticizes both Beling and Kelsen by contending that the fashionable jurisprudence of the day is really conservative or static in character, unequipped to deal with DEVELOPMENT in the law. "There can be no more incorrect view", he says, "than the opinion that the basic element of revolution stands opposed as alien or even inimical to law."[44] His explanation of this seemingly paradoxical statement is in terms of the one kind of theory that Kelsen had been most concerned to avoid, namely natural law. From the true legal standpoint, according to Laserson, revolution appears as a hurtling together (*Zusammenstoß*) of the positive and natural laws, which had become too widely separated in a given state because of a failure of adaptability on the side of the old positive legal system. Laserson recalls older philosophical justifications of the 'right to revolution'. Of his kind of natural law, however, there are no trans-temporal formulations: "Such a law... we can call intuitive or, if one wishes, immanent."[45]

To attempt a critique or a full synthesis of these four positions would require an expenditure of space not commensurate with its probable value, for most of this book will be concerned with approaches to the concept of fundamental change in law and society that differ considerably from the above. I have presented them simply as being suggestive and as helping to illustrate both the sorts of difficulties into which the Kelsenian approach can lead and some possible ways of escaping from it. Sander's theoretical position concerning international law and the problem of revolution is the one that is closest to Kelsen's, but Sander

[42] *Ibid.*, p. 508. Tr. mine.
[43] Max Laserson, "Revolution und Recht", *Zeitschrift für öffentliches Recht* 8 (1929), pp. 553-570.
[44] *Ibid.*, p. 557. Tr. mine.
[45] *Ibid.*, p. 563. Tr. mine.

also has the merit of being more generous than Kelsen in drawing parallels from the histories of philosophy and of natural science to his own and opponents' perspectives. Sometimes the parallels strike us as amusing or far-fetched; at other times, notably in the references to Kant, they are very illuminating in showing the still largely unrejected philosophical heritage common to both Sander and Kelsen, a heritage that manifests itself most pervasively of all, perhaps, in the very language in which their theories are couched.[46] Beling tries valiantly to escape from the Kelsenian-Sanderian universe by the route of sociology, that is, by at least rejecting Kelsen's treatment of the state as simply the personification of its legal system; but he continues to adhere to Kelsen's hypothetico-deductive 'levels' model, and he draws the conclusion that legal science itself cannot treat of the problem of fundamental change (though sociology and political theory, the higher levels of legal realism, and, ultimately, value theory can). Merkl's reaction to Sander, though still well within the boundaries of Kelsenism, contains many of the basic elements that the dominant British and American philosophies of law – as well, I suppose, as most ordinary British and American lawyers – are most likely to raise in criticism of the Kelsenian model as I have presented it: it is too formalistic, too 'pure', not in conformity with the facts of law as they 'really' are. Laserson's conclusion partly confirms a point that has frequently been made, for example, by students of mine who have for the first time become acquainted with Kelsen: namely, that his most vigorous protestations against natural law theory, all its works, and all its pomps, cannot but make one suspect all the more strongly that basic aspects of his own thought could easily lend themselves to some sort of a non-positivist, ideal-oriented interpretation. In addition, Laserson does well to note the potential danger of conservatism which lurks behind any political theory that places greater stress on the concept of 'order' than on that of 'development', and which thus remains ever-present, for obvious reasons, in the philosophy of law.

Kelsen's influence, as the last section of this chapter has contributed to demonstrating, has continued strong on the Continent. Laserson was an exception among the four writers mentioned above in upholding the view that revolution is itself some form of law, and not just a fact.

[46] Cf. Norberto Bobbio, *Giusnaturalismo e positivismo giuridico* (Milano, Edizioni di Comunità, 1965) for an interesting reference to the influence, unhappy as far as Professor Bobbio is concerned, of neo-Kantianism in leading Kelsen to regard "the *sollen*, instead of more simply and more correctly as a modal verb proper to normative propositions, as a transcendental category of our knowledge". – pp. 40-41. Tr. mine.

The expression 'normative fact', which sounds paradoxical and yet is a keystone of the Kelsenian doctrine, retains a much more widespread currency than have some of the other Kelsenian views that we have had occasion to examine. Arguing that their adhesion to a society implies not merely that "the subjects *obey*", but that "the subjects *must obey*", Orazio Condorelli advanced the doctrine of normative facts as the basis of law in a celebrated article fittingly entitled "Ex Facto Oritur Jus".[47] One of Norberto Bobbio's works is entitled *La consuetudine come fatto normativo*. Pierandrei, while finding the ultimate justification of law in a kind of consent which he calls the " 'opinio juris et necessitatis' of the social group",[48] still maintains the view of revolution as 'fatto normativo'. Cattaneo, to whom I have already referred, also finds this expression in the end to be the most precise. But at least one group of legal thinkers has traditionally stressed the greater importance of the noun, 'fact', than of the adjective, 'normative', in understanding both fundamental changes in law and law itself. These are the Scandinavians, and they demand a new chapter.

[47] *Rivista internazionale de filosofia del diritto* 11 (1931), pp. 585-600.

[48] Franco Pierandrei, "La rivoluzione e il diritto", *Nuova rivista di diritto commerciale*, etc. 5 (1952), p. 144. Tr. mine.

3

SCANDINAVIA

The title of Karl Olivecrona's *magnum opus*, *Law as Fact*, is a striking illustration of the predominantly empiricist bent of a sizable group of contemporary Scandinavian legal philosophers. Their treatment of the concept of fundamental change in law is most closely connected with their analysis, strongly psychological in its orientation, of legal obligation. Of the two with whom I shall chiefly deal in this transitional chapter, namely Olivecrona and Alf Ross, the former, the earlier writer, may be regarded as the more uncompromising empiricist. The subtle differences that exist even between Ross and Hart, however, may serve as a useful introduction to the legal thought of the English analyst.

One thinker of an earlier generation, Axel Hägerström, is held in especially high esteem by the entire 'Scandinavian school'.[1] Painstaking scholarship had led Hägerström to discover numerous examples of ritual practices, or what he called 'magic', in the legal transactions of classical Rome. In the conveyance of property, for instance, Hägerström noted that certain forms of words and gestures were considered necessary before the transaction acquired legally binding status. Traces of 'magic' were still to be found in contemporary law, Hägerström thought; as Olivecrona expresses it in making the same point, "Modern thinking in legal matters is far from being wholly rational."[2] Hägerström's conclusion, as his use of the rather pejorative term 'magic' suggests, is that such traces should be extirpated.

Hart takes Hägerström to task both on a superficial level, for his unfortunate use of 'magical' to denote elements common to all legal systems, and, more importantly, for the error which is behind Hägerström's usage here, the belief that ritual and rule may be treated as something

[1] Notable among the many published tributes to Hägerström is that of one of his earliest and best-known disciples, Anders Vilhelm Lundstedt. Cf. his posthumously-published *Legal Thinking Revised: My Views on Law* (Stockholm, 1956), esp. pp. 6-10.

[2] Karl Olivecrona, *Law as Fact* (Copenhagen, Einar Munksgaard, 1939), p. 115.

relatively external to what is essential in legal forms. On the contrary, for Hart, "the rules not merely account for the legal efficacy of the words, but show what their function or, in a wide sense, their meaning is." [3] Hart's criticism is very fundamental; as Hobbes,[4] Hume,[5] Rousseau,[6] and Marx, among others, have all recognized, it is questionable whether even such elementary forms as 'property' would retain much meaning if completely severed from their ties to the rules and ritualistic practices of a given legal system or group of such systems. In short, while no one would want to contend that modern man should be ruled by superstition and 'magic', Hägerström's inclination to condemn certain legal rules as 'magical' renders suspect the very concept of legal 'convention'. But a refusal to allow for convention would greatly diminish the intelligibility of the concept of law – unless one were to try to compensate by insisting, as Hägerström at one point does, "that natural law or moral notions must enter into a legal system contrary to the legal positivists".[7]

One moral notion with which Hägerström wrestles most mightily is that of obligation, or the sense of duty.[8] His successor, Olivecrona,

[3] Hart, review of Hägerström's *Inquiries into the Nature of Law and Morals* (ed. by Olivecrona, tr. by C. D. Broad), *Philosophy* 30, 115 (Oct. 1955), p. 372.

[4] "Where there is no coercive power erected, that is, where there is no commonwealth, there is no propriety." Thomas Hobbes, *Leviathan* I, 15 (ed. by M. Oakeshott) (Oxford, Basil Blackwell, 1960), p. 94.

[5] "After this convention, concerning abstinence from the possessions of others, is enter'd into, and every one has acquir'd a stability in his possessions, there immediately arise the ideas of justice and injustice; as also those of *property, right*, and *obligation*. The latter are altogether unintelligible without first understanding the former. Our property is nothing but those goods, whose constant possession is establish'd by the laws of society." David Hume, *A Treatise of Human Nature* III, 2 (ed. by L. A. Selby-Bigge) (Oxford, At the Clarendon Press, 10th ed., 1958), pp. 490-491.

[6] "Telle fut ou dut être l'origine de la société et des lois, qui donnèrent de nouvelles entraves au foible et du nouvelles forces au riche, détruisirent sans retour la liberté naturelle, fixèrent pour jamais la loi de la propriété et de l'inégalité, d'une adroite usurpation firent un droit irrévocable, et, pour le profit de quelques ambitieux, assujettirent désormais tout le genre humain au travail, à la servitude, et à la misère." Jean-Jacques Rousseau, "Discours sur cette question proposée par l'Académie de Dijon: Quelle est l'origine de l'inégalité parmi les hommes et si elle est autorisée par la loi naturelle?" from *Du Contrat Social etc.* (Paris, Éditions Garnier Frères), pp. 78-79.

[7] Hart, review of Hägerström's *Inquiries into the Nature of Law and Morals*, p. 373. The preceding suggestion as to exactly WHY Hägerström might feel a theoretical need to resort to such notions, however, is my own; Hart merely says that he does not fully understand Hägerström's point here.

[8] Cf. C. D. Broad, "Hägerström's Account of Sense of Duty and Certain Allied Experiences", *Philosophy* 26, 97 (Apr. 1951), pp. 99-113. Hägerström develops the supposed analogy between deontic experiences and the experience of receiving a

shares this interest and makes use of Hägerström's insight (misleading though it may be) into the 'magical' character of legal ritual in order to wage a full-scale attack upon proponents, of whom he regards Kelsen as a prime example, of 'the concept of law as binding force'. It is irrational and superstitious, according to Olivecrona, to speak with reverence about the law's 'validity', its 'normative' character, or the dependence of lower upon higher norms. If by 'validity' we really mean 'effectiveness', then we are in fact referring to the habit of obedience which a given legal system continues to command in a sufficiently large number, usually the vast majority, of its subjects. The dominant cause, Olivecrona maintains, of this habit of obedience is fear; physical might and political propaganda, not some binding force in the concept of law itself,[9] are what keep a given system effective; our moral conceptions are shaped by law and are no more altruistic than or different in kind from other considerations of expediency; and duty is a purely subjective category.[10]

The predominantly psychological perspective from which Olivecrona looks at law and morality enables him to re-examine the concept of revolution and to draw conclusions about it quite opposite to those of Kelsen. Revolution is a large problem for legal philosophy, he says, only as long as the '"binding force" superstition' is retained. Once it is seen that constitutions, or fundamental laws, have as their purpose the promotion of respect and obedience for the legal system, and that in certain historical situations that purpose is thwarted, it is no longer a mystery (as it was with Kelsen) why a constitution may sometimes be changed and the rest of the legal system left intact. Olivecrona preserves a large amount of continuity in his account of fundamental change in law: he denies that any "absolutely sharp line can be drawn between revolution and ordinary legislation", and comes to the following conclusion: "Thus a revolution is only one step in the long development of

---

command. Broad is forced to admit that Hägerström's solution to the further problem of how we can talk about the RIGHTNESS of obeying a certain command is very obscure (p. 110).

9 *"Law chiefly consists of rules about force." Law as Fact*, p. 134.

10 Lundstedt is, if anything, even blunter than Olivecrona in stating the ultimate conclusions of the most extreme version of Scandinavian empiricism: "There is no justice. Neither is there any objective 'ought,' consequently neither any material law, i.e., legal commands. Thus the entire legal ideology – including legal rights and duties, wrongfulness and lawfulness – goes up in smoke." – "Law and Justice: A Criticism of the Method of Justice", in Paul Sayre, ed., *Interpretations of Modern Legal Philosophies* (New York, Oxford University Press, 1947), pp. 450-451.

the law."[11] It must be remembered that the essential presupposition of Olivecrona's treatment of fundamental change and indeed of the entire concept of law is his simple behaviorist psychology and his belief that it is applicable to human nature at any time and under any circumstances. Consider the following excerpt:

> When the constitution has broken down, however, the inveterate habit of obedience to a set of rules of government is a source of strength to the new constitution. The attitude is simply transferred from one set of rules to another. . . . Paradoxical as it may seem, success in the revolution depends upon the working of those human characteristics which make for law-abiding.[12]

In Karl Olivecrona, then, we find the most perfect proponent to be introduced in this book of what might be called an Hobbesian approach to legal obligation. The position is a powerful one because of its straightforwardness and consistency. And it offers a forceful antidote to Kelsen's ultimately untenable attempt to keep legal theory 'pure' by making it in no way dependent on non-legal facts or disciplines; where Kelsen saw a complete void created by the rejection of a state's constitution (if for the moment we set aside his later solution in terms of the 'higher norms' of international law, much of which Olivecrona believes can be called 'law' only in the nonsensical metaphysical sense),[13] there Olivecrona sees only a relatively slight change and great continuity because of certain habitual characteristics of human behavior. But the old objections to such a theory still have weight. It amounts to an oversimplification, and even a suppression, of some of the relevant phenomena. There are times when some legal systems are consciously and deliberately ACCEPTED as authoritative, not merely passively obeyed, by large numbers of their subjects; at least, there is nothing inconceivable about such a situation. Is fear always the dominant motive in obedience to the law?[14] Unless fear were the ONLY human motive, there would be no logical necessity for it always to be so. Hasn't the old conflict between expediency and altruism[15] by now resulted in some agreement, among those who have studied it, that the reduction of either one to the other is a falsification of the complexities of human psychology? Is it not simply

[11] *Law as Fact*, p. 73.
[12] *Ibid.*, pp. 70-71.
[13] *Ibid.*, p. 206.
[14] Olivecrona admits that introspection does not always point to the dominance of fear– at first. But he is confident that a more careful examination will confirm his conclusions. *Ibid.*, pp. 134 ff.
[15] Olivecrona denies that there is any such thing as altruism. *Ibid.*, p. 169.

incorrect to hold that justice, as a motive for conduct, is fundamentally no different from expediency? Finally, is there quite as wide an area of stability and unchangeableness about the human mind as Olivecrona, in his account of revolutions as simply steps 'in the long development of the law', steps not very different from some other kinds of new legislation, is forced to presuppose?

Olivecrona's legal philosophy depends, for much of its force and originality, upon certain very dubious doctrines both in psychology and in philosophical method. In his equating, following Hägerström, of abstract entities and concepts with kinds of magic, he has denied any autonomy to the studies of politics,[16] of morality, and, perhaps it could ultimately be said, even of law itself. At least, this last criticism is the one which Alf Ross offers of what he calls the 'psychological realism' of Olivecrona and others. By conceiving of law as being so heavily dependent upon individual psychology, says Ross, Olivecrona has made it impossible to define a legal system as what it is, an 'intersubjective phenomenon'.[17] Ross makes very few allusions to his Swedish predecessor, but it is obvious even from this one reference that there are significant differences between the two men.

Perhaps these differences may be better focused if we turn for a moment to some brief allusions made in *On Law and Justice* to the problem of fundamental change. Ross agrees with Olivecrona that law normally has an 'ideologically motivating function', that is, that legal systems usually promote pro-attitudes towards themselves on the part of their subjects.[18] Such attitudes can be called 'moral' attitudes, he says, but there is an ambiguity in the term 'moral'. Here Ross departs from Olivecrona by distinguishing a pro-attitude of this first kind, which he calls a '"formal" or "institutional" legal consciousness', from what he calls 'the genuine "moral" attitude'. This distinction, of capital importance, then enables Ross to account for the growth of 'revolutionary consciousness'.[19] For it is in terms of too great a widening of the gap

[16] Olivecrona agrees with Kelsen that the state cannot be thought of as an entity existing independently of the law. *Ibid.*, p. 40.

[17] Alf Ross, *On Law and Justice* (Berkeley & Los Angeles, University of California Press, 1959), p. 72.

[18] My use of the active voice here is intended to bring out the sense in which, as the Scandinavians have seen, the mere existence of a legal system can sometimes be said to exert considerable force over individuals' conduct ... Ross speaks of 'attitudes', not of 'pro-attitudes', but I have used Nowell-Smith's locution for brevity's sake.

[19] *On Law and Justice*, pp. 54-55.

between those two attitudes of legal consciousness, the 'institutional' and the 'moral', that Ross can explain the impulse to bring about a fundamental change in a legal system on the part of (at least some of) its subjects. Ross then goes on to say that the decision as to how to effect such a change in a given situation is a tactical one, and that it is possible for minorities within given bodies of people to bring about changes not approved of by the others. What I wish primarily to call attention to here, however, is the way in which Ross has succeeded in modifying Olivecrona's position. Olivecrona had spoken rather vaguely in terms of the 'thwarting' of the habit of obedience to law in certain 'historical situations', but his psychological behaviorism had prevented him from bringing moral categories to bear in his analysis of such situations. Ross not only points out that Olivecrona's account is too individualistic, or subjective, to explain the intersubjective, sociological phenomenon that is law, but he also goes on to place more emphasis than had his predecessor on the 'genuine "moral" attitude' with regard to law and changes therein. Olivecrona had insisted on the subordination of 'morality' to force and to particular legal systems, on the dominance of fear as a motive for obedience, and on the notion that the purpose of constitutions is to promote respect for, and obedience to, their legal systems; for Ross, on the contrary, "Fear and respect, the two motive components which are characteristic of the experience of the law, are RECIPROCALLY related to each other,"[20] Indeed, on the very next page, he goes even further by maintaining that force is never ultimately dominant: "In the final analysis all power has an ideological authoritative basis."[21]

On the other hand, Ross does not, either in his account of fundamental change or elsewhere, represent a return to Kelsen.[22] While

[20] *Ibid.*, p. 56. Emphasis mine.

[21] *Ibid.*, p. 57. In a footnote, he quotes with approval R. M. MacIver, *The Web of Government*: "In all constituted government authority of some sort lies back of force." Cattaneo (*op. cit.*, p. 78) is therefore justified in claiming that, for Ross, the supreme authority of a legal system is a meta- (Cattaneo calls it 'pre-') juridical political ideology. But Cattaneo may be assimilating Ross's treatment too closely to a Kelsenian hypothetico-deductive model of normative levels... Two pages later in his book (p. 59), somewhat characteristically, Ross reverts to Olivecrona's definition, stating that "the law consists of rules concerning the exercise of force".

[22] It should be noted at this point that another contemporary Scandinavian philosopher, the Norwegian Harald Ofstad, is the author of one of the most devastating attacks yet made on Kelsen, in "The descriptive definition of the concept 'legal norm' proposed by Hans Kelsen", *Theoria* 16 (1950), pp. 118-151 and 211-246. Ofstad finds Kelsen's intentions unclear and constructs several rival definitions on the basis of Kelsen's text. He concludes that Kelsen is an authoritarian and that his

acknowledging his tremendous debt to the latter, Ross explicitly rejects the possibility of talking about 'a norm in the descriptive sense',[23] the hypothesis of the *Grundnorm*, and the ideal of the methodological 'purity' (independence of all other disciplines) of legal science.[24] He calls Kelsen a 'formal idealist' for regarding legal thinking as being in terms of 'what ought to be' (*sollen*) and not of 'what is' (*sein*);[25] Ross wants his own legal philosophy to be a 'realistic' one. One crucial issue in Ross's disputes both with Kelsen and with Hart is the meaning of the word 'validity'. His critique of Kelsen here is fairly clear: he charges Kelsen with "making validity an internormative relation (deriving the validity of one norm from the validity of another)", instead of admitting that the concept of the validity of law must be considered in relation to 'the social reality'.[26] But Ross's own conception of 'validity' is far from clear; let us consider a few of his comments concerning it.

In his account of moral attitudes and their relevance to fundamental changes, Ross admits the possibility of some regimes' not being experienced as valid: his native Denmark under German occupation during World War II is an example. But 'valid' in this context, he claims, is a purely subjective category, not an 'objective' one of the sort that can be attached to a legal system and that can thus be dealt with by jurisprudence. He sees this subjective, emotionally-colored meaning of 'validity' as "the source of the metaphysical notion of 'validity' as a moral-spiritual quality ascribed to a 'legal order' in contrast to a 'regime of violence' ";[27] and any SUCH notion apparently merits the same disdain, from the point of view of a scientific treatment of law, as Ross accords to 'justice' in his emotivist analysis of the latter concept further on. Elsewhere, however, Ross has used the term 'validity' in a quite different sense, as one of the central concepts of his theory:

> The point from which we set out is the hypothesis that a system of norms is 'valid' if it is able to serve as a scheme of interpretation for a corresponding set of social actions in such a way that it becomes possible for us to com-

---

definition of 'legal norm' is an attitude-colored, persuasive one (p. 242). He also criticizes both Kelsen and Ross, the latter in his early writings, for being so limited by 'Aristotelian class-logic' as not to see that " *'general legal norm' (or 'law') is not a thing name, but a relational term designating certain objects (prescriptions) standing in certain relations to certain other objects (actual performance)*" (p. 244).

23 *On Law and Justice*, p. 10.

24 *Ibid.*, pp. 338-339.

25 *Ibid.*, p. 66.

26 *Ibid.*, p. 70.

27 *Ibid.*, p. 56.

prehend this set of actions as a coherent whole of meaning and motivation, and within certain limits to predict them.[28]

He then proceeds, in the discussion which follows, to omit the quotation-marks around 'valid' and 'validity'. The 'set of social actions' turns out, in Ross's view, to be mainly the actions of the courts, and thus the continuing validity of the law seems to depend (and here we note Ross's obvious concession to American legal realism) on predictions as to what the judges will do: "The concept of the validity of the law rests, according to the explanation offered in this section, on hypotheses concerning the spiritual life of the judge." [29] But the spiritual life of the judge is itself dependent on something internal, 'a normative ideology of a known content', and not simply on 'external' custom and habit; it is on the grounds of an alleged failure to see this that Ross criticizes the 'behaviourism' of Justice Holmes' form of realism.[30]

Setting aside the question as to whether Ross's brief critique does justice to the theories of Holmes, we note that there seems to be a great deal of confusion in Ross's various treatments of the concept of legal 'validity'. We may attempt to treat 'validity' in complete abstraction from 'social reality'. But of what 'social reality' are we to speak? In the formal definition given just above, it is obviously the life of the courts and judges that is referred to, and that determines Ross's concept of validity. In his treatment of the growth of 'revolutionary consciousness', which is the necessary first step towards at least certain kinds of fundamental changes in 'valid legal systems', however, Ross is clearly speaking about the consciousness of the general citizenry, of all those subject to given legal systems. So perhaps, after all, Ross's concept of validity will have to rest on a broader base than just 'hypotheses concerning the spiritual life of the judge'. But in this same section on revolutionary consciousness, Ross speaks of a DIFFERENT concept of 'validity' (in quotation-marks), the emotional, metaphysical sort, which cannot be dealt with by jurisprudence because it is subjective, has no objectivity. Quite a few critics, however, might want to characterize 'the spiritual life of the judge' as rather 'subjective-sounding', too; and they might want to point out further that even if the 'normative ideology of a known content', which sounds like something rather more 'objective', because known, and which Ross regards as the basis of the judges' spiritual lives, could in principle be known fully at a given time for a

[28] *Ibid.*, p. 34.
[29] *Ibid.*, p. 37.
[30] *Ibid.*, pp. 73-74.

given set of judges, this would still not guarantee that the said normative ideology might not change radically within a short space of time – as, indeed, Ross fully admits.

My point in this last criticism is not to argue that there IS some mysterious way of guaranteeing accuracy of prediction concerning what judges and other individuals are going to think, and how they are going to act, with respect to a given legal system, but simply that Ross's explanation of how we are to interpret the meaning of 'validity' that he accepts may show this meaning to be no less 'subjective' (though 'subjective' need not mean 'irrational') than the other meaning of 'validity' that he considers in his account of fundamental change and that he rejects. And in fact it does seem rather strange, *prima facie*, to say that intelligent people frequently use and confuse the same word, 'validity', with respect to the same class of objects, legal systems, in two senses that are in fact so radically different as apparently to bear almost no family resemblances to one another; yet this is in effect what Ross has said. But the final linguistic puzzle concerning Ross's use of 'validity' is yet to come: in his brief review of Hart's *Concept of Law*, Ross says (alluding to a few short footnote references to him by Hart) that Hart has misunderstood him. Ross now admits that he was misled by the Danish, in which 'validity' is synonymous with 'mere existence' when applied to a legal system, into thinking that usage was the same in English! Therefore, Ross charges Hart with confusion in thinking that his own legal theory differs very significantly from Ross's, once we substitute 'existent' for 'valid' in the latter and allow for a few minor disagreements.[31]

Hart does well to distinguish his own position from Ross's, despite the latter's announced adherence to 'logical analysis' as the only justifiable method of legal philosophy and jurisprudence.[32] Ross's analyses are often profound but not always, as I have shown in the discussion of 'validity', as clear or consistent as one would wish. In an article written prior to the publication of *The Concept of Law* and devoted to the Scandinavians, Hart criticizes Ross, *inter alia*, for the latter's emphasis on PREDICTION in his definition of a legal system, for his misplacing of the distinction, which Hart is going to develop in great detail, between the internal and external aspects of rules, and, of course, for his queer use or uses of the term 'legally valid'. I consider the first criticism important and correct, but there is not a sufficient reason for

[31] Ross, review, *Yale Law Journal* 71, 6 (May 1962), p. 1190.

[32] *On Law and Justice*, p. 25.

developing it at length here. As to the second, this relates partly to the problem of 'objectivity' and 'subjectivity' treated above. Hart thinks that the central use of 'legally valid' is an 'internal' one, exemplified by the judge or ordinary citizen who accepts a legal system as his own, and a given law as a part of that system;[33] for Ross, on the other hand, pronouncements of judges in accordance with a given set of legal rules, though not SUBJECTIVE questions about whether citizens regard their legal system as 'valid' in the moral-spiritual sense, can be treated with scientific OBJECTIVITY and are therefore regarded by him as being 'external' comments about 'valid' (in the acceptable sense) systems. Thus both Hart and Ross want to talk of 'externality' and 'internality' with respect to legal systems, but they want to draw the line between the two in different places. Hart's is the subtler distinction. It is perhaps significant that Ross, in his review, admits to a disagreement with Hart at least on this question of 'internalization', and that the gist of his objection is that Hart has transferred to his concept of a legal system in ordinary times a phenomenon, that of 'acceptance' or 'an attitude of allegiance', the occurrence of which Ross is only willing to allow in 'extraordinary situations', notably in times of fundamental changes in legal systems.[34]

[33] Hart, "Scandinavian Realism", *Cambridge Law Journal*, Nov. 1959, pp. 237-238 . . . Another Scandinavian, Anders Wedberg, has formalized the paradigm case of what Hart means by 'internal' statements about legal rules in his "Axiom of Naive Jurisprudence": If *P* is a legal rule and *S* a legal system, "For all *P* if *P* is in force in *S* at *t*, then *P*" – at least in the special case of a given historical epoch and country! ("Some Problems in the Logical Analysis of Legal Science", *Theoria* 17, 1951, p. 259.)

[34] Ross, review, p. 1189.

4

HART

I have examined some recent legal philosophies, particularly with respect to whatever their values may be in clarifying the concept of fundamental change in law, that have had an especially strong influence on H. L. A. Hart's thinking. We are now in a position to concentrate on Hart's own account, the clarifications that it may contribute, and the problems that it may raise. In the present chapter, I shall give a brief résumé of what seem to me to be the most important elements in Hart's 'crude survey of the pathology and embryology of legal systems'.[1] In *The Concept of Law*, it is crude and short, but it is also suggestive. Here, I shall be concerned neither with criticizing Hart nor even with elucidating very much what he has to say; these things will come later.

The first point to be noted is the apparently obvious one that a legal system and fundamental change in law are distinct concepts. We may recall, however, that it was not so obvious to Olivecrona, who saw revolution as 'only one step in the long development of the law'. Hart makes his point at the end of his lengthy criticism of the classical 'command' or 'sovereignty' model in legal and political theory. The last defense of this theory is to claim that it is the people as a whole who 'command'; what are we to say then, asks Hart, of a legal system whose constitution contains provisions that some part of it may not be amended?[2] Proponents of the command theory, he says, would have to argue in this case that the fact that the people have not revolted shows that they have 'tacitly' given themselves the command embodied in this

[1] *The Concept of Law*, p. 118.

[2] The United States legal system is an example. Article V of the Constitution provides for the methods of amendment and contains an implied 'extremal clause' to the effect that these are the only constitutional methods of amendment. It also mentions two matters not subject to amendment, of which the second is that "No state, without its consent, shall be deprived of its equal suffrage in the Senate".

provision, along with the others. "That this would make the distinction between revolution and legislation untenable is perhaps a sufficient reason for rejecting it", he concludes.[3]

One of the struggles in which Hart is principally engaged, and for which the analytic method that he employs is admirably suited, is the fight against the excessive simplicity characteristic of so much of legal philosophy, including the writings of all the command theorists such as Austin and Kelsen. A good remedy for this defect, according to Hart, is to think of legal systems in terms of their similarities to human beings: they are born, usually enjoy periods of great health, may be somewhat or very sick at times, may recover, and eventually die.[4] It is with this suggestion in mind that he entitles the section in which he deals with fundamental changes "The Pathology of a Legal System".[5]

The EXTERNAL statement of fact that a legal system exists at a given time and place is, under normal conditions, one which the observer can make with a great deal of confidence. But a legal system is usually, in point of fact, a very complex entity; the external observer (external, *qua* observer, whether or not he happens to be living in the country in question) is most likely to be made aware of this complexity at those extraordinary times when a legal system begins to break down, to undergo fundamental change, and the observer is unable to say with confidence whether a given system exists, is dying, or has ceased to exist entirely. One principal means advocated by Hart for understanding the complexity of an advanced legal system is in terms of the distinction, to which we shall return later, between 'primary rules' of obligation and 'secondary rules' of recognition, change, and adjudication. In primitive societies, which may lack secondary rules, a conscious (though probably not highly reflective) 'acceptance' of the legal (or, more correctly, 'pre-legal') system by the greater part of the group which observes the rules is requisite to prevent breakdown and fundamental change. In a more advanced society, however, a legal system may continue to be said to exist if only the OFFICIALS truly 'accept' the rules and the rest of the citizenry simply observes them in a passive manner; a system of this sort might be utterly deplorable, it would probably be a most 'unhealthy' one, but it would still be an existing legal system.

Of the various kinds of breakdowns possible in legal systems, revolution is only one. Other outstanding examples are belligerent occupation

[3] *The Concept of Law*, p. 76.
[4] *Ibid.*, p. 109.
[5] *Ibid.*, pp. 114-120.

of a territory by an enemy from without, "and the simple breakdown of ordered legal control in the face of anarchy or banditry without political pretensions to govern".[6] (Here it should be recalled that Ross had judged it impossible, from the point of view of legal philosophy, to distinguish between a 'legal order' and a 'regime of violence', since judgments about this would always have to be predicated on Ross's unacceptable 'subjective' meaning of 'validity'.) In fact there may be 'revolutions', says Hart, in which only the identity of the officials, not that of the constitution or legal system, changes.[7] In any case, given the complexity of what we mean by 'law' and 'legal system', there may also be 'half-way stages' of partial breakdown. During civil wars, for example, rival systems may be effective in adjacent parts of the same country. Governments-in-exile may claim to be the legitimate governments in territories that are in fact, from the external observer's point of view, under a different legal system entirely.

These factual examples, and others that Hart gives, may appear completely obvious when enunciated; nevertheless, their philosophical relevance is very great. For they illustrate Adolf Merkl's point that elegantly simple theories cannot always eliminate stubborn, empirical facts, and they show why, in legal philosophy, such basic concepts as 'legal system', 'rule', 'validity', and 'revolution' should not be drastically distorted to fit the requirements of a particular model used in a particular philosophical system.

The range of possibilities contained in the concept 'fundamental change in law' is wider still when we go beyond the cases of breakdown and consider the more 'positive' aspect of this concept. A government-in-exile may later return and may declare, by means of 'retrospective laws', that its own legal system "is deemed" to have been in effect during the period of exile; from a moral viewpoint, this will often seem

[6] *Ibid.*, p. 115.

[7] I think that there is a slight confusion in Hart here, due to his failure to consider the differences in meaning between 'revolution' and '*coup d'état*'. Cattaneo (*op. cit.*), to whose book Hart refers in his footnote on this section of *The Concept of Law*, does discuss these differences, which he decides are largely emotive. He asks (p. 70) whether, if a *coup d'état* is illegal, it is not therefore a revolution. However, to leave the matter at that would be the death of linguistic analysis, because any ordinary criminal act is illegal, and yet we would not usually want to call it revolutionary.

For an interesting discussion of the differences between revolutions and *coups d'état*, including a criticism of Kelsen similar to my present criticism of Hart, cf. David C. Rapoport, "*Coup d'état*: The View of the Men Firing Pistols", in Carl J. Friedrich, ed., *Revolution* (*Nomos* VIII) (New York, Atherton Press, 1966), pp. 53-74.

to be a highly dubious procedure, but its logic must be regarded as impeccable once we note along with Hart the difference in logical status between external statements of empirical fact about the existence of a legal system, and statements internal to a legal system itself. Again, a colony may break away from its mother country (and here we may observe the evidence from ordinary language in favor of Hart's metaphor of 'pathology and embryology') and become independent, thereby developing an independent legal system. This suggests a set of problems of particular interest to an Englishman in jurisprudence: for instance, what could be said if the British Parliament were to revoke the Statute of Westminster, whereby certain parts of the Commonwealth were given Dominion status? The factual results would of course be chaotic, but it is both logically and legally (in terms of British law) possible for Parliament to do so. Lastly, in his treatment of fundamental change in law, Hart takes up the possibility of differences of interpretation, even concerning 'the ultimate rule of recognition' of a system itself, among the officials of the system.[8] What would happen next in such a situation cannot, of course, be decided *a priori*, but any philosophy that purports to deal with modern legal systems must take account of such potentialities for fundamental as well as non-fundamental changes of the most varying kinds that are inherent in the complexities of law and that are at least partly explicable in terms of the phenomenon which Hart goes on to treat in the following section of his book: law's 'open texture'.

The preceding résumé has deliberately been made quite brief, but I believe that it conveys the essential points as well as something of the flavor of that small section of *The Concept of Law* where Hart is most directly concerned with analyzing what I have called 'the concept of fundamental change in law'. It contains, moreover, all the elements that I wish to subject to further analysis and discussion in the remainder of the first section of this book. They are: the analytic methodology that Hart espouses, his use of analogies and models as a further aspect of his method, the notion of law as a system of rules (including Hart's more specific notions of primary and secondary rules and the rule of recognition), his concept of 'acceptance' of law (involving the related problems of obligation and morality), and finally his obviously un- Kelsenian view of law as a sociological phenomenon.

[8] Hart mentions an example of this, the case of *Harris v. Dönges* in South Africa. The courts invalidated some measures passed by the legislature, whereupon the legislature created a special appellate 'court' which overrode the ordinary courts. But the latter invalidated the creation of the special 'court'. This situation of legal anarchy (in one area of the system) was resolved when the legislature retreated.

5

ANALYSIS

Hart's preferred method of philosophizing is that of linguistic analysis, as was noted in Chapter One of this section. His book is about *the concept* of 'law', that is, about the various subtle shadings of meaning that the word 'law', as it is used in our language, connotes, and that even a very elaborate dictionary definition would fail to contain. But Hart does not and could not confine his philosophy MERELY to language (whatever that would mean), of course,[1] for words refer to 'things', and therefore, as he says on the first page of his preface, "the suggestion that inquiries into the meanings of words merely throw light on words is false".[2] In saying this, we have begun to analyze the concept of 'analysis', insofar as this refers to Hart's philosophical methodology.

The analytic method, then, begins by inquiring into the meanings of words, though it does not end there. It is, at least at its inception, an exercise in definition. But it turns out to be a fact about language that the definitions of interesting concepts are not easy to give. The classical model of definition, that *per genus et differentiam*, may work for simple concepts, but it will not work for the more profound ones, as Hart points out in his inaugural lecture[3] and again in *The Concept of Law*. One can readily see why this should be so, if one considers the phenomenon of language: it is the 'interesting' and 'profound' concepts which play, in any language, the most complex, variegated, and sometimes

[1] However, Peter Winch attributes such a language-world dichotomy, in terms of which philosophy could deal only with the former, to T. D. Weldon. (*The Idea of a Social Science and its Relation to Philosophy* (London, Routledge & Kegan Paul; New York, The Humanities Press, 1958), p. 13.) Weldon does leave himself open to this charge, when he begins by saying that many philosophical problems "arose not from anything mysterious or inexplicable in the world but from the eccentricities of the language". *The Vocabulary of Politics* (Baltimore, Penguin Books, 3rd ed., 1960), p. 9.

[2] *The Concept of Law*, p. vii.

[3] Hart, "Definition and Theory in Jurisprudence", *The Law Quarterly Review* 70, 277 (Jan. 1954), p. 46.

even mysterious-seeming roles. And yet most of us, to some extent, continue to be influenced by the *per-genus-et-differentiam* model of definition into thinking that such a definition, if it can be found, will assist more than it will mislead; Hart strews the first few pages of *The Concept of Law* with examples of such attempts at definition of 'law'. In the case of the concept of law, Hart suggests a further reason why the traditional form of definition will not suffice: there is no higher *genus* of which law is obviously a species. 'The general family of *rules of behaviour*' is the best candidate for this, but the obscurity of the concept of a rule is so great, as we shall have some occasion to see later, that it would be of no help in an initial definition of 'law'.[4]

Similar considerations may be used in approaching the compound concept of 'fundamental change'. 'Change' by itself is one of the most 'profound' and all-pervasive of concepts; of what *genus* are we to say that 'change' is a member – that of 'metaphysical primitives', perhaps? The adjective 'fundamental' introduces some principle of limitation, though surely not a decisive one: a 'fundamental change' is not an 'absolute change', and the latter is strictly inconceivable except as an ideal limit of thought. Yet 'fundamental change' seems comparatively clear-cut if it is compared with the omnibus term for which I have been substituting it, 'revolution'.

Prima facie, therefore, the analysis of complex concepts does not seem at all to resemble a mechanical procedure of finding and stating a simple definition. There often occur situations, in the process of analysis, where it is open to the analyst to take alternative paths: I have already noted one such example, near the beginning of my discussion of Kelsen, where Hart explained why he did not follow a certain old natural law procedure of refusing to regard 'bad laws' as being truly laws. Hart defended his 'reasoned choice' on PRAGMATIC grounds, in that he believed that his own analysis would better serve to advance the theoretical inquiry. He would doubtless give the same argument, among other reasons, for not accepting the solutions offered by Kelsen, Sander, and Laserson to their problem of fundamental change in law. The question now arises, on another level, as to why a philosopher may choose to adopt the analytic method itself. The answer here must obviously be similar: analysis is of practical value for the philosophic enterprise. Perhaps the best way of specifying the principal value of analysis as a method is to reconsider my reference, above, to the 'mys-

[4] *The Concept of Law*, pp. 14-15.

terious-seeming roles' that the philosophically interesting concepts sometimes play in language.

What I want to suggest is that the analytic method is like any other method of philosophy, inasmuch as it does not in fact, and should not in the light of an analysis of its own very concept, really "leave everything the way it was" or "state what everyone admits", as Wittgenstein's celebrated aphorisms would have it; and that what it does accomplish, if carried out well, is to get below (or beyond) the appearances of MYSTERY (or bewitchment, or puzzlement, or obscurity) that 'everyone' ordinarily accepts. I take as some support for my point a comment by the celebrated J. L. Austin, Hart's erstwhile close colleague, prematurely deceased, who is regarded by many as a leading advocate of the view that analytic philosophy "makes no contribution to knowledge", whatever THAT may mean: "Definition, I would add, EXPLANATORY definition, should stand high among our aims: it is not enough to show how clever we are by showing how obscure everything is." [5] Compare this with another Wittgensteinian aphorism: "We must do away with all *explanation*, and description alone must take its place." [6] At first glance, I submit, these two statements of purpose are contradictory; though the fact that it is later in the same passage that Wittgenstein gives his famous explanatory description of philosophy as 'a battle against the bewitchment of our intelligence by means of language' goes to show that, once again, Wittgenstein was deliberately speaking paradoxically in order to indicate the paradoxical nature of the philosophic enterprise.

Thus the analytic method (or METHODS, if another of Wittgenstein's aphorisms [7] is to be taken seriously) cannot be definitely distinguished from other philosophical methods by claiming that the latter have been purely prescriptive in intent, aiming at certain in fact unattainable goals, whereas the former is purely descriptive – or by an attempted dichotomy along any similar lines. Analysis, too, has its aims: high among them, as I have pointed out, is the elimination, or at least the reduction, of mystery. This is not a new aim in the history of philosophy, though a failure to think enough about the importance of language may have diverted many past philosophers from fully realizing its significance. The concluding sentences of Hart's inaugural address, though directly

[5] J. L. Austin, "A Plea for Excuses", The Presidential Address, *Proceedings of the Aristotelian Society*, NS 58 (1956/57), p. 15. Emphasis mine.

[6] Wittgenstein, *op. cit.*, #109, p. 47e.

[7] "There is not *a* philosophical method, though there are indeed methods, like different therapies." *Ibid.*, #133, p. 51e.

concerned with the philosophy of law, may serve as a final clarification of what we have just observed about the analytic method:[8]

But though the subject of legal definition has this history, it is only since the beneficial turn of philosophical attention towards language that the general features have emerged of that whole style of human thought and discourse which is concerned with rules and their application to conduct. I at least could not see how much of this was visible in the works of our predecessors until I was taught how to look by my contemporaries.[9]

But we are immediately confronted with a serious, new paradox, when we reflect further on the concepts of 'mystery' or 'bewitchment by language'. I deliberately hedged above in stating that one aim of analysis "is the elimination, or at least the reduction, of mystery". Elimination and reduction are not the same thing, and 'clarification', for example, is a different concept from either. Granted that the analytic method should aim at CLARIFYING, and thereby, if only BY MEANS OF this clarifying procedure, REDUCING mysteries that common sense ordinarily simply accepts, should analysis aim at altogether ELIMINATING the mysteries? This first statement of the problem may sound very vague, but, happily enough, we have an example of it right at hand, in Chapter Three of this section. Axel Hägerström was one of the greatest iconoclasts among the legal philosophers with whom we have dealt. He favored ELIMINATING all that was 'magical', as he put it, about even contemporary legal practice. This sounds like a thoroughly laudable purpose, to which every enlightened individual must subscribe. Why, then, does Hart voice such a cautionary note about this in his review of Hägerström's book? He does so because he feels that Hägerström has failed to see that many of the ritual practices which he wishes to eliminate are so intimately connected with given elements in the concept of law, that is, with the words (such as 'property') which are most central to the legal systems that Hägerström is examining, that the complete abolition of 'ritual' would render the legal systems themselves meaningless. Hart's demurrer to Hägerström's iconoclasm seems even less shocking or unenlightened when we reflect on the intimate relation between the two concepts of 'ritual' and 'rule', and on the close connection between the latter concept and 'law'.

But now, in making these last observations, I seem to have gotten

[8] Peter Winch (*op. cit.*, pp. 1-10) makes some rather similar points in his attack on what, borrowing a phrase from Locke, he calls 'the underlabourer conception of philosophy'.

[9] Hart, "Definition and Theory in Jurisprudence", p. 60.

myself into a position in which my earlier point, namely that philosophical analysis not only does not, but indeed SHOULD not, "leave everything the way it was", is put into question. For it seems that, if a philosopher like Hägerström tampers too much with things 'the way they are', some FUNDAMENTAL CHANGE may ensue, and it may be a disaster – a theoretical disaster in the form of meaninglessness, and a practical disaster if he or other individuals act on the basis of his recommendations. On the other hand, such a revolutionary breakthrough COULD be a highly desirable one. We cannot make an abstract generalization about the goodness or badness of ALL analytic demystifications, just as we cannot, without presupposing a rigid theoretical framework such as that of Kant's legal philosophy, pass a general judgment about the desirability or undesirability of all revolutions as such. At any rate, Herbert Marcuse's contention, cited at the beginning of this book, to the effect that analytic philosophy is intrinsically incapable of generating negative criticism of the existing socio-political order has not been substantiated. On the contrary, demystification seems to be one of the primary possible uses of linguistic analysis. But not ALL 'demystification', as we have seen, makes equally good sense, for the process may sometimes threaten the preservation of 'sense', or meaning, itself.

I wish, for the moment, to continue to focus on this problem in analytic method by raising some other considerations about it that analytic philosophers have brought to light. It has often been stressed that, in order to make sense, the analyst needs to insist on 'contexts'. As I noted in my preface to this section, a concept cannot be considered in complete isolation, since it summarizes – to recall Ryle's expression, which I quoted, and which itself has a rather well-known Wittgensteinian ancestry – 'general statements about families of propositions'. A. I. Melden makes a similar point in a discussion of 'promises', a point which also recalls Hart's observations about definition, when he says that instead of trying to give a DEFINITION of a 'promise' on the terms demanded, for example, by many intuitionists in ethics, we should look for the roles played by promises IN THEIR CONTEXTS.[10] This emphasis on contexts, 'ways of life', and 'systems', on the one hand, and 'roles', 'principles', and 'practices'[11] on the other, has become so much of a com-

[10] A. I. Melden, "On Promising", *Mind* 65, 257 (Jan. 1956), p. 56.

[11] I am thinking most specifically here, of course, of the ethical theories of Nowell-Smith, Hare, and Toulmin. But in fact Hart's theory about the 'internal aspect of rules', which we have seen used, in the preceding chapter, to demonstrate

monplace in contemporary analytic discussion that there is no need for me to dwell on it any further. But I do wish to point out its relevance to the fact that much of Hart's account of 'fundamental change in law' as reported in the preceding chapter would be quite unintelligible or at least completely unilluminating if considered in isolation, not only from what we know as ordinary men about laws and legal systems, but even from the special ways in which Hart has used certain terms – 'rules', 'rule of recognition', 'acceptance', 'internal and external aspects', etc. – in order to develop OTHER elements of his theory about law. Outside of its own context, in other words, the account could not be fully understood.

The distinction between our ordinary language about law and that which we find in Hart's theory is important, because it brings us to what, if anything, is the crux of our problem as to whether the analytic method can and should ELIMINATE, or only DESCRIBE, the 'bewitchments' created by language. Is Hart, to use as our main example the man on whom I have chosen to concentrate, an 'ordinary language philosopher' merely? And if he were, would that be a bad thing? As far as Hart's book is concerned, I have already begun to answer the first question in the negative. But there is a great (perhaps a 'systematic') ambiguity in the expression 'ordinary language', just as there is in the expression 'our language'. What language is meant? Surely not just the language of a certain circle of people in Oxford, nor just English as it is spoken in Great Britain (though an American might find Hart's use of a phrase like 'municipal legal system' somewhat unfamiliar), nor just English in all its varieties and dialects, either (though, to judge from Ross's unhappy experience in translating in the other direction, a Dane might be somewhat confused by what Hart has to say about 'validity'). L. J. Cohen, in criticizing Hart's use of the word 'power', tries another tack by noting that Hart has expressed his desire to elucidate professional lawyers' concepts,[12] which are definitely not those of the ordinary man, though they ARE the ordinary professional language of the ordinary lawyer. But Cohen has misrepresented Hart here: in the very next sentence on the page to which Cohen refers,[13] Hart goes on to say that his analysis should also elucidate certain concepts in political theory.

the non-contradiction between legal statements and statements of fact, and to which we shall be returning later, is of an analogous sort.

[12] Cohen, review of *The Concept of Law*, p. 399.

[13] *The Concept of Law*, p. 95.

And law and political theory are not the only two technical (non-ordinary) areas of language with which Hart is concerned. One of Cohen's own works begins with the premise that, in trying to define 'legal system', we must use NON-TECHNICAL language;[14] but his own principal conclusion, that we owe supreme allegiance to a world legal system, not to any national one,[15] is surely not non-technical in the sense that it would seem immediately plausible to the ordinary Englishman. The conclusion to which I am drawn by all this is that neither Hart nor Cohen (I am not concerned for the moment with others) is 'merely' a 'philosopher of ordinary language' in any sense not hopelessly ambiguous, that it would indeed be a bad thing if either of them were such a philosopher, and that, more importantly, given the interests and aims of each of them, it would be an IMPOSSIBLE thing. "The Pathology of a Legal System", for example, is simply not explicable in terms of strictly 'ordinary' language.

Cohen, in his review, makes a further important point against Hart in connection with the latter's strong claims about the value of his distinction between primary and secondary rules. He remarks:

> Indeed there may be room for doubt about how far Hart's philosophical ideal of elucidating legal concepts as they are is compatible with the discovery of any single principle as the key to the science of jurisprudence.[16]

Whether Hart can consistently make so strong a claim for his primary-secondary distinction is not the issue here, though I shall discuss it in Chapter Seven. The new issue that is raised, over and above the original one of whether analysis "leaves everything the way it was", is about the extent to which the analytic method, at least as Hart uses it, is SYSTEMATIC. It might be thought that on this question, if anywhere, a perfectly clear boundary could be drawn to distinguish the analytic method from at least many other traditional methods of philosophizing. Hart himself, in his article on the Scandinavians, encourages such hopes by saying that one of the things that English legal theory shares with Scandinavian thought "is a general disbelief in the capacity of philosophical

[14] Cohen, *The Principles of World Citizenship* (Oxford, Basil Blackwell, 1954), p. 5.

[15] *Ibid.*, p. 71. I do not intend to ridicule or contradict this conclusion, but only to show how, in attempting to alter existing reasoning patterns (as Cohen admits that it does), it parts company with the non-technical language of today (though perhaps not of the future).

[16] Cohen, review of *The Concept of Law*, p. 411.

systems to throw light either on what law is or ought to be".[17] Whatever Hart's method of philosophy was, then, it would NOT be systematic. I consider even this conclusion invalid, however, and indeed it would be surprising if it were valid, in the light of our earlier observation that what Hart says in his analysis of fundamental change is in a large measure dependent, for its quality of being illuminating, on some of the special terms (such as 'internal and external aspects' and 'rule of recognition' that he has developed to cope with problems throughout the rest of *The Concept of Law*.

Much of the difficulty, of course, concerns the question as to what the word 'systematic' means. The very first sentence of Cohen's review calls *The Concept of Law* a 'systematic treatment of problems',[18] but this may just be a very casual, conventional reviewer's use of the word. Certainly the impression left by a reading of Hart is far less one of formal structure in thought-content than is that left, let us say, by a reading of Kelsen. This could clearly be seen, too, in my résumé of Hart's account of fundamental change. But it would not be a misuse of language to say that Hart has actually constructed something of a philosophical system of his own, of which the systematically-employed distinction between primary and secondary rules is but one element, in order more illuminatingly to analyze the concepts of legal systems with which he is concerned. Once one has begun even to group concepts according to their family resemblances, one has begun to do something that is 'systematic' in philosophy. And Hart's systematizing has gone considerably further than this.[19]

But Hart's philosophy, insofar as it can be considered a system, is certainly a system with a great deal of free play in it. One way in which he guarantees this is by stressing Waismann's notion of 'open texture' in its application to the law. Legal rules, like concepts in a natural language, serve their purposes well enough most of the time. This contention entails no intuitionism or 'conceptualism'[20] in the sense of an

[17] Hart, "Scandinavian Realism", p. 233.

[18] Cohen, review of *The Concept of Law*, p. 395.

[19] There has been considerable discussion in recent German jurisprudence about the alleged inferiority of systematic thought, of which Kelsenism is a noteworthy example, to what is called the 'topical' way of analyzing legal concepts. For a short critique of the 'topics' approach along lines with which I am generally sympathetic, cf. U. Diederichsen, "Topisches und systematisches Denken in der Jurisprudenz", *Neue Juristische Wochenschrift* 19 (April 21, 1966), pp. 697 ff.

[20] Hart defends himself against the charge of 'conceptualism', though mainly as it would be levelled by realist critics in jurisprudence, on pp. 126-127 of *The Concept of Law*.

epistemological theory which claims that there exist natural 'meanings' capable of being perceived by 'the eye of the mind'. But legal rules and concepts are such as, not to be inherently vague, but to have '*possibility of vagueness*';[21] at times there occur BORDERLINE CASES, which are often the most interesting sort, in which we cannot be sure which rule or concept best applies. If we take 'law' as a concept, surely 'fundamental change in law' is a rather natural candidate for being, both from the point of view of legal theory, and in actual fact when such a change takes place, a borderline case.

One of Hart's main reasons for introducing his discussion of open texture, of borderline cases, and of the 'core' of certain meaning contained in most concepts is to combat scepticism. He is most concerned with 'rule-scepticism' of the type represented by extreme positions in American legal realism, but his arguments could be directed against scepticism concerning the possible achievements of philosophical analysis, as well. It is true that borderline cases are baffling, but it is not true that analytic philosophy can say nothing about them: Hart's very treating of fundamental change in law shows this. Is it not precisely the borderline cases, though, that best illustrate the mysteries, the bewitchments, into which language can lead us? John Wisdom, another noted analytic philosopher to whom Hart refers, brings us back to the first point made in this chapter by insisting that "the line between a question of fact and a question as to the application of a name is not so simple...", and he goes on to draw the conclusion from this that a consideration of the baffling cases will cause different persons to see different patterns in the same phenomena.[22] To discover an 'unconventional' pattern, however, as the analytic philosopher is apparently encouraged by Wisdom to do, is in one sense "to leave things the way they were", because the philosopher has observed what can in some basic way be called the same phenomena as have other people, and yet it is in another sense to 'change things', too, because in discovering the new pattern he may well have reduced (though, logically, he might even have increased) the appearance of mystery about these phenomena. There is nothing about the concept of analysis as a methodology that would make it logically impossible for an analytic philosopher to discover some radically new pattern capable of effecting even a FUNDA-

[21] Friedrich Waismann, "Verifiability", in A. Flew, ed., *Essays on Logic and Language* (New York, Philosophical Library, 1951), p. 120.
[22] John Wisdom, *Philosophy and Psycho-Analysis* (New York, Philosophical Library, 1953), pp. 152-153 (from "Gods").

MENTAL CHANGE in our ways of seeing things! Nevertheless, one might advance some very good reasons against his doing so in particular cases.

The main problem of this chapter, that concerning the nature and function of analysis as a philosophical method, especially as Hart uses it, thus remains in a partly unresolved state. Not all the mysteries about it, that is, have been eliminated, but perhaps some have been reduced. The claim has been made that analysis is merely descriptive, and yet we have seen that it cannot be MERELY so; the claim has been made that analysis can confine itself to ordinary language, and yet we have seen that it cannot profitably do so; and the claim has been made that analysis is radically non-systematic, and yet we have seen that this is exaggerated. And yet – though this is probably a paradox of the sort in which Wittgenstein would have delighted – there is something distinctive about analysis as a philosophical method, so that Hart, for example, can be identified as an analytic philosopher by something more than the fact that he teaches at Oxford. Hart's own antisceptic metaphor about a 'hard core of meaning' may be helpful here: the concept of analysis, as a philosophical methodology, has some hard core of meaning.

But a metaphor is 'only' an analogy, and often not a very scientific one. One of the greatest sceptics in the analytic movement, Margaret Macdonald, has maintained that "Philosophic remarks resemble poetic imagery rather than scientific analogy." [23] This may be a serious charge, especially since the use of analogy is so pervasive in Hart's writing. We must examine this technique in a new chapter.

[23] M. Macdonald, "The Language of Political Theory" in Flew, ed., *op. cit.*, p. 176.

6

ANALOGY

In his note on analogy and allied figures in *The Concept of Law*,[1] Hart refers to Aristotle and John Austin on the subject of analogies proper, to Aristotle for examples of 'paronyms' ('different relationships to a central case'), and to Wittgenstein for the notion of 'family resemblances'. He does not himself attempt to define 'analogy', though he gives as an example the ascription of 'foot' to both a man and a mountain.[2] However, the noun 'analogy' and the adjective 'analogous' are generally used by Hart in a quite loose sense, one often only analogous to the central one suggested by the example.

It would be contrary to the spirit of Hart, who has waged such an effective campaign against using classical models of definition in defining complex terms, to try to formulate a concise and rigorous definition of 'analogy' against which to measure the interesting analogies, pertinent to the concept of fundamental change in law, which he offers. If the concepts 'law' or 'game' can suggest whole families of related propositions, then surely so can the concept 'analogy'. Analogies of proportionality, paronyms, models, helpful though paradoxical metaphors, resemblances and similarities of all sorts short of outright identity – all these, while surely differing in connotations from one another, are sufficiently closely related so as to be locatable in adjacent areas on any atlas of logical geography. That is why Margaret Macdonald's remark, as cited at the end of the preceding chapter, cannot be taken as a devastating one for philosophy at least until a very careful survey, of the sort in which J. L. Austin was interested, has been made of the entire terrain. It is with these considerations in mind that I have entitled the present chapter simply 'Analogy'.

Such a survey as the one just mentioned cannot be a task of this present study. However, it will be well to introduce the discussion of

[1] *The Concept of Law*, p. 234.
[2] *Ibid.*, p. 15.

analogies in connection with the concept of fundamental change in law by noting a few points made by John Austin and Aristotle, Hart's two authorities on the subject. Austin begins his treatment by saying that "every metaphor springs from an analogy; and every analogical extension given to a term is a metaphor or figure of speech". The suggestion here is that analogy, strictly speaking, is some quality inherent 'in things', whereas metaphor has to do with speech. However, Austin goes on to say, the use of the terms 'analogy' and 'metaphor' is different in ordinary language ('in common parlance', to use Austin's language), where "Analogy is a species of resemblance",[3] and 'metaphor' is taken to be a fainter kind of analogy.[4] Austin's formal definition of analogy in this second sense is as follows:

> Two resembling subjects are said ... to be *analogous*, when *one* of them belongs to some class expressly or tacitly referred to, and the *other* does *not*: when one possesses all the properties common to the class and the other only some of them.[5]

To this may be compared Aristotle's view that "analogically identical things... are not only different for different things but also apply in different ways to them".[6]

Several conclusions may be drawn. One is that Austin's fairly rigid view of language, the world, and the relationship between them is incompatible with the flexibility allowed by Wisdom's dicta concerning the possibility of seeing quite different patterns in the same phenomena, or by Hart's observations on definition and family resemblances. Austin's concept of a 'class' appears especially inflexible in this excerpt: he seems to think that, in every class, there is a certain number of qualities that are common to all its *bona fide* members; by comparison, Aristotle's doctrine of analogy is very much closer to what Wittgenstein meant by family resemblances. Austin's clear-cut classification procedure leaves little to the imagination: he will conclude that (1) the laws of God, (2) positive human laws, and (3) positive morality constitute laws properly so called, that opinions or sentiments with regard to conduct are laws by analogy,[7] and that natural ('scientific') laws are called laws only by a loose use of metaphor. What if someone were to chal-

[3] John Austin, *The Province of Jurisprudence Determined Etc.*, introd. by H. L. A. Hart (London, Weidenfeld & Nicolson, 1954), p. 119.
[4] *Ibid.*, p. 121.
[5] *Ibid.*, p. 119.
[6] Aristotle, *Metaphysics* XII, 5 (1071a5-7), tr. by W. D. Ross, ed. by R. McKeon (New York, Random House, 1941).
[7] John Austin, *op. cit.*, p. 123.

lenge Austin on the grounds that either the laws of God, or the laws of positive morality, or both, were improperly called laws? What if, finally, a person wanted to challenge a legal system in a given country at a given time on the grounds that this system was so 'degenerate' (I am extending Hart's metaphor of 'pathology' here) that its laws hardly merited the name 'laws' any more? As long as he remained faithful to the notion of 'class' which he sets forth above, Austin would be hard pressed to meet a clever challenge with reasoned argument.

With Aristotle, on the other hand, we have an opposite problem. In the passage cited he is concerned with the analogical use of the principles of actuality and potentiality, and in other notable passages he discusses the importance of analogy with respect to the terms 'being' and 'good'. In fact, he makes extensive use of analogy in many areas, and his use of it sometimes seems fully as loose as a very broad interpretation of the quoted passage might suggest. For example, as I noted in the preface to this section. Aristotle draws an analogy between the self-sufficiency of the ideal city-state and that of the prime mover; he draws further analogies between the prime mover and the 'god-like ruler' who alone justifies monarchy as a form of government, and between the law of a harmonious and well-ordered commonwealth, which ought to be based on justice and equity, and the law of the gods, to whom the categories of justice and friendship cannot apply, which governs the universe. Although these problems in Aristotle's use of analogy cannot here be given the detailed treatment that they require, the point of my mentioning them is obvious enough: there are some fundamental, not merely superficial, discrepancies among the various analogies that Aristotle employs. This does not imply that any one of these analogies fails to be suggestive, but only that they cannot all be taken equally literally, and that there is a strong possibility that all of them, while helpful for advancing philosophical understanding, are potentially misleading. The same *caveat* may be extended, by analogy, to the analogies employed by Kelsen and Hart.

It is interesting to note that Kelsen has apparently been influenced by Aristotle's account of fundamental change, even though, in arriving at his solution to his problem of continuity in terms of international law, he repudiates Aristotle's view. According to the latter, a change in kind in the constitution, or fundamental law, entails a change in identity of the polis.[8] Kelsen makes reference to this doctrine and declares it an

[8] *Politics* III, 3 (1276b1-3), tr. by E. Barker (Oxford, At the Clarendon Press, 2nd ed., 1948).

'inevitable' one "if one tries, as Aristotle did, to comprehend the nature of the State without regard to international law".[9] Now, Aristotle's conclusion may in some sense have been inevitable in terms of the rest of his political theory, but it would be anachronistic and misleading to place the main responsibility for it on his failure to understand international law. Indeed, the influence of ANALOGIES on Aristotle's thought is excellently illustrated in the section of the *Politics* referred to. In his deliberations, Aristotle sees as his main alternative the view that "the state retains its identity as long as the stock of its inhabitants continues to be the same".[10] This, he says, would be to apply to the state the analogy of the stream, which is said to remain the same despite the constant flow of water. When Aristotle rejects this and arrives at the opposite conclusion in the next paragraph, he immediately draws an analogy between the change in nature of a state, due to a fundamental change in its constitution, and the change in a chorus, the members of which remain the same, but which appears at one time as comic and at another as tragic. He then goes on to apply to this example his more fundamental analogy of a compound, a whole made up of parts, which can be said to differ according to the 'scheme' of its composition. As if for good measure, he further illustrates his point by means of an analogy with two harmonies, made up of the same notes, but composed in different modes, the Dorian and the Phrygian.

In all this abundance of analogies that Aristotle supplies, it is that of the compound that is most significant: the organic theory of the state, which dominates his political philosophy, is strongly dependent on the view that a state is a whole made up of parts, its citizens. The idea of the self-sufficiency of the whole is a further basic analogy for Aristotle. For Kelsen, on the contrary, even if we omit from consideration his mature views on international law, the dominant analogy is very different. Kelsen identifies the state with its legal system, and by this he means a set of *Rechtssätze*, which have as their source his hypothetical *Grundnorm*. For Kelsen, as we have seen, the constitution taken in its 'material sense' seems to mean little more than the postulate "that one ought to behave as the individual, or the individuals, who laid down the first constitution [in the more 'ordinary' sense] have ordained"; whereas for Aristotle, as Barker clearly indicates, the word usually translated as 'constitution' (πολιτεία) means "a way of life, or a system of social

[9] Kelsen, *General Theory of Law and State*, p. 369.
[10] *Politics* III, 3 (1276a36).

ethics, as well as a way of assigning political offices"[11] – a definition that would be anathema to the proponents of the 'pure theory' of law. Kelsen's theory, it will be recalled, concerns only norms, never 'patterns of actual behavior' or any sort of ethics.

In the chapter on Kelsen, I have already discussed at some length the extent to which what I have called his hypothetico-deductive model of a legal system colors his entire theory. All the norms are traceable back, across various levels of generality, to the one basic norm, which is said to be the 'source of validity' of the rest. Sander waxes even more eloquent than Kelsen himself in explaining this model, and in defending it against charges of being unable to cope with facts of law 'in the real world':

> Every level of the legal system signifies only abstract possibility – 'hypothesis' – in relation to the lower-order level. . . . Every form of legal ordinance is an a posteriori (matter of fact) over against the forms of legal ordinance of higher levels, an a priori (legal ordinance) over against the forms of legal ordinance of lower levels. Legal ordinance and matter of fact are identical concepts.[12]

That there are serious criticisms to be made of at least Kelsen's formulation of this model even from the perspective of the formal logician is abundantly proved by Ofstad's and Wedberg's articles.[13] I can summarize the other criticism of it that I have previously suggested by saying that Kelsen, as a result of certain methodological commitments and prejudices, has given a very incomplete and one-sided view of the law and of fundamental change. He has permitted his model, or 'analogy' in the broad sense, to exert too great an influence over his thought. It would be much too simple merely to say that Kelsen's model is 'incorrect'. It is in some ways most suggestive, especially perhaps for those who use logical formalization as a means of making legal systems more intelligible; but it may also be highly misleading.

Hart's analogy of 'pathology' and 'embryology', used by him primarily in his account of fundamental change in law, is intended as a pedagogical device to combat the harmful effects of misleading and oversimplified models, notably the "command" theory of law that is to

[11] *Politics*, introd. by E. Barker, p. lxvi.

[12] Sander, *op. cit.*, pp. 148 and 150. Tr. mine.

[13] Wedberg, for instance, finds tremendous obscurity in Kelsen's contention that P, a legal rule, is somehow entailed by other rules and ultimately by the *Grundnorm*. He asks why we could not, for example, define a system as "P_1 & . . . P_n" and call this the basic norm (*op. cit.*, p. 256).

be found in various forms in Austin, Kelsen, and many others. The comparison of a legal system with a human being, who is born, suffers, and eventually dies, is made as a challenge to "take off the spectacles... and look at the facts".[14] Surely it would not be amiss briefly to note some of the implications and shortcomings of this analogy as an account of legal systems and fundamental changes therein – nor would it in any way constitute a 'refutation' of Hart's methods, for one cannot 'refute' pedagogical devices.

First, it may be remarked that Hart's analogy represents something of a return to Aristotle, by comparison with Kelsen, because a human being is a paradigm case of an organic compound, in Aristotle's sense. Then, too, human beings have personalities, and so Hart's legal systems will have distinctive characteristics; this image, likewise, is closer to Aristotle's view of a constitution, intimately related to a way of life, than it is to Kelsen's. On the other hand, to say that a legal system IS LIKE an organism is not to say that it IS an organism; Hart would be rightly horrified if anyone attempted to attribute the latter theory to him.

The discussion of 'embryology' in connection with new legal systems that are spawned from old, as in the case of former colonies which become independent, suggests a most intriguing question about fundamental change: is there any way in which new legal systems 'born' of revolution or belligerent occupation can be said ultimately to have been 'born' of other legal systems? In cases of belligerent occupation, an affirmative answer is certainly plausible, but in cases of revolutions (other than *coups d'état*) the analogy becomes much less clear. We might say that the IDEOLOGIES of revolutionary parties are never formulated *in vacuo*, but somehow grow out of conditions in older societies; but it would be more far-fetched, and certainly less helpful, to say this of revolutionary LEGAL SYSTEMS. No one disputes the fact that revolutionary governments usually utilize many of the minor provisions of the old law, but it is also a fact that it is certainly possible for the more fundamental laws to be abrogated; can the new fundamental laws really be said to be the offspring, albeit ungrateful offspring, of the old?

The analogy with human beings is most helpful in understanding Hart's distinction between the 'internal' and 'external' aspects of rules, but I am not sure exactly how it applies to that between primary and secondary rules. The fact that primitive societies lack the latter, though, might suggest that their development is similar to the (human) growth

[14] *The Concept of Law*, p. 109.

of consciousness and maturity; with adulthood, however, come more acute psychological tensions, and so Hart's example of an unhealthy system in which the 'officials' ACCEPT the rules, and the rest of the citizens merely OBEY, might be regarded as an extremely serious form of neurosis, doubtless psycho-somatic, whereas the case of South Africa, where two groups of officials were divided in their interpretations of the ultimate 'rule of recognition', seems a perfect specimen of split personality. The case of a government-in-exile, which later returns to its territory and may even 'deem' its legal system to have been effective all along, seems a particularly sticky one for the pathology and embryology analogy: would we want to say that such a legal system had been born again, and, if it deems itself to have been effective, that it is now claiming never to have been dead at all? Or would we rather want to say that it had simply 'been away' for a long time, or that it had been in a lengthy coma? And if the latter, will it not seem extremely difficult in some instances for the observer ever to determine whether the patient is really dead? [15]

But in carrying out these speculations we are indeed approaching the sort of 'poetic imagery' to which Margaret Macdonald sternly consigns all 'philosophic remarks'. I shall make one final observation, however, about Hart's use of the word 'pathology' in connection with fundamental change: the word often has certain negative emotional connotations which an individual in a particular case might want completely to discard, either as an external observer of a dying legal system about the demise of which he could exclaim, "Good riddance!" or even as a citizen subject to an 'unhealthy' system which he obeyed but could no longer accept. In other words, 'pathology', when applied to a legal system under attack by some revolutionary movement or other, need not signify 'tragedy', except from the strictly internal point of view; from the viewpoint of the legal philosopher, the 'pathology of a legal system' as a general concept may be called 'interesting' rather than mainly 'tragic', and of course there are occasions when fundamental changes in law may seem 'encouraging' to many. Hart would certainly not deny any of these points, but I make them in order to indicate one more way in which his analogy of a legal system to a human being, and his use of the term

[15] Hart's several allusions to the possibility that Russian exiles might still regard the Tsarist constitution as somehow 'valid', and his reference to the further possibility, in his account of 'the pathology', of the British Parliament's declaring "that the law of Tsarist Russia was still the law of Russian territory" (*The Concept of Law*, p. 116), suggest that he would agree to some extent about the uncertainty of death warrants.

'pathology' to designate the destructive aspects of fundamental changes in law, might mislead.[16] Analogies are particularly susceptible, as we have seen, to misleading interpretations and erroneous conclusions.

A number of other analogies can be found in Hart's writings. One of the most interesting is his 'mercantile analogy', the inadequacy of which he immediately admits, which is developed in an article in which Hart defends the category of legal responsibility as a means of safeguarding certain ethical values. According to the mercantile analogy, law may be regarded as "a *choosing* system, in which individuals can find out, in general terms at least, the costs they have to pay if they act in certain ways".[17] But since this has less immediate relevance to the analysis of fundamental change, where the choosing systems themselves are in question, I shall refrain from developing its implications any further here and instead turn to the legal analogy for which analytic philosophy is perhaps best known, that of games.

Hart, of course, is by no means the first to show the usefulness of our familiar notions about games, in all their varieties and with all their different kinds of rules, in understanding important points about languages, legal systems, and conventions of all sorts. Wittgenstein's influence is especially strong in this respect. Alf Ross, among the other legal philosophers with whom I have dealt, makes extensive use of the analogy between a legal system and a game of chess. Hart's use of the games analogy is even more extensive: it serves his purposes in opposing the 'command' theory, even in the case of Ross, in pointing out the wide variety of possible legal systems and the absurdity of trying to give a concise definition *per genus et differentiam* of 'law', and generally in stressing certain complexities that earlier theorists overlooked. One of the most brilliant uses of analogy in the entire *Concept of Law* is Hart's comparison of extreme formulations of American legal realism with an imaginary game which might justly be called 'scorer's discretion'.[18]

The analogy of a game is of some value, too, in understanding the

[16] Crane Brinton, in his sociological and historical account of revolutions, uses an analogy similar to Hart's and is sensitive to this particular problem. He says: "Though it has one very grave defect, the best conceptual scheme for our purposes would seem to be one borrowed from pathology. We shall regard revolutions – wholly, be it understood, for convenience, and with no implications of eternal and absolute validity, and with no moral overtones – as a kind of fever." *The Anatomy of Revolution* (New York, Vintage Books, 1958), p. 17.

[17] Hart, "Legal Responsibility and Excuses", in S. Hook, ed., *Determinism and Freedom in the Age of Modern Science* (New York, New York University Press, 1958), p. 96.

[18] *The Concept of Law*, pp. 138-141.

meaning of fundamental change in law. Just as it is logically conceivable that the rules of a game might be radically altered even while "a" game (or would it then be two successive games, with no time in between?) is going on, so "the society may cease to accept the rule".[19] One of the most total revolutions during the last two centuries in England, for example, took place in just this way, when the Rugby boy "picked up the ball and ran".[20]

But there seem to be severe limitations on the games analogy as applied to fundamental change, limitations which may help to account for Hart's adoption of the quite different metaphor of pathology to explain more fully this particular feature of the concept of law. One of these limitations, I would suggest, is due to historical circumstances, namely, to the unfortunate and indeed rather patently false use to which T. D. Weldon put this analogy in his widely-read *The Vocabulary of Politics*:

> To ask 'Why should I obey the laws of England?' is the same sort of pointless question as 'Why should I obey the laws of cricket?' It looks rather different because 'law' has had a number of different uses and has a lot of religious and semi-mystical ingredients.[21]

The first question is clearly NOT pointless, at least not under all circumstances; neither, in fact, is the second. Even the English public schoolboy is capable of asking himself why and whether he should take part in compulsory games, and of deciding that there is no sufficient reason and that he therefore should not – though he would be well advised to bear in mind the possible consequences of such a decision.

Weldon was right in one respect, however, if by 'religious and semi-mystical ingredients' he REALLY meant certain emotion-laden ethical questions. For it is in fact not as easy for any individual to opt out of a legal system as it is for most to decide not to play a particular game at a particular time. And indeed it is virtually impossible – this is simply an empirical fact about the world today – for anyone to decide not to be subject to any legal system whatever without running the risk of incurring the severest penalties, whereas it is perfectly possible not to be much of a gamesman (using 'games' in the ordinary sense).[22] Hart is correct in saying that "society may cease to accept a rule", but the

[19] *Ibid.*, p. 58.
[20] This celebrated event is used by Winch (*op. cit.*, p. 93) as an example of an unpredictable revolution.
[21] Weldon, *op. cit.*, pp. 61-62.
[22] A. P. d'Entrèves, in "The Case for Natural Law Re-Examined", I, *Natural Law Forum* 1 (1956), p. 13, makes the same point.

problem is that 'society' is a very vague term, and that in almost every potentially revolutionary situation 'society' itself is divided. Decisions, when the occasion for them arises, concerning whether one ought to accept a given legal system are intimately related, as I shall discuss in more detail later, to important questions about individual and social ethics. That is why, basically, the analogy between legal systems and games seems less apt when the concept of fundamental change in legal systems is being analyzed: legal systems are much more SERIOUS phenomena, particularly for the individuals who are parts of them, than are games.

The greatest single value of the analogy between law and games derives from the tremendous similarities between the uses of 'rules' in both. It would only be fair to Weldon's memory to close this chapter and to introduce the next by quoting from him again to show that he recognized this, though even the following statement must remain subject to possible later qualification:

> There are important differences between politics and games but the function of RULES in both of them is the same. There is no point in attempting to distinguish between the laws of England and the laws of croquet from this point of view.[23]

[23] Weldon, *op. cit.*, p. 67. Emphasis mine.

7

RULES

While it would be to correct to say that there is an interesting analogy (though, like all analogies, a not thoroughly satisfactory one) to be drawn between legal systems and games, it would seem odd to say that there is an ANALOGY between laws and rules. Laws (the laws of legal systems, that is) ARE kinds of rules (though law as such may consist of much more than SIMPLY rules).[1] It will be recalled that, in his discussion of definitions *per genus et differentiam*, Hart noted that 'rule' (of behavior) was the most plausible candidate for being the genus of which 'law' was a species; he rejected the attempt to define 'law' by this means, however, chiefly because of the complexity and obscurity of the concept of 'rule' itself.

At the outset, Hart points out that practically everyone will agree to the unexciting claim that legal systems are made up of rules of some sort or another:

> Both those who have found the key to the understanding of law in the notion of orders backed by threats, and those who have found it in its relation to morality or justice, alike speak of law as containing, if not consisting largely of, rules.[2]

He goes on to say that controversies of the most heated kind arise, however, as soon as attempts are made to specify what rules are, what the origin of legal rules is, etc. Among the varieties of rules besides legal rules that he mentions here are 'rules of etiquette and language, rules of games and clubs';[3] but he notes further that there are great varieties of kind even among legal rules themselves.

If we accept Hart's account, then, the analysis of 'the concept of

[1] For further discussion of this point, cf. Michel Villey, "Une définition du droit", *Archives de Philosophie du Droit* 4 (1959), pp. 47-65.

[2] *The Concept of Law*, p. 8.

[3] *Ibid.*

rule' could occupy an entire volume, of which 'the concept of law' might be one chapter. This is why it seems extraordinarily difficult to say anything significant about Hart's extremely pervasive employment of the concept of 'rules'; if we were to follow the example of one reviewer of *The Concept of Law*, for instance, by showing that the respective roles of 'rules' and of 'standards' are developed in different and not fully compatible ways in different parts of the book,[4] we could be met by a reply from Hart to the effect that such criticism is irrelevant. Hart uses the concept 'rule' to explain so many phenomena, that for him there would be nothing strange about the possibility that 'rule' and 'standard' sometimes have the same meaning, and that, when they differ, 'rules' sometimes create standards.[5] Nevertheless, we can at least ask ourselves, particularly in the light of the concept of fundamental change in law, what explanatory value the notion of 'rules' retains in view of the rather promiscuous use that Hart makes of it. This will be the first task of the present chapter, and then two more specific uses to which Hart puts 'rules' in his own account of fundamental change, namely his distinction between primary and secondary rules, and his so-called 'rule of recognition', will be investigated.

To repeat a familiar philosophical paradox, if rules explained everything unequivocally, then they would explain nothing. That is, if all the apparent varieties of rules could be reduced to one which governed all phenomena, then no clearer understanding of the phenomena would result. Is Hart in danger of finding himself in this dilemma? No, first because of his already-mentioned distinctions among different kinds of rules, which seem to resemble each other again rather as a 'family' than as a single type of entity, and secondly because he clearly admits that there are 'fields of experience' other than that of rules.[6] One such field of experience, with which Hart is especially anxious to contrast rules, is that of habits.

In insisting on the contrast between rules and habits, Hart is of course expressing his opposition to the Scandinavian view, especially that of Olivecrona, to the effect that laws are simply empirical facts. On the contrary, Hart wants to maintain, there are essential logical differences between rule-governed and merely habitual behavior.[7] It is in

[4] Morris, *op. cit.*, pp. 1452-1456. Sometimes, according to Morris, Hart identifies rules with standards, sometimes he indicates that there exists a clear distinction between them, and sometimes he sees rules as creative of standards.

[5] *Ibid.*, p. 1455.

[6] *The Concept of Law*, p. 123.

[7] *Ibid.*, pp. 54-55.

this connection that Hart first discusses the 'internal aspect of rules', a subject to which I shall return in the next chapter. Merely habitual behavior can be described in terms of causal antecedents and in terms of statistical generalizations; so can rule-governed behavior, but an account which stops at this point is not an adequate account of what it means to follow a rule. A parallel can be drawn between Hart's distinction and that made by Wittgenstein, in his discussion of the uses of rules, between "being causally determined and being logically determined".[8] It does not make sense to speak of merely habitual behavior in terms of the latter type of determination.

Witttgenstein's discussion also brings out the interesting facts, concerning rule-governed behavior, that the possibility of obeying a rule also implies the possibility of 'going against it', and that to ask for a JUSTIFICATION for one's continuing to follow a rule (i.e., for NOT going against it) is quite different from asking for a causal explanation of why one follows it. It is here that the concept of fundamental change sheds considerable light on the complexes of rules which constitute legal systems. True, as Hart points out, any sophisticated legal system will contain 'rules of change', to allow for the elimination of some individual rules and the addition of others while still leaving the system as a whole unchallenged.[9] But those who bring about a FUNDAMENTAL change in law are not following any such legal 'rules of change'; on the contrary, their decision is that the observance of the rules of a given system as a whole is no longer JUSTIFIED.

Does this mean that fundamental changes in law, involving the substitution (usually) of one system of legal rules for another, are not themselves rule-governed? If he were forced to such a conclusion, Hart could truly be said to have developed a *Katastrophentheorie* of the kind that Sander found so deplorable. But the fact that no rules OF LAW, not even (at least in any helpful sense) the rules of international law, govern changes of legal systems, does not imply, for Hart, that no rules at all are followed at such times. We are led to recall the point made at the beginning of this chapter, to the effect that the concept of 'rules' is a very broad one indeed for Hart, one which covers many varieties of human experience. Peter Winch, who like Hart draws considerable inspiration from Wittgenstein, makes a stronger statement than any that I have found in *The Concept of Law* concerning the omnibus nature of 'rules': "All behaviour which is meaningful (therefore all specifically

[8] Wittgenstein, *op. cit.*, #220, p. 85e.
[9] *The Concept of Law*, pp. 93-94.

human behaviour) is *ipso facto* rule-governed." [10] If this is true, then there must be some rules governing even fundamental changes in systems of legal rules; and the two (or more) kinds of rules involved must at least bear family resemblances to one another. The leading candidate for the non-legal type of rules that IS involved here, namely moral rules, will be the subject of the following chapter of this section.

The question as to whether the concept of 'rules' retains any explanatory value when used as widely as it is by Hart has thus been answered in the affirmative, and its use in the analysis of the concept of fundamental change in law has helped to establish this. But Winch's equation of rule-governed behavior with 'specifically human behaviour' serves to emphasize the fact that some way or ways must be found to differentiate legal rules from other members of the 'family' of rules, or else not only politics and croquet, as Weldon has suggested, but even etiquette, language, and morality (for Hart also speaks of 'moral rules') will all have to be regarded as being indistinguishable from the viewpoint of the function of rules in them; and this would seem to be a surrender of the claims of analysis to elucidate concepts. The next problem, then, is to discover what is distinctive about LEGAL rules.[11]

In a sense, of course, Hart's entire book is an attempt to meet this problem of analysis. In part, his method of going about answering it is a *via negativa*: legal rules are NOT necessarily the same as, for example, social rules, commands of a sovereign, moral rules, etc., for certain reasons that he elaborates. In part, as Cohen's remark cited in Chapter Five of this section indicates, 'Hart's philosophical ideal of elucidating legal concepts as they are' militates against his holding that any single characteristic definitively distinguishes legal rules from all other kinds of rules; indeed, the view that jurisprudence must have as its subject-matter something quite distinct from any other science is a methodo-

[10] Winch, *op. cit.*, p. 52. This allows Winch to regard as being rule-governed even the one kind of fundamental change mentioned by Hart in his account, in which no new legal system comes into being, namely 'the simple breakdown of ordered legal control in the face of anarchy . . .'. For Winch points out, on the next page (p. 53) of his book, that according to his view even the anarchist is rule-governed.

[11] One way of dealing with this problem is exemplified in Kurt Baier, *The Moral Point of View: A Rational Basis of Ethics* (Ithaca, Cornell University Press, 1958). Baier claims (p. 123) that there are six senses of the word 'rule' (regulations, mores, maxims and principles, canons, regularities, and rules of procedure). Law, morality, social custom, etc., can then be sub-classified under one of these labels. This may be a helpful approach at times, but it seems somewhat arbitrary and minimizes the difficulties of definition which the 'family resemblances' approach to rules is better able to meet.

logical prejudice that I have attributed to Kelsen and shown that analytic philosophy can avoid. But there is no logical reason why the analyst should be forced to choose between two mutually exclusive alternatives, represented by Kelsen and his 'pure normative science' of law on the one hand, and by Weldon and his surrender of all attempts to find something distinctive about legal rules on the other. The analyst might, in other words, find that the concept of 'legal rules' had some 'hard core' of certain meaning, surrounded by an area of doubtful meaning and of borderline cases of the sort that the occurrence of fundamental change especially raises.

Hart's own preferred candidate for the hard-core characteristic which best distinguishes legal rules from other kinds, however, is a rather surprising one; surprising, too, as Cohen's comment also indicates, is the unwonted assurance with which Hart singles it out. It is, of course, the combination of 'primary' and 'secondary' rules:

> ... we shall make the general claim that in the combination of these two types of rule there lies what Austin wrongly claimed to have found in the notion of coercive orders, namely, 'the key to the science of jurisprudence'.[12]

Primary rules, for Hart, are rules of imposed obligations; as such, they resemble more closely than do secondary rules the notion of laws as 'coercive orders' which Hart is combatting. Hart says that primitive societies, which may be called 'pre-legal' rather than, strictly speaking, legal, have rules only of the primary type.[13] Such pre-legal social orders suffer from at least three important deficiencies, namely UNCERTAINTY, a STATIC quality, and INEFFICIENCY, which it is the function of secondary rules to remedy. Secondary rules are "on a different level from primary rules, for they are all *about* such rules".[14] To remedy uncertainty, secondary 'rules of recognition', the first historical step towards which may be the writing down of legal codes, are introduced. The 'rules of change' mentioned earlier are of course a remedy for the inflexibility of primary rules; in addition to the rules of change connected with legislation, however, Hart also includes 'power-conferring rules', which make individuals capable of legislating in such legal areas as those of wills, marriage contracts, and property transfers, under this

[12] *The Concept of Law*, p. 79.

[13] He later says that "it is indeed arguable" that international law also consists merely of primary rules. This is one way of expressing the doubt as to whether international law should truly be called 'law'. *Ibid.*, p. 209.

[14] *Ibid.*, p. 92.

second category of secondary rule. Finally, inefficiency is lessened by introducing secondary 'rules of adjudication', good examples of which would be rules establishing and regulating a court system.

This summarizes Hart's distinctive combination of primary and secondary rules, in which he claims to have found 'the key to the science of jurisprudence'. The major part of Cohen's review in *Mind* consists of a lengthy and masterful critique of this particular doctrine in *The Concept of Law*. It would be unnecessary and pointless to go over this same ground in detail again; Cohen is correct, for example, when he challenges Hart's secondary 'power-conferring rules' on the grounds that certain of them, notably the power to contract marriages in some sort of formal way, are to be found even in very primitive societies, that it is not very illuminating to think of these rules as making petty legislators of individual citizens, and that Hart does not explain his use of the word 'power' here very satisfactorily; Cohen is also correct in showing that the 'rules of recognition' seem to be a very disparate sort of rule from the other two kinds of secondary rules mentioned by Hart. What I am more concerned with is, first, whether Hart's combination of primary and secondary rules really fulfills the role that was tentatively assigned to it, namely that of distinguishing legal rules from all other kinds of rules, and secondly, what its use in Hart's analysis of the concept of fundamental change may show.

One parenthetical admission by Hart in his discussion of the secondary rules of change is particularly damaging to the claim that the primary-secondary rule combination is a peculiar characteristic of LEGAL rules. "Of course", he says, "an elementary form of power-conferring rule also underlies the moral institution of a promise." [15] Now, morality is usually thought of as consisting primarily of rules of obligation – primary rules in Hart's sense. Here, Hart rightly points out that there is at least one kind of secondary, power-conferring rule that is involved in promise-making, which is not (always) a legal activity. Therefore, morality, like law, must also consist of a combination of primary and secondary rules; but moral rules were one of the kinds of rules from which legal rules were supposed to be distinguished, notably by the combination, peculiar to the latter, of primary and secondary rules! Furthermore, in developing his analogy between legal systems and games, Hart quite readily allows for "the addition to the game of secondary rules".[16] This helps him to make his point, indeed, against the

[15] *Ibid.*, p. 94.
[16] *Ibid.*, p. 138.

American legal realists, but does it leave much special significance to the entry under "Rules" in the index of his book which reads "law as combination of primary and secondary"? [17] For now, it seems, the same could be said of morality and of games, though NOT of primitive pre-legal social orders, and perhaps not of international law.

The brief use to which Hart puts his distinction between primary and secondary rules in introducing his analysis of fundamental change is revealing. He says, it will be recalled, that in primitive societies, which lack secondary rules, 'acceptance' of the system by most of the social group is an essential requisite for the avoidance of fundamental change. However, an 'unhealthy' modern society is conceivable, he adds, in which only the OFFICIALS truly accept the legal system, and the others merely obey. Now, how important is the conception of the modern legal system as a combination of primary and secondary rules for understanding what Hart says here? By 'officials' Hart can only mean members of the various branches of government, and then what more can he be implying than that modern legal systems are parts of modern states, with their various branches of government, whereas primitive societies lacked such machinery, and that consequently it is theoretically possible for a modern government to continue to function (unchanged) without the consent of the majority of the social group that it governs? If my conclusions concerning the shortcomings of Hart's characterization of the combination of primary and secondary rules as 'the key to the science of jurisprudence' are correct, I have found agreement both with Cohen and with A. P. d'Entrèves. Cohen argues that, if the highly questionable 'power-conferring' rules concerning marriage, contract, etc., are eliminated from Hart's list of secondary rules, then what we are left with are really rules concerning legislative, executive, and judicial functions.[18] D'Entrèves points out that what is distinctive about a legal order as compared with, for instance, the rules of a game or the laws of a church organization, is precisely the peculiar connection of the modern legal order with a unique institution, the State.[19] In his

[17] *Ibid.*, p. 262.

[18] Cohen, review, p. 410. Cohen says that Hart is then left with the 'unexciting' proposition that the most important element in passing from a pre-legal to a legal system is the development of legislative, executive, and judicial rules. This proposition would certainly be unoriginal, but it is not therefore 'unexciting' or uninteresting. Hart may unwittingly have demonstrated here the necessarily intimate connection between legal theory and political theory.

[19] d'Entrèves, *La dottrina dello stato* (Torino, G. Giappichelli, 1962), p. 185. d'Entrèves here vindicates the continuing importance of Hobbes's old concept of sovereignty against excessively pluralist views of legal orders. He does not thereby

determination to destroy Austin's model of 'coercive orders' as explanatory of the concept of law, Hart has perhaps been too completely captivated by his own new model; the combination of primary and secondary rules, at least in the form in which he has developed it, is inadequate by itself as the basis for an analysis of legal systems or of fundamental changes therein.

To conclude the present chapter on rules, some further mention is needed of the peculiar kind of secondary rule which Hart calls a 'rule of recognition'. This is, of course, Hart's substitute for Kelsen's basic norm, and the differences between the two are quite substantial. The very fact that Hart regards the rules of recognition as 'secondary rules', developed to overcome the uncertainty characteristic, according to him, of systems containing only primary rules, is proof of the extent of his departure from Kelsen's hypothetico-deductive model of legal systems. In the latter, the 'validity' of the subordinate rules of the legal system was said to be 'derived' from the postulated validity of the *Grundnorm*. Hart carefully distinguishes SUBORDINATION from DERIVATION,[20] and furthermore attempts to avoid the profound confusions that Kelsen's and even Ross's uses of 'validity' in this connection have caused.[21] Hart's rule (or rules) of recognition is an especially peculiar sort of legal rule for an advanced society to have, in that "in the day-to-day life of a legal system" it "is very seldom expressly formulated as a rule".[22] (This obser-

---

deny the meaningfulness of fundamental changes in sovereignties or the possibility of the supersession of the modern nation-state by a world order. His characterization of 'the relation of command and obedience' as one of the unique attributes of a state organization (p. 184), however, might fall under some of the criticisms that Hart levels particularly against the Austinian and Kelsenian versions of the command theory.

[20] *The Concept of Law*, p. 98. Rules of recognition may in some sense be subordinate, as we shall see below, and yet not the 'sources' of other rules. This echoes both Ago's devastating critique of Kelsen on this point in connection with international law, and Wedberg's critique from the viewpoint of formal logic.

[21] In a long footnote (*ibid.*, pp. 245-246), parts of which have already been referred to in this section, Hart lists four 'major respects' in which he differs from Kelsen on this matter; all may be focused around the question of validity. (1) The 'criteria of validity' of any given system are an empirical question for Hart; Kelsen's talk of empirical norms muddies this problem. (2) Kelsen must "presuppose the *validity*" of his basic norm; Hart is not forced to use such misleading language. (3) The content of this norm must in a sense always be the same for Kelsen, as we have already seen. (4) For Kelsen, but not for Hart, "it is logically impossible to regard a particular rule of law as valid and at the same time to accept, as morally binding, a moral rule forbidding the behaviour required by the legal rule." This last point demonstrates the concealed moral appeal in Kelsen's use of the word 'validity', despite his protestations to the contrary.

[22] *Ibid.*, p. 98.

vation is particularly appropriate as applied to England, where there is no written constitution.) Since Hart has previously said that the historical act of writing down a legal code for the first time is often the first, though not the crucial, step towards the development of secondary rules of recognition and the passage from pre-legal to legal society, and now we see that the explicit formulation of the rule of recognition may be a rare occurrence even in modern legal systems, we are led to wonder whether any organized society, however primitive, can really be said to lack any sort of rule of recognition, in the widest meaning of that term. At any rate, Hart returns to a similar problem in his last chapter, concerning international law, and it is here that he attacks Kelsen's claim to have found the basic norm of international law in the phrase "*pacta sunt servanda*". Hart expresses doubt as to whether, at the present time, international law can really be said to have any very definite rules of recognition. He points out that Kelsen's concern to find one such may stem from "the obstinate search for unity and system where these desirable elements are not in fact to be found".[23]

This suggests a most important point about rules in general and about rules of law in particular: I, following Hart's and others' general usage, have frequently spoken about 'legal systems'; this entails that groups of legal rules must somehow or other be 'systematic'. But 'groups', 'sets', 'structures', or 'systems' of legal rules need not be closed logical systems of the sort that Kelsen's model might have suggested. There are degrees of systematization, as was demonstrated by the discussion in Chapter Five of the sense in which Hart's own analytic philosophy of law could be called systematic. The analytic method can cope with this fact; in some other methods of philosophizing, it may be more difficult to do so. What Hart takes to be the element that renders modern municipal legal systems more systematic than international law, primitive societies, and many other varieties of rules is, precisely, the greater definiteness of the municipal systems' ULTIMATE rule or rules of recognition; this was part of the core of truth about Kelsen's doctrine of the *Grundnorm*, and in this, surely, regardless of other defects in his views about particular kinds of legal rules, Hart is correct.

But borderline cases of uncertainty are always possible even with the high degree of definiteness attached to present-day 'rules of recognition'. Hart's allusion, in his treatment of "The Pathology of a Legal System", to the case where officials might reach an impasse concerning the interpretation of their system's rules of recognition (as exemplified by the

[23] *Ibid.*, p. 230.

recent experience of South Africa), is very instructive in this regard. This MAY be, and sometimes is, the prelude to a fundamental change in law. For Hart has made it clear that, even in modern legal systems, which can theoretically dispense with more than a passive obedience on the part of the majority of the subjects of the laws, an ACCEPTANCE of the system, and notably of its rules of recognition, on the part at least of its OFFICIALS is absolutely essential for the continuance of that system. Kelsen's account of revolution centered around the nullification of the *Grundnorm*; Hart's account of fundamental change, purged as it is of many of the dubious elements of Kelsen's legal philosophy, centers around the non-acceptance of the ultimate rule of recognition of the old legal system. A closer examination of 'acceptance', therefore, should be the next step in the present analysis.

8

ACCEPTANCE

Ross's last mentioned criticism of Hart (in Chapter Three) was that the latter, in using "the word 'acceptance' or even 'voluntary acceptance' to depict the internalization of the rule", was misleadingly transferring to his analysis of everyday legal situations a phenomenon that might plausibly be said to occur often only in revolutionary situations, in times of fundamental change in law. Ross pointed out that the language of 'acceptance' suggests the concept "of a deliberate decision", of a choice.[1] I think that Ross is correct in what he has pointed out; the question now is whether it constitutes a criticism of Hart.

There are two issues involved here. One concerns the factual question of what attitudes individuals governed by legal rules have towards those rules both in normal times and in situations of fundamental change in law. The other has to do with the logic of rule-governed behavior in the case of legal rules. The two issues may be separated for purposes of analysis, but in fact, as they pertain to actual legal systems and living human beings, they are inextricably bound up with one another.

What is required for the external observer to be able to speak of a given legal system as the legal system of a particular country at a particular time? In a word – effectiveness, the fact that it is in effect, that it is GENERALLY obeyed (not UNIVERSALLY obeyed, for then we would be dealing with an erewhon without law-breakers), that it is IN FORCE. Some writers, such as Kelsen and many Continental positivists following him, have equated this quality of being in force with the word 'validity'; but either they intend thereby to express approval of those legal systems that are in force, in which case they have resorted to an ethical pronouncement and this judgment may now be examined on ethical grounds, or else they do not intend to express any such approval, in which case they have distorted the previous meaning and logic of the word 'validity' so that it is now left with no independent role in their

[1] Ross, review of *The Concept of Law*, p. 1189.

language.[2] Other writers, including many earlier theorists of natural law, would deny that the effectiveness of a given system is sufficient ground for denominating it a system of LAW; they take the 'true legal system' of a given country at a given time to be an ideal system of a certain content, and they then regard the extent to which the system actually in force conforms to that ideal as the criterion for judging whether the actual legal system is to be called truly a legal system. A parallel criticism may be made of such theorists: either they intend by this device to express approval or disapproval of those legal systems that are in force, in which case they have resorted to an ethical pronouncement and this judgment may now be examined on ethical grounds, or else they do not intend primarily to express such an ethical judgment (i.e., they claim that their position rests on an ontological fact,[3] rather than a deontological evaluation), in which case they have distorted the previous meaning and logic of the term 'legal system'. At any rate, the effectiveness of a given legal system is empirically ascertainable, though not always, as Hart's account of 'the pathology' of legal systems very commendably shows, with as much ease, precision, or certitude as might at first be thought. There are always law-breakers, there are usually some law-breakers who "get away with it", there are sometimes law-breakers who manage to take control of governments illegally (in *coups d'état*) but then continue to govern otherwise according to the established legal system, there are occasionally large groups of law-breakers who manage to prevent a given legal system from being effective either among a certain segment of a country's population or even in a certain part of a country's territory, etc., etc., on up to the case of a complete overthrow of a once-effective legal system, either by violence or by mutual consent or by a combination of both.

These are the kinds of consideration appropriate to what Hart calls the 'external aspect' of legal rules; do they, taken by themselves, furnish adequate conceptual tools for understanding the general way in which legal systems function? Kelsen is sure that they do; as he says, "Normative jurisprudence describes law from an external point of view although its statements are ought-statements."[4] Olivecrona believes that they do, if supplemented by a psychology based on fear as the motive

[2] Cattaneo freely admits this last result, as I noted in Chapter Two.

[3] Such a view, which maintains that the ideal legal system for a given place and time really exists in some non-empirical realm, and that only this system merits the name 'legal system', is in effect another variety of positivism, "Gesetz ist Gesetz" – a positivism of natural law!

[4] *General Theory of Law and State*, p. 164.

for obedience to legal rules. Ross believes, first, that Olivecrona has placed too much stress on individual psychology instead of emphasizing the inter-subjective, or societal, character of the habit of obedience to legal rules; furthermore, Ross admits 'respect' as another motive, equally as important as fear; but he shies away (except in his account of the growth of 'revolutionary consciousness' and fundamental change) from discussion of what he calls 'subjective categories', which for him are non-external, in understanding law because he feels that such categories are immune to 'scientific' treatment. Hart maintains, on the contrary, that the functioning of legal systems is ultimately unintelligible if their 'internal aspect' is not admitted along with the external, and that the explanation of this new aspect is logically dependent neither on a behavioristic view of habitual obedience nor on non-scientific guessing about purely subjective and in principle unobservable preferences. A given legal system has a special contextual logic of its own, according to Hart, a logic which is not the same as that of the external, empirical facts about it; if this were not so, legal peculiarities of the sort exemplified by the returned government-in-exile which 'deems' its legal system to have been effective during the period of exile would be simply factual errors of the most elementary kind.

It is under the rubric of this second, internal aspect of legal rules, which concerns the logic of behavior in accordance with a legal system, that Hart introduces the term 'acceptance' to designate that attitude which, in its paradigmatic form, is expressed in Wedberg's 'Axiom of Naive Jurisprudence'. Thus far, his distinction between the two aspects of rules, which I have recounted and elaborated upon, seems both important and extremely well-founded. But now, mainly because the two aspects are so inextricably connected, there arise difficulties in analysis of which Hart does not always successfully steer clear. For 'acceptance' usually means something more than a necessary presupposition for the logical analysis of rules; the more basic reference of the word is to human psychology, both individual and intersubjective. Here, 'acceptance' may designate either (a) a long-term, perhaps life-long, perhaps highly unreflected, dispositional attitude towards a legal system or (b) an act of choice (here, of a legal system as one meriting allegiance) occurring at a given time, though surely capable of being repeated at any other given time, or (c) any of the gamut of shorter-term dispositions or long-term series of acts of decision and choice that may be regarded as intermediate possibilities between the extremes of (a) and (b). But suppose now that we examine the phenomena of modern societies and the individuals of whom they are composed, with relation to their legal systems; can we make any *a priori* assumptions about the extent to which the 'acceptance' of the legal system in any particular such society will be, AS A GENERAL RULE, closer to (a) or to (b)?

We may note, once again, that this question is partly an empirical one and partly one concerning the logic of rule-governed behavior; it is the latter that the Scandinavian empiricists have for the most part neglected and that Hart has very rightly brought to the fore in his distinction between the internal and external aspects of rules. Hart himself has not always been clear as to which question he was dealing with. Olivecrona's picture of a modern society is (I say this at the risk of caricature and over-simplification) of a fear-dominated 'nation of sheep', psychologically conditioned to obey its legal system out of force of habit and without reflection. Even revolutions, times of fundamental change in law, do not seem to have much effect on the bulk of Olivecrona's populace: they simply "transfer their habits of obedience" to the new system, so that he can conclude that revolution is just 'one step in the long development of the law'. Hart is quite correctly repelled by such a picture, as his lengthy defense of the essential distinction between rule-governed behavior and habitual behavior shows; but there are several DIFFERENT grounds on which this view can be attacked. One ground, the only one which Olivecrona would recognize as valid, is, precisely, the empirical one: is Olivecrona's picture a true picture of the modern societies with which we are familiar? Presumably on the basis of his own experience and readings, Hart would tend to answer "No." So would I. But we must concede that there is some plausibility to Olivecrona's account as an empirical account if we reflect on the comparatively PASSIVE role that the ordinary citizen plays in modern legal systems. This highly contingent condition, however, obviously varies from one country to another; the degree of passivity towards the law among citizens of pre-World War II Sweden may well have been higher than that among citizens of present-day England. But a conclusion of this kind is likely to be accurate only if arrived at on the basis of very extended and complex empirical observations. A philosophy of law should not be dependent on such national differences for its validity.

In brief, then, to answer the question posed as to the nature of the 'acceptance' required for the functioning of legal systems in modern societies, it would seem that empirical generalizations about it may be made only with the greatest care, that in fact in most modern societies there is a more 'active' kind of acceptance (i.e., not SIMPLY an unreflective, long-term disposition) than Olivecrona is willing to allow, and yet that a society is CONCEIVABLE in which the bulk of the citizenry behaves more or less in accordance with his image of societies in general. This MAY be true even at times of fundamental change, as Olivecrona has suggested. In a 1958 article entitled "Legal and Moral Obligation", Hart wrote as if an 'active' (occurrent, episodic) 'recognition of an obligation to obey *the law*' were a quite ordinary practice among citizens of modern states, and a necessary practice for the coming into existence of a new legal system at a time of fundamental change.[5] Graham Hughes, in his article two years later, pointed out that Hart's language there seemed to presuppose a detailed knowledge of the legal system, and particularly of its ultimate rule(s) of recognition, that it was 'artificial' to assume among the generality of citizens of ANY country today. In connection with the specific concept of fundamental change, Hughes asked what legal positivism had to say about how the insurgent regime acquires 'the quality of validity' (or of being in force, to use our more neutral terminology); he answered as follows:

> The healthy positivist answer has been that the only empirical explanation that makes sense is the de facto acceptance by the bulk of the population of the new source of prescriptions as authoritative. But this explanation, though free of the charge of mystique, is unsatisfying, for it postulates a sophistication in the citizen which is implausible.[6]

In *The Concept of Law*, Hart modifies his position on this empirical question. He admits that, in the ordinary modern society (as distinguished from the primitive one, which supposedly lacked 'secondary rules' and in which, consequently, a rather active acceptance of the social order was required of all members in order to maintain stability), "the ordinary citizen manifests his acceptance largely by acquiescence in the results of... official operations".[7] Hart now acknowledges Hughes' criticism of his language in the 1958 article to have been justified;[8] even at times of fundamental change, it would seem, an ACTIVE attitude of acceptance toward either the old or the new system on the part of the majority of the population MAY NOT play a crucial role, though the attitude of the OFFICIALS, on the contrary, always

[5] Hart, "Legal and Moral Obligation", in Melden, ed., *Essays in Moral Philosophy* (Seattle, University of Washington Press, 1958), esp. p. 104.
[6] Graham Hughes, "The Existence of a Legal System", 35, *New York University Law Review* 5 (May 1960), pp. 1012-1013.
[7] *The Concept of Law*, p. 60.
[8] *Ibid.*, p. 248 (note).

makes an empirical difference at such times. A legal system about the acceptance of whose rules the OFFICIALS have begun to doubt, to disagree, or even to be simply passive is necessarily one which is in the process of going out of existence; a legal system about the acceptance of whose rules the same can be said of the ORDINARY CITIZENS is not necessarily in the same situation.

This is the extent of the concession that, as I see it, Hart can make to Olivecrona on the concept of 'acceptance' with respect to legal systems. Hughes' article was of value in recalling to Hart and to the rest of us that many people, even at times of crisis, do not engage either in a detailed examination of the intricacies of their legal system and especially of its rule(s) of recognition, or in a highly reflective and conscientious appraisal of the relative merits and demerits of that system with a view to deciding whether or not they shall continue to choose to accept it. But this concession is not very damaging to Hart. It does not rule out the strong possibility that many ordinary citizens even in modern societies sometimes DO make personal decisions of the short-term, episodic type concerning accepting – or rejecting – a part or the whole of their legal system; even on this strictly empirical question, anyone holding a position such as Olivecrona's must plainly take the defensive.[9] Nor does it at all rule out the relatively passive, long-term, dispositional variety of 'acceptance' that is a logically necessary presupposition for the continued behavior of human beings in accordance with rules rather than with mere animal habit. Once even this minimal kind of acceptance begins to be lacking among a segment of those previously subject to a given legal system, then that legal system may be said to have ceased to be operative in that segment of the population, and a fundamental change in law may be said to have begun.

The preceding analysis has been an attempt, based principally on Hart's distinction between the internal and external aspects of rules and on my own examination of possible meanings and uses of the word 'acceptance', to clarify confusions, surrounding Hart's use of the word, of the sort exemplified by the criticism by Ross to which we reverted at the beginning of this chapter. But surely neither Hart nor anyone else dedicated to the advancement of human aspirations by means of law could find much satisfaction in a legal system towards which the attitude of acceptance of the generality of its subjects was of the merely passive,

[9] This contention is strengthened if we recall Olivecrona's admission that the simple empirical test of introspection will not always IMMEDIATELY convince us that we obey laws solely out of fear.

dispositional kind which we have found to be the minimal requirement. Hart's analogy to a human being is particularly helpful here: such a system would not be HEALTHY. Hart, like many other people, has certain ideals concerning the values that legal systems should seek to preserve. The value in which he seems most interested, which is intimately connected with the more episodic, 'active' kind of acceptance that I have mentioned, is that of individual responsibility. He advocates fresh thinking about the concept of responsibility, and retention of it in law (despite some contemporary attempts to extend the use of 'strict liability', whereby wrongdoers are held guilty regardless of their prior knowledge or intentions), as a means of safeguarding the 'underlying assumptions or our whole morality'.[10] I would further point out, on the basis of the preceding analysis, that the retention of at least some MINIMAL concept of responsibility in any legal system is required to safeguard the 'underlying assumptions' of that whole system, i.e., to prevent fundamental change.

To have responsibility means to be able to choose, to accept or to reject; we may recall my earlier mention of Hart's suggestion that a legal system be thought of as a mercantile 'choosing system'. Now it is evident that Hart is not arguing for an extreme legal individualism of the sort that would require everyone to make a highly reflective personal decision before observing, or failing to observe, each individual law. For such a view would remove all independent meaning from Hart's key concept of 'legal obligation' (since a person could then never be said to have an obligation to observe a legal rule AS legal rule, but only as a moral law that he had prescribed to himself),[11] and would make even of MORAL obligation a far less societal phenomenon than Hart believes it to be.[12] Hart, speaking as a moralist, is concerned not to destroy the special status of law as creative of semi-autonomous obligations that he, speaking as an analyst of legal concepts, has been able to discern.

[10] Hart, *Punishment and the Elimination of Responsibility* (London, The Athlone Press, 1962), p. 30.

[11] "The recognition of an obligation to obey *the law* must as a minimum imply that there is at least some area of conduct regulated by law in which we are not free to judge the moral merits of particular laws and to make our obedience conditional on this judgment." Hart, "Legal and Moral Obligation", p. 104.

[12] The following amusing criticism of R. M. Hare illustrates Hart's societal orientation in ethics: "To characterize morality (as, e.g., R. M. Hare does in his illuminating book, *The Language of Morals*), as PRIMARILY a matter of the application to conduct of those ultimate principles which the individual accepts or to which he commits himself for the conduct of his life seems to me an excessively Protestant approach." *Ibid.*, p. 100.

(Of course, not all moralists would agree on the value of law as such: the antinomian implications of Sartre's Marxism, for example, will be one of the themes of the second half of this book.)[13] Nevertheless, it would seem that in his emphasis both on responsibility as a value that legal theory should seek to safeguard and on acceptance as the healthy attitude for the subjects of a legal system to maintain, Hart has strikingly reaffirmed the close connection between law and morality. I say 'the CLOSE connection', not 'the NECESSARY' one, for the latter formulation is what Hart finds objectionable about most theories of natural law.

It is in his treatment of those unusual, borderline cases which constitute the 'pathology' of legal systems, the times of fundamental change in law, that Hart, as I see it, best demonstrates the intimate connection between law and morality. It is at such times, much more than during the normal, healthy functioning of an effective legal system, that the concept of 'acceptance' in the sense of 'a deliberate decision', of reflective, personal choice, plays its most important role in determining the actual course of legal history. On this point Ross is correct, though he has misinterpreted its implications.

In looking to the concept of fundamental change as being most enlightening in connection with the ancient controversy about law and morality, however, I am taking a course in some ways quite opposite to that followed by Lon Fuller in his celebrated debate with Hart over the merits of natural law theory. Fuller, it may be remembered, entitled his reply "Positivism and Fidelity to Law". His argument was that Hart, as a positivist, shared with him the conviction that law was something deserving of loyalty, or fidelity,[14] and that therefore Hart admitted the existence of an 'inner morality of law itself'.[15] True, Fuller noted that the issue of fidelity to law became most important in times of crisis; but it was at such times, he said, that legal positivism was of little help.[16] Now there is obviously a great ambiguity about the word 'law' as Fuller

[13] For a slightly more detailed discussion of the implications of advocating (as Hart himself does NOT) the MAXIMUM exercise of responsibility at all times with respect to the choice of accepting or rejecting laws, cf. my "The Acceptance of a Legal System", *The Monist* 49, 3 (July 1965), pp. 388-389. On the idea of maximizing responsibility as a prime social value, treated from a different perspective from that of the philosophy of law, cf. my "Voluntary Association: The Basis of an Ideal Model, and the 'Democratic' Failure", in J. W. Chapman and J. R. Pennock, eds., *Voluntary Associations* (*Nomos* XI) (New York, Atherton Press, 1969), pp. 202-232.

[14] Fuller, *op. cit.*, p. 632.

[15] *Ibid.*, p. 660.

[16] *Ibid.*, p. 634.

uses it here. Everyone, not only Hart, shares Fuller's 'fidelity to law' if this means, as is sometimes suggested, the desire for laws to be enacted which promote or at least safeguard certain human values that cannot adequately be promoted or safeguarded by individual efforts alone. But if the emphasis on the virtue of fidelity to law, understood in this broad sense, is taken to imply that some 'inner morality of law itself' [17] requires individuals necessarily to transfer this general attitude of 'fidelity' to any particular legal system, then of course it is precisely the times of crisis, the times when there is a possibility of fundamental change in law, that show that 'fidelity to law' need not be a virtue or a desirable attitude at all. And Hart's 'positivist' analysis of legal systems and of their 'pathology' IS of considerable help in showing why this is so. It is in his insistence on the possibility of INfidelity to law, both in his controversy with Fuller (where both disputants concur in approving of actions taken by individuals in defiance of the Nazi regime in Germany, but disagree concerning the legality of these actions), and in his analysis of the concept of fundamental change, that Hart best shows the intimacy of the connection between law and morality.

Exactly how is this connection brought out by the possibility of fundamental change in law? It is brought out by the fact that individuals and social groups can put into question their supposed obligation, not just to a particular legal rule, but to a whole system of such rules. But it is only from the perspective of the obligations of MORALITY, which Hart chooses to regard as also consisting of rules, that a serious questioning of LEGAL obligation seems reasonable. This suggests a certain logical dependence, despite etymological and historical evidences for the legal origins of the word 'obligation', of the concept of legal obligation

[17] Fuller sometimes reduces his claim concerning the 'inner morality of law' to the fact that legal rules must always accord with some minimal standards of ORDER; he is willing to allow for the possibility of there being a dictatorship so arbitrary as to cease to meet these standards, and therefore to have no law. Hart's comment on this is similar to Fuller's criticism of positivism noted above: if that is all that Fuller's natural law theory can say, then it is of little help. "Indeed, one critic of positivism has seen in these aspects of control by rules, something amounting to a necessary connexion between law and morality, and suggested that they be called 'the inner morality of law.' Again, if this is what the necessary connexion of law and morality means, we may accept it. It is unfortunately compatible with very great iniquity." (*The Concept of Law*, p. 202.)

Fuller has expanded on his view, which bears some striking resemblances to the legal philosophy of Kant, in his more recent *The Morality of Law* (New Haven, Yale University Press, 1964). Here (p. 96), he labels his kind of approach a 'procedural version of natural law'.

on that of moral obligation; or as Benn and Peters express it, revolutionary questioning implies "that the question of obligation is ultimately a moral one".[18] This is seen to be the case just BECAUSE, in modern societies, law and morality are regarded as being distinct. In pre-legal societies, which lacked Hart's 'rules of recognition', the meaning of the word 'obligation' may well have been univocal. But Hart is right in holding that nowadays, theoretically speaking, a set of legal rules and a set of moral rules need not contain any similarities of content (though of course a legal system which entirely failed to conform to the moral attitudes of its subjects could not survive very long). There IS, therefore, a certain autonomy about the phenomenon of law, and it is this autonomy that it is Hart's primary concern to insist upon in his talk of 'positivism and the separation of law and morals'. While we saw, in the previous chapter, that he is not completely successful in showing the peculiarities of LEGAL rules as distinguished from all other kinds, he does make an interesting attempt at showing the peculiarities of MORAL rules (as distinguished "not only from legal rules but from other forms of social rule") by listing four of their 'cardinal related features'.[19] At any rate, the whole enterprise of analyzing 'the concept of law' may be taken, to the extent to which it is successful, as being some evidence for the autonomy of law as a phenomenon. But the autonomy, the distinctness, of law and of legal obligation turns out to be only a semi-autonomy particularly when we reflect on the concept of fundamental change in law, when we reflect on those occasions when one's legal rules and one's moral rules appear most different from one another and when, therefore, the former can best be challenged by reference to the latter. At

[18] S. I. Benn and R. S. Peters, *Social Principles and the Democratic State* (London, George Allen & Unwin Ltd., 1959), p. 318. This is an interesting reference because Hart cites this book with approval on several matters.

[19] These are: the IMPORTANCE of moral rules, their immunity from alteration by simple FIAT, the fact that a moral offense is ALWAYS voluntary (whereas, according to the notion of 'strict liability' in law, there may be non-voluntary legal offenses), and the typical form of moral pressure, which is usually not physical (*The Concept of Law*, pp. 169-176). A detailed criticism of these characteristics singled out by Hart would be beyond the scope of this chapter, though it is interesting to note the similarity of the first characteristic, the fact that moral rules are always thought of as being about IMPORTANT matters whereas legal rules need not always be, to the quality of SERIOUSNESS which Hart has elsewhere (p. 84) pointed to as being the primary distinguishing mark of all rules, moral, legal, or whatever, that "are thought of as giving rise to OBLIGATIONS". (Emphasis mine.) Once again, the concept of legal obligation seems logically to point back to that of moral obligation and to the distinctive features of moral rules.

such times, legal obligation may always be rejected in favor of moral obligation.[20]

It has not been my purpose here to become very deeply enmeshed in the long and acerbic debate over the question of 'natural law'. But it

[20] This raises the further question, more appropriate to an essay in moral than in legal philosophy, as to whether and how systems of moral rules can themselves be challenged and undergo fundamental change. This question is close enough to my subject here to warrant a brief survey of the answers given to it by three of Hart's outstanding contemporaries in the field of ethics. Stephen Toulmin places special stress on the grounding of morality in social custom and is therefore highly sceptical about the possibility of any very fundamental change from one system of moral rules to another. In a section entitled "The Limited Scope of Comparisons between Social Practices", he says: "In general, then, if one is to *reason* about social practices, the only occasions on which one can discuss the question which of two practices is the better are those on which they are genuine alternatives: when it would be practicable to change from one to the other *within one society* ... But, if this condition is not satisfied, there is, morally speaking, *no* reasoning about the question, and pretended arguments about the merits of rival systems – personal preferences apart – are of value only as rhetoric." (*An Examination of the Place of Reason in Ethics* (Cambridge, Cambridge University Press, 2nd ed., 1961), p. 153.) The sticking point here, as I see it, is the problem of what Toulmin means by 'within one society'. Surely there are many senses in which a SOCIETY as such may also be said to be capable of undergoing fundamental change, as the following section of this book will show. Therefore, it would seem that Toulmin's limitation on comparisons between practices is a bit precipitate. P. H. Nowell-Smith, in his *Ethics* (London, Penguin Books, 1st ed., 1954), emphasizes the logical necessity for those cases to be RARE in which individuals adopt rules that conflict with ACCEPTED, or customary, ones (p. 257); to this extent his line of thought is similar to Toulmin's. When, in discussing legal obligation, Nowell-Smith says that "disobeying the law of the land is thought to be morally wrong as such" (p. 210), he is indicating the close connection between law and morality, but at the expense of overlooking, for the moment, the situation that arises at times of questioning legal and moral systems. Later on, however, he rectifies this first, limited perspective. He says that while it is very difficult, it is never logically impossible for a man to change his fundamental principles; "but", Nowell-Smith concludes, "the one thing that he cannot do is to try to alter his conception of the Good Life; for it is ultimately by reference to this conception that all his choices are made" (pp. 312-314). From Toulmin to Nowell-Smith, then, there is some movement in the direction of allowing greater scope to the possibility of reasoned fundamental change in morality as well as in law, and of doing so by decreasing the role of society and increasing that of the individual as morally decisive. In R. M. Hare, of course, the mild criticism of whom by Hart I have already noted, there is the greatest insistence on the factor of individual decision in determining moral 'ways of life'. Hare sharply criticizes Toulmin for leaving out this factor and for attempting to assimilate moral judgments, prescriptions, too closely to empirical propositions, descriptions. (*The Language of Morals* (Oxford, At the Clarendon Press, 1952), p. 46.) At the end of the first half of his book, Hare gives a most striking account of periods of fundamental change in morality, when old principles cease to be accepted and society enters an era of moral instability. Interestingly enough, Hare at one point uses a metaphor very similar to Hart's of 'pathology' when he says, "It may take several generations for this disease to play itself out" (p. 73). Hare's account also mentions

would have been inadvisable to avoid it entirely, especially since Hart himself, who remains the central figure of this first section of the present study, has participated so actively in this debate, and since the role played by 'acceptance' in Hart's analysis of fundamental change in law seems to me to make a considerable contribution, when it has itself been clarified and analyzed, to an understanding of the relationship between law and morality and consequently of the meaning of 'natural law'. For a relationship (between law and morality) there certainly is, despite the best efforts of some legal positivisms, of which Kelsen's is probably the outstanding example, to develop a legal theory in isolation from it. All of Hart's writings point to his tremendous concern with that relationship, a concern which is no longer merely negative, seeking to deny it. What Hart does deny is that there is a NECESSARY connection between law and morality, meaning by this not the subject-matters of law and ethics, but rather particular legal and moral systems. We have seen in what way this is correct. This is very damaging to some versions of natural law theory, but it does not seem to me to be in any fundamental opposition to the 'deontological' concept of natural law held, for example, by A. P. d'Entrèves, who explains it as follows:

---

elements not likely to be altered in any moral change, though he is much more tentative about these than Nowell-Smith is concerning his 'conception of the Good Life': "No doubt there are among these old principles certain very general ones", Hare says, "which will remain acceptable unless human nature and the state of the world undergo a most fundamental change" (p. 72). This point closely resembles what Hart says about 'the minimum content of natural law', which will be introduced at the end of this chapter. At any rate, Hare is the most helpful of the three in answering my original question as to whether and how moral rules themselves, on the basis of which revolutionary questioning of legal rules was seen to be possible, could be challenged. His explanation, which is given in terms of a widespread refusal of many individuals in society to decide to accept the old principles of preceding generations, clearly shows that he is not so excessively and exclusively individualistic as Hart's criticism might have led one to suppose, though Hare certainly, and quite rightly, places greater stress on the individual in his account of ethics than does Toulmin.

All three of these approaches, including Toulmin's, to the matter of fundamental change in moral rules may be contrasted with an influential treatise dating from an earlier generation in British moral thought, F. H. Bradley's *Ethical Studies* (London, Henry S. King & Co., 1876). Here, the questioning of the established moral system is regarded as being worse than merely bad philosophy: indeed, "to wish to be better than the world is to be already on the threshold of immorality" (p. 180). "The knowledge that as members of the system we are real, and not otherwise, encourages us more and more to identify ourselves with that system" (p. 165). In short, according to Bradley, "there is nothing better than my station and its duties, nor anything higher or more truly beautiful" (p. 182).

It is clear that the notion of natural law can retain a meaning only if the notion of it as an 'ontology' of law is abandoned, and it is conceived 'de-ontologically', not as a fact, but as a value. In this sense the natural law will be nothing other than the indication of the value or of the disvalue attributed to the 'existing' law.[21]

Hart opened his debate with Fuller by referring critically to a passage in which d'Entrèves, defending the concept of natural law against its positivist opponents, had spoken of 'the point of intersection between law and morals'.[22] Hart's criticism here is misdirected; the way in which it is misdirected may be seen more clearly by referring back to the distinctions that I made at the beginning of this chapter in examining Hart's use of the word 'acceptance'.

Once again, there are two issues involved, one empirical, the other concerning the logic of concepts; once again, while the two issues are separable for purposes of analysis, they are inextricably bound up with one another in actual human experience. We have granted the theoretical possibility that a particular legal system might be found, the content of whose rules was completely dissimilar from the content of a given set of moral rules. We have granted the further possibility that some legal system, however unhealthy, might exist, the 'acceptance' of which by the majority of its subjects was of an almost completely passive sort; in such a situation, there might be almost no intersection between these legal rules and the moral rules of the same people. But here we begin to approach the limits of credence, the limits of conceivable empirical situations. Can we really conceive, for example, of governmental officials, who by their continued ACTIVE 'acceptance' of a given legal system preserve it from undergoing a fundamental change, and who at the same time adhere to a set of moral rules which have no content in common with any aspect of that legal system? This becomes difficult, if not utterly impossible, to imagine in any case but that in which the officials in question had completely split personalities. And the reason WHY it is difficult to conceive of such a possibility, of the possibility, that is, of there being a specific society in which there was no empirical 'point of intersection between law and morals', is not hard to discover: it lies in the very logic of the concepts of law, morality, acceptance, etc., considered as general terms. Both law and morals have to do with human conduct. Their respective areas of interest may differ considerably in modern society, so that law can be treated as a

[21] d'Entrèves, *La dottrina dello stato*, p. 321. Tr. mine.
[22] Hart, "Positivism and the Separation of Law and Morals", p. 594.

relatively autonomous field. But we have seen in how many different ways, as for example in this chapter in analyzing the significance of 'acceptance' for the concepts of law and of fundamental change in law, they inevitably DO intersect. To insist on a 'point of intersection' between law and morality is not to lapse into a natural law ontology of the kind that we have criticized; it is rather, *pace* Hart, to make a very minimal claim indeed, one that is obviously correct.

The practice of making minimal claims about 'natural law', however, has been gaining in popularity since the Hart-Fuller controversy. In *The Concept of Law*, Hart himself indulges in it. The considerations which he singles out for inclusion in his section on "The Minimum Content of Natural Law" are contingent facts about 'human beings and the world they live in'.[23] In the next chapter, I shall make a few final observations about these sorts of considerations.

[23] *The Concept of Law*, p. 195.

9

SOCIOLOGY

Hart lists five elementary facts about men and their world which ought always to serve as valid reasons for enacting certain laws rather than other possible laws, and which thus, taken together, constitute the basis for his 'modest but important' minimum content of natural law. He concedes that even in order for this minimum to be accepted, however, at least one goal, or ideal, of law must be presupposed: that of human survival.[1] The five salient truisms are: (1) men's vulnerability to bodily attacks by their fellows; (2) their approximate equality to one another; (3) their limited but real (Olivecrona's psychology to the contrary notwithstanding) altruism; (4) their limited resources; (5) their limited understanding and strength of will. The first three facts, according to Hart, are the bases of STATIC rules, that is, of rules having to do with permanent obligations among all the individuals in a legal system. The fourth suggests the need for a division of labor, and therefore for DYNAMIC rules, varying for different individuals. The fifth fact serves as the reason for there being SANCTIONS in legal systems.[2]

What is of interest for us here is not to inquire whether or not Hart's list is definitive or can be improved upon, but to understand the nature of the facts that he is presenting. He says that these truths belong neither to the category of definitions nor to that of 'ordinary statements of fact',[3] but rather to a third category. This somewhat dark saying may be clarified by pointing out that, whereas the facts referred to are by no means analytic truths, since there is no logical necessity for human nature and the world to be the way they are, yet they seem too funda-

[1] A. P. d'Entrèves, in an excellent article entitled "'Un noyau de bon sens' (à propos de la théorie du droit naturel chez H. Hart)" (*Revue internationale de Philosophie* 65 (1963, Fasc. 3), p. 323), insists on the fact that it is only this 'judgment of value' which permits Hart to argue in favor even of his attenuated natural law theory.

[2] *The Concept of Law*, pp. 189-195.

[3] *Ibid.*, p. 195.

mental to be regarded as merely complex empirical descriptive reports. It is these facts themselves that are the PRESUPPOSITIONS for any special internal logic of law, of politics, and even of morality, that may be discovered by philosophers. But it is possible for us to conceive of a world, as indeed Hart attempts to show in every case, in which these five basic conditions did not obtain. For example, the relative scarcity of the resources needed to support human life is nothing more than a contingent fact about the planet Earth and human physiology, considered in their interrelationship.

In short, Hart is now bringing out most clearly, in his discussion of the 'minimum content of natural law' near the close of his analysis of the concept of law, a point that he has attempted to bear in mind throughout, namely, that law is an essentially sociological phenomenon. I use 'sociology' in a very broad sense here, to designate the actual behavior of human beings in society. That this is not as obvious or as harmless a point as it might at first seem, becomes apparent when we recall the basic prejudice of Kelsen's whole program of 'normative jurisprudence'. Kelsen wanted deliberately to divorce pure *Rechtswissenschaft* from all considerations of actual behavior, and to confine it to the study of legal norms. I have already shown, in the chapter on "Analogy", how Kelsen was misled by his hypothetico-deductive model in attempting to understand legal phenomena; I wish now to point out once again, as I first did in the chapter on Kelsen, the related danger involved in his admittedly heroic efforts to segregate the pure science of law from all other disciplines. If we once overlook or forget the artificiality involved in such attempts at segregation, bizarre results are certain to ensue.

The phenomenon of fundamental change in law provides an excellent test-case for this contention. For example, we have noted the bizarre nature of Kelsen's effort to overcome, by resorting to international law as a 'higher level' of norms, the complete void in law that, according to his theory, a revolution must create. Even Max Laserson's explanation of revolution as the 'hurtling together' of the two sets of laws, positive and natural, that have become too widely separated in a given country, completely opposed as it is to Kelsen's account in most basic respects, shares with the latter the tendency artificially to divorce the science of law from all other disciplines. But there is no need to go over all the old ground again. The important point is that the phenomenon of fundamental change in law provides the most obvious possible demonstration of the dependence of law on certain non-legal factors. This is why the phrase 'normative fact', as applied to revolution, has so great a significance especially for those who wish to continue to follow Kelsen's ideal of rigidly separating 'normative jurisprudence' from the other sciences, and who at the same time naturally recognize, as Kelsen himself does, that legal systems do not come into existence apart from the occurrence of other events that can be called, broadly speaking, 'sociological'.

The great merit of Hart's analysis of the concept of fundamental change in law, an exploration of some of the details of which has been the central theme of this section, is to have avoided much of the artificiality of the accounts of some of his immediate predecessors. True, Hart is well known for his support of the positivist thesis that there is no necessary connection between law and morality; but in the preceding chapter I have shown how Hart's treatment of fundamental change is especially valuable in indicating the extent to which he has qualified the dogmatic and artificial positions on this issue that have been taken by Kelsen and by the Scandinavian empiricists. Regarding Hart's disavowal of Kelsen's artificial separation of legal science from SOCIOLOGY, however, there is no need for me even to make a detailed case. The point is too obvious. It is made particularly obvious by the way in which Hart, in his account of 'the pathology of a legal system', insists on the complexities involved in making 'the external statement of fact that a legal system exists' or has begun to break down. Such times of fundamental change, as Hart shows, often involve fascinating LEGAL issues – issues, that is, which are truly related to the concept of law, and which yet do not arise out of the internal logic either of the particular legal system that is ceasing to exist or of that which may be coming into existence. Phenomena, such as that of fundamental change in law, for the understanding of which both legal and non-legal factors must be taken into consideration and cannot be separated, cannot be convincingly dealt with by a legal theory which seeks to maintain a 'pure' point of view, independent of sociology; they CAN be dealt with by the analytic method.

"Jurisprudence, ethics, economics, politics, and sociology are distinct enough at the core, but shade out into each other." [4] This judicious conclusion drawn many years before by Roscoe Pound is an anticipation of Hart's theory of the core meaning of concepts and of borderline cases. But there is another meaning of sociology, the one that I have used

[4] Roscoe Pound, *Law and Morals* (Chapel Hill, The University of North Carolina Press, 1924), p. 123.

above, which would make of it a very broad concept of which 'jurisprudence' was one special aspect. Hart himself seems to support this meaning in his Preface when he says, "Notwithstanding its concern with analysis the book may also be regarded as an essay in descriptive sociology."[5] If this is so, and if, further, fundamental change in law is a borderline phenomenon that is not fully explicable in terms strictly of the concept of law, then, regardless of whether law is a part of sociology or separate from it, we are justified at this point in going on to view our phenomenon from a new perspective, one from which the importance of the law itself will be diminished, though not entirely overlooked.

Furthermore, in the sentence just quoted, Hart draws a distinction between two approaches to phenomena, that of analysis and that of description. He seems confident concerning the possibility of their coexisting. In line with this, we may now consider a treatment of fundamental social change that not only occupies a new perspective, but also employs a different philosophical methodology from that of analysis.

[5] *The Concept of Law*, p. vii.

II

INTERLUDE

INTERLUDE

Hart whose analysis of fundamental change in law we have just completed examining, is essentially (leaving aside for the moment all the qualifications which our own examination will have induced us to add to this statement) a philosopher of common sense; the same is unlikely to be said of Sartre (whether this is for better or for worse). It would be foolish to underestimate the enormous differences that exist between the two authors – differences in background, in philosophical formation, in style, in interests, and, generally, in way of life. The fact of their being contemporaries and sharing a common commitment to the enterprise of philosophy seems hardly sufficient to bridge such a tremendous gap.

Indeed, it is as much for their obvious dissimilarities as for whatever resemblances a common historical era, a common subject-matter, a common concern with the nature of human activity, etc., may suggest, that I have chosen to compare and contrast Sartre's treatment of revolution with Hart's. I feel, of course, that both treatments have something to contribute to an understanding of our subject, and I feel that both can, at a minimum, be brought into the same 'universe of discourse'. But warning should be given, here and now, that a transition from the philosophy of Hart to the philosophy of Sartre bears many of the characteristics of a fundamental change.

First of all, it is desirable briefly to recapitulate some of the principal contributions to explaining and justifying fundamental change in law and society that the section just concluded has produced. After making a preliminary bow to Hart, we turned to an examination of a few of Hart's immediate predecessors in legal philosophy, whose views are perhaps less generally well known and are especially relevant for an examination of the concept of fundamental change in law. Kelsen was the first and most important of these predecessors to be discussed, and fundamental change turned out to pose a peculiar and especially serious problem for his system. For it was Kelsen who proposed that we regard as fundamental only those changes which result in the substitution of one legal system for another, and that we define such substitution as the replacement of one 'basic law' by another. Kelsen, I showed, was so bound by his adherence to certain methodological principles, such as that of the complete separation of the subject-matter of legal science from the subject-matters of all other disciplines, that revolutionary change threatened to introduce an artificially radical discontinuity into his theoretical world. The empiricism of the Scandinavian legal theorists, on the other hand, reached its crescendo in the thought of Karl Olivecrona, for whom revolution was 'only one step in the long development of the law'. The legal philosophy of H. L. A. Hart, notably with respect to his treatment of fundamental change, may be seen as occupying in some ways a middle ground between these two positions.

The title given by Hart to the several pages in his book in which he directly discussed fundamental change was, we saw, "The Pathology of a Legal System". Common sense, as I have already noted, predominated in this account, which stressed the necessity of avoiding the excessive simplicity characteristic of so much past legal philosophy, suggested the usefulness of looking at the deaths of legal systems in terms of analogies with human pathology, and attempted to make clear the fact that political revolution was only one of several ways in which fundamental changes in law could take place. But the account relied on something more than simply ordinary language, we noted: the incessant probing into the meaning of law as a system of certain types of rules, the crucial distinction between the external and internal aspects of legal systems, and the use of the concept of 'acceptance' to explain the occurrence or non-occurrence of fundamental change – all these elements in Hart's account depended for their plausibility, we sensed, on some more or less systematic positions that he had established elsewhere in *The Concept of Law*.

We then had a basis for beginning to answer some of the questions raised in the Introduction. We first probed into some of the sources, the meaning, the possible values, and the alleged uniqueness of Hart's philosophical method of linguistic analysis. We found that this method had been helpful in analyzing fundamental change (thus implicitly refuting the view of Marcuse's which I had quoted at the very outset of this book) primarily for the reason that Hart himself had emphasized, to wit, that it was a good antidote to the facile, misleading simplicity to which much of past legal philosophy, heavily dependent on definitions *per genus et differentiam*, had been excessively prone. We found it impossible to give a concise statement, on the other hand, of what precisely constituted the 'hard core' distinctiveness of the analytic method as we had seen it applied to the concept of fundamental change, since none of the possible distinctive characteristics that I suggested (the precept that philosophy must leave everything the way it was, the glorification of ordinary language, the disdain for systematization) seemed quite accurately to fit the case at hand.

We then continued our examination of how Hart had gone about explaining fundamental change in law by considering the ANALOGIES on which he had relied in making many of his points. A brief excursus into the past served to remind us of how the use of analogy had both abetted and placed limitations on the accounts of fundamental change, as well as of other legal and political phenomena, to be found in Kelsen and Aristotle. We noted the dangers inherent in Hart's analogies both of pathology and of games in the explanation of fundamental change in law.

Our next set of problems was that raised by Hart's pervasive employment of the concept of 'rules'. We first had to satisfy ourselves by allaying the gnawing suspicion that his employment of the concept was so all-pervasive that it actually lacked explanatory value. We noted Hart's distinction between rule-governed and habitual human behavior, which was the most essential point of difference between him and the Scandinavian empiricists (Olivecrona, especially) in the analysis of law and fundamental change. In examining the notion of rule-governed behavior, we found the concept of JUSTIFICATION (the justification for following or for refusing to follow a given set of rules) arising for the first time. Our attempt to become clear about what distinguished LEGAL rules from all other kinds of rules led us to conclude that Hart's proposal on this matter, to the effect that law was characterized by a 'unique combination of primary and secondary rules', was neither adequate (for, among other defects, it neither excluded moral rules nor, in all likelihood, included international law) nor strikingly original (for, after certain corrections, it could be reduced to a demonstration of the intimate connection between modern law and the modern state). Finally, we found that Hart's secondary 'rule of recognition' was playing the role in Hart's analysis of fundamental change that most closely paralleled the role of Kelsen's 'basic norm'.

Our continued uncertainty about the exact relationship between legal and other types of rules, the introduction of questions concerning justification, and references to the secondary 'rule of recognition' – these were among the many indications that it was necessary to investigate further one of Hart's key concepts in analyzing fundamental change, the concept of 'acceptance'. We began by discussing Hart's distinction between the internal and external aspects of legal systems, and we found that an attitude of acceptance was essential to considerations of a legal system from an internal point of view. We also examined in detail the problem of how acceptance could come to mean primarily an ATTITUDE for Hart, when it so often refers to, in Ross's words, 'a deliberate decision'. Our own principal concern in this matter, namely the use to which Hart had put the possibility of non-acceptance of a legal system (especially by its OFFICIALS, but also, to a lesser degree and in any 'unhealthy' system, by its other subjects) in his explanation of fundamental change, led us to a recognition of the importance of MORAL rules in accounting for acceptance and non-acceptance. In this regard, I had occasion to take issue with Hart over certain formulations of his views concerning 'the separation of law and morals'. The subject of 'natural law' was raised briefly. In opposition to Hart's sometime antagonist, Lon Fuller, I showed that it was times of fundamental change and of the possibility of 'INfidelity to law' that best demonstrated the necessarily intimate connection between law and morality which Fuller had been anxious to uphold.

Lastly, I brought to the surface a certain uneasiness that had remained present but unexpressed throughout most of our examination of Hart's treatment of fundamental change in law, and that the introduction of problems of justification, first in our considerations regarding 'acceptance', and now in Hart's somewhat peculiar and unexpected effort at reconciling himself with the natural law tradition in terms of a few salient but contingent 'truisms' about human nature, had finally forced us to contend with. Law, in point of fact, is only one kind of social phenomenon. Law may be so defined, as it is by Kelsen, that extra-legal sociological factors need not be taken into account by legal science; but especially when fundamental change in law is under consideration, the artificiality of this procedure *saute aux yeux*. It is this fact which has brought us to the point at which we now find ourselves, ready to plunge into the essentially simple profundities and the logically unassailable neologisms of our French author, Jean-Paul Sartre. What has he to offer us?

Sartre can offer us alternatives to some of the limitations that we may feel as long as we continue to work within a framework that is not radically different from Hart's own. It may indeed prove to be true that greater genuine freedom of philosophical action is possible within the so-called 'limitations' (in method, in the manner of explaining social activity, and in subject-matter) of a Hartean framework than within the violently free atmosphere of a Sartrean perspective, and thus that the Hegelian (AND, paradoxically, the Sartrean) way of reconciling liberty with necessity will once again have been vindicated; but this remains to be seen. We cannot at this point REALLY anticipate in detail what conclusions may emerge from our forthcoming examination of Sartre's explanation of fundamental social change within the framework of an abstract theory of social structures, for such conclusions can fairly be drawn only on the basis of that examination. However, I consider myself entitled at present to provide at least a subjective [1] explanation of why, on the basis both of the problems that I raised in the Introduction and of the Hartean contributions to their solution that I have just summarized, I regard it as being reasonable to turn now to Sartre's social philosophy.

The Concept of Law left us, as every book must, with many unanswered questions. For one thing, it pretended to be nothing more grandiose than an analysis of the concept of law (though there are some who might consider this in itself to be sufficiently pretentious); but it did not demonstrate the IMPOSSIBILITY of a more grandiose approach to political, social, and legal philosophy, either. Now, it would certainly be false to say that the French have a monopoly in *grandeur*, but it happens to be the case that Sartre's *Critique de la raison dialectique*, Tome I, is one of the best-published recent attempts at resolving, with the rigor of thought essential to a serious work in philosophy, and from a perspective considerably more grandiose than that chosen by Hart, some of the problems with which we have been most concerned. Furthermore, as I have already mentioned in the Introduction, Sartre now regards himself as a Marxist, and this ought to imply, among other things, that he cherishes some sort of vision of a definitive 'revolution' which would put a decisive end to all fundamental changes of the sorts with which we are at present familiar, would abolish the 'alienations' which are alleged to be characteristic of the relations of production in contemporary capitalist society, and would bring in its wake the gradual

[1] I am here thinking of Hegel's attitude: "... As a preface, its only business has been to make some external and SUBJECTIVE remarks about the standpoint of the book it produces. If a topic is to be discussed philosophically, it spurns any but a scientific and objective treatment ..." (Emphasis mine.) *Op. cit.*, p. 13.

elimination of all political and legal 'superstructures' as we know them – thus, as a side-effect, rendering rather outdated all that Hart has done and all that we have concluded from our examination of Hart.

Recent developments in Marxist theory in France are not nearly so widely discussed as are the basic Marxist tenets themselves, from which Sartre and many others draw much of their inspiration. Consequently, I shall preface my examination of Sartre's views with a recapitulation of some of these recent developments, rather than with a summary of Marx's own philosophy with reference to the concept of fundamental change. The highly systematic character of the entire Sartrean social theory, as well as the non-self-explanatory nature of some of his key technical terms, will compel me to recount Sartre's explanation of fundamental change at greater length than was necessary in the case of Hart's analysis. Sartre's explanation will be seen to be a highly abstract, widely applicable account of the transition from one basic form of social collective to another, the difference between the two forms consisting in the relative 'activity' or 'passivity', with respect to the results produced by the common effort, of the individuals who compose them.

The first question then to be raised about Sartre's account, just as it had to be raised about Hart's analysis, will be a 'question of method'. This last phrase, interestingly enough, is Sartre's own title for the introductory essay which precedes the *Critique* proper. We shall see Sartre make the claim that his method alone has the comprehensiveness, internality, and progressiveness needed to provide an adequate social philosophy along the lines that he thinks a systematic social philosophy should take. Furthermore, we shall have to consider his particularly audacious claim that this method alone is able to account for novelty, such as fundamental social change. We shall want to challenge these claims, and we shall find it most convenient to do so by referring back to some of the methodological contrasts that we have already established as existing between Hart and Hans Kelsen. We shall then want to ask ourselves whether, since Sartre is indeed serious in making the claims for his method that I have just noted, he proposes to make good on them by resorting to the 'philosophically dubious premises' of collectivism and historical determinism, and to the dubious practice of explaining by means of myth, that I mentioned in my Introduction and that are sometimes laid (often with more than a little unfairness) to the charge of Marxism; we shall find that he does not.

But, however strongly Sartre may inveigh against 'mystification', we shall discover that there are certain terms that play crucial roles in his account of fundamental change and throughout his social theory and that have the appearance, on the other hand, of referring to something suspiciously like mystical entities. It will be quite obvious to us that, if Sartre hopes in any way to convince us that his is the 'true' account of fundamental social change (although the meaning of such a claim will still not have become completely clear to us at this point), he will have to show that it is permissible for him to rely on these suspect concepts. We shall find that the concepts refer, in fact, to abstractions; how Sartre has arrived at, in particular, the two abstractions which we shall have selected as being the most basic to his account of fundamental change, and precisely what their ontological or other status is, will be the next set of problems to occupy our attention. In the course of this examination, we shall begin to see the notions of ALIENATION and of PROJECT or PURPOSE introduced into our considerations of the human activity that brings about fundamental social change.

We shall by this point have noticed that a very weird neologism, 'totalizations' ,'*totalisations*'), seems to play nearly as pervasive a role in Sartre's social philosophy as did the concept of 'rules' in Hart's. We shall want to ask ourselves what totalizations are, and we shall find that the best way of answering this will be to consider first precisely how Sartre tries to explain fundamental change in terms of them. But there is a sort of absolutism about the notion of 'totalizations' which, combined with the weirdness of the term, will induce us to perform a rather weird, slightly satirical, and yet potentially valuable thought experiment by examining the concept of 'totalization' at its absolute conceptual limit; the value of the experiment will be measurable in terms of our increased ability to appreciate the limitations of any attempt to explain fundamental change exclusively in terms of 'totalizations'. This, in turn, will lead us to re-evaluate the importance of Hartean rules in explaining fundamental change, and on this basis to put into question Marxist and neo-Marxist claims concerning the possibility of radically altering human nature and of bringing about a state of affairs, in a 'world without scarcity', in which alienations will have been permanently abolished and the possibility of there occurring future fundamental changes in the direction of a regression to 'passive' social structures will have been permanently eliminated.

It will next be important to consider the Sartrean counterpart of Hart's concept of 'acceptance', which Sartre calls 'the oath', and which he regards as the logically necessary basis of all PERMANENT social structures. Given the permanently binding nature of the oath, however, it will at first appear difficult to see how Sartre can either explain or justify fundamental change OUT OF a presently existing 'active' social structure, except by means of outside interference. The imperfections and indeed the practical 'contradictions' of any such structure will be found to serve as the basis of Sartre's account of fundamental change in this context, but we shall begin to wonder whether Sartre is not trapping himself into a radically pessimistic view according to which social institutions would be deplorable *per se*. The question of JUSTIFICATION, on the other hand, will turn out to be an especially peculiar one here, since the issue will not be whether Sartre, if he can account for fundamental changes, can also justify them, but rather whether he has left himself any basis for approving of some and for disapproving of others instead of simply justifying indiscriminately any and all that may take place. A reference to desirable FUTURE states of affairs will be seen to be essential for preventing a Sartrean ethics from being relativistic in an utterly futile way. This will bring us back, once again, to a consideration of the nature of the future that Sartre, as a Marxist, envisions as attainable by fundamental social change, and to a verdict of caution and mild scepticism vis-à-vis the 'teleological optimism' characteristic of much of Marxist thought on this subject.

Finally, just as the limitations of the perspectives of legal philosophy were what originally led us to begin to investigate Sartre's social philosophy, so at the conclusion of our treatment of Sartre we shall have reached the point of wondering why there is no little discussion, within the framework of the *Critique*, of the law. We shall examine the reasons for this, and we shall end by administering another mild dose of scepticism to ourselves, this time concerning the more specific suggestion that the legal 'superstructure' might conceivably be abolished by some future change of an especially fundamental kind.

The upshot of our lengthy retreat from Sartrean 'totalizations' may well prove to be a return to Hartean common sense; but if so, it will be a chastened common sense, a common sense that will have walked with the Poet, passed through the fire, and been 'taken up' – whether into the Seventh Heaven or elsewhere it may be difficult to say –, a common sense that will no longer be the same as it once had been. But this has already been an unusual Interlude, inasmuch as, during it, one has acquired a great deal of advance information about the forthcoming act; it is now time to begin in earnest to contemplate the spectacle that Jean-Paul Sartre proposes to present to us.

III

A THEORETICAL ACCOUNT OF THE PHENOMENON OF FUNDAMENTAL CHANGE IN SOCIETY

1

INTRODUCTION

It is not unfitting that one organizational stronghold of contemporary analytically-inclined philosophers bears the name 'Aristotelian Society'. Of the two greatest figures of ancient philosophy, it is Aristotle whose method seems more akin to that of analysis as portrayed in Chapter Five of the preceding section.[1] Aristotle's predecessor and counterpart, Plato, on the other hand, himself often calls his own method 'dialectic'.[2] This latter word has undergone many shifts of meaning in the history of philosophy; today, it evokes the names of Hegel and Marx as readily as it does that of Plato.

Jean-Paul Sartre is an eminent contemporary French philosopher who has in the past allowed at least two very important 'labels' to be attached to his thought. In *L'être et le néant* he asserted, even in his subtitle ("Essai d'ontologie phénoménologique"),[3] that he was using the method of PHENOMENOLOGY developed by Husserl. And it was also Sartre who, perhaps more than any other single person, succeeded in popularizing the word 'existentialism'. But in his most recent serious work, the word 'phenomenology' goes almost entirely unmentioned, and existentialism is explicitly dealt with only in the introductory essay. Sartre now claims to be examining and adhering to the method of dialectic, to which he opposes analysis, and to be writing in the shadow of his dialectically-inclined predecessor, Karl Marx.

Sartre has entitled this work *Critique de la raison dialectique*; the

[1] Cf. *Politics* I, 1 (1252a19-22), where Aristotle speaks of 'our normal method of analysis', the analysis of a compound "until we reach its simple and uncompounded elements".

[2] Cf. *Republic* VII (532a) (tr. by B. Jowett) (New York, Random House, 1937), where Plato begins his 'hymn of dialectic', 'the discovery of the absolute by the light of reason only'. In 537c, he equates the dialectical mind with the synoptic or comprehensive one. Elsewhere, as in *Phaedrus* 265e, he appears to regard dialectics as the combined 'processes of division and generalization'.

[3] Paris, Librairie Gallimard, 1943.

volume thus far published, the first of two projected volumes, bears the subtitle "Théorie des ensembles pratiques", and is preceded by an essay, originally written as an article for a Polish journal and revised to serve as an introduction to the *Critique*, entitled "Question de Méthode".[4] At the very outset of this introductory essay, he sketches out a theory of the history of philosophy according to which "the epochs of philosophical creation are few", the three most recent having been those of Descartes and Locke, of Kant and Hegel, and of Marx, and the only philosophers in the fullest sense of the word are those few great geniuses who have set the tone for all philosophical discussion that has taken place during a given epoch.[5] One need not, and I think cannot, take this theory too seriously in its detail; what is interesting about it is that it enables Sartre to label himself a Marxist almost by definition (since this is the era of Marx, and Sartre wants to add to, rather than to react against, the philosophy of this era); his existentialism, he says, is an example of "an *ideology*: it is a parasite system" which at first opposes, and then attempts to become integrated with, the philosophy of the epoch.[6]

Critique de la raison dialectique, then, pretends to be an illustration[7] of how Marxism, and the dialectical method of philosophy, can deal with certain phenomena – in the case of this first volume, with the phenomena of societal groupings, or wholes. Is it a good illustration?

[4] Paris, Librairie Gallimard, 1960. This essay has been translated into English under the title, *Search for a Method* (tr. by Hazel E. Barnes) (New York, Alfred A. Knopf, 1963).

[5] *Critique de la raison dialectique*, p. 17. ALL TRANSLATIONS FROM THE FRENCH IN THIS SECTION AND IN THE CONCLUSION OF THIS BOOK ARE MINE, UNLESS OTHERWISE NOTED.

[6] *Ibid.*, p. 18. It is clear that at least on this point Sartre is 'revising' Marx; we have only to recall the highly pejorative connotation given by the latter to the word 'ideology'. In *The German Ideology*, for instance, this passage occurs: "In direct contrast to German philosophy ... we set out from real, active men ... Morality, religion, metaphysics, all the rest of ideology and their corresponding forms of consciousness, thus no longer retain the semblance of independence. They have no history, no development" (ed. by R. Pascal) (New York, International Publishers, 1947).

[7] At times, at least, Sartre's claims seem to be as modest as the word 'illustration' suggests: "What is dialectical rationality, what are its limits and its basis? The very slight position of detachment that we have assumed in relation to the letter of Marxist doctrine ... permits us to grasp the meaning of this question ... But I am far from believing that the isolated effort of an individual can provide a satisfactory answer – however partial – to such a broad demand and one which brings into question the totality of History. If only these first investigations have permitted me to clarify the problem, ... I shall consider myself satisfied." *Critique de la raison dialectique*, p. 135.

The easiest and most obvious method, though it is a highly fallible one, of beginning to determine the answer to such a question is to turn to reputable critics who might be expected to favor such an enterprise. In the case of Hart's *Concept of Law*, regarded as an illustration of how philosophical analysis can deal with problems of legal philosophy, some of the critics whom I cited were, if anything, excessively effusive in hailing Hart's success. For Sartre's *Critique*, however, the early auguries are not so uniformly auspicious. *Prima facie*, it might be thought that friendly critics of Sartre's should be found among fellow 'ideologists' (in Sartre's sense) of Marxism; but a great number, and in some countries the majority, of avowedly Marxist thinkers are members of a political organization, the Communist Party, which is apt to regard with disfavor writings in political theory by non-members. Thus it is not surprising that Adam Schaff, a leading Polish Marxist and Communist, replied to the original version of Sartre's introductory essay, "Question de Méthode", by contending that there was in fact a complete opposition between Marxism and existentialism, the crucial point of which was 'the way of treating the conception of the individual, central problem of every existentialist tendency'.[8] Schaff's criticisms have since been expanded in later publications, and his voice is by no means the harshest among Communist writers. (Indeed, recent unhappy events in Poland have resulted in serious challenges to Schaff's orthodox credentials on the part of his Party colleagues.) Theodor Schwarz, who constantly speaks of Sartre's "idealism" and of the bourgeois ancestry of some of his central non-Marxian concepts,[9] is perhaps more typical of Party members.

But other critics, too, have made very similar comments, tending to denigrate one or more of the main aims announced by Sartre for this book. The comment that "the attempted union of Existentialism and Marxism seems both desperate and forced"[10] is by no means atypical. One of the first long reviews of the *Critique* by a Continental philosopher, that of De Waelhens, is highly unfavorable; he begins by referring

[8] Adam Schaff, "Sur le marxisme et l'existentialisme", *Temps Modernes* 173-174 (Aug.-Sept. 1960), p. 400. (Translator into French not named.) Schaff does adopt a more conciliatory attitude in the end, arguing that Sartre's individualism at least points up a lacuna in Marxism that orthodox Marxists should now attempt to fill on their own terms.

[9] Theodor Shwarz, *Jean-Paul Sartres 'Kritik der dialektischen Vernunft'* (Berlin, D.D.R., Veb Deutscher Verlag der Wissenschaften, 1967).

[10] Richard J. Bernstein, "Summary and Comment" on *Critique de la raison dialectique*, Tome I, *Review of Metaphysics* XV, 3 (Mar. 1962), p. 529.

to "this huge, dense book, badly composed – or not composed at all –, badly written, almost constantly irritating by its appearance, which seems, as it were, deliberate, of making the task painful for its reader." [11] A somewhat later French reaction, that of Claude Lévi-Strauss (one of the few writers to whom Sartre refers in the text of the *Critique*), has become a central rallying-point for the so-called "structuralist" opposition to Sartre among a large segment of the French intellectual community.[12] A rather shallow American review characterizes Sartre's doctrine as 'Metaphysical Stalinism'.[13] This list could easily be expanded.

The method of appeal to authorities, then, is hardly very reassuring for the contention that the *Critique de la raison dialectique* is a good example of how Marxism or neo-Marxism can deal with the problem of social philosophy, and specifically with our central concept of fundamental change.[14] But at least it can be said to be a serious attempt at doing this, and one of relatively few such attempts in recent times that attain to the degree of precision, rigor, and formalization often thought necessary to distinguish a philosophical from a literary essay. For the rest, we must reserve our own judgments until some of Sartre's arguments have been presented and analyzed here.

At any rate, fundamental change in the structures of society is one of Sartre's chief preoccupations in this book. The *Critique* fairly bristles with a great variety of French expressions for this basic concept, considered in its variety of aspects. On p. 384, for example, Sartre speaks of the 'bouleversement qui déchire le collectif par l'éclair d'une *praxis* commune', which is 'une transformation synthétique'. Previously, on the same page, he had spoken of this *praxis* as being 'révolutionnaire'. Later in the same paragraph, he uses the words 'changement', 'restructuration', and 'dépassement' to refer to the same phenomenon, which he sees as happening in the 'groupes fondamentaux de la société', and in a footnote on the next page he calls this phenomenon the 'fait fondamental de groupement comme conquête ou reconquête de la *praxis* sur le collectif'. The use made by Sartre of several of these terms, notably *praxis*, group,

[11] Alphonse De Waelhens, "Sartre et la raison dialectique", *Revue Philosophique de Louvain* 60 (1962), p. 79. De Waelhens' concluding remarks, p. 99, are scarcely more sanguine.

[12] Claude Lévi-Strauss, chapter entitled "Histoire et dialectique", in *La Pensée Sauvage* (Paris, Plon, 1962), pp. 324-357.

[13] Lionel Abel, "Metaphysical Stalinism", *Dissent* 8, 2 (spring 1961), pp. 137-152.

[14] On the other side, however, at least one favorable review ought to be mentioned. It is by Mikel Dufrenne, who concludes: "One cannot ignore this amazing book, and one awaits the sequel with impatience." *Esprit* 19, 294 (Apr. 1961), p. 692.

and collectif, will be examined later. At present, it should only be noted that, while Sartre's whole effort is an attempt to describe both the basic structures of society and their transformations, so that change is a constant concern, yet the most fundamental change for him is the abovementioned passage from the serial collective, or series, to the group; it is on his account of this that I shall concentrate.

The chapters of the present section of this study will follow a sequence rather similar to that of the first section. In the next chapter (which will correspond to Chapters Two and Three of the first section), I shall provide a rough sketch of some aspects of the post-World War II awakening of interest in Marxism among French philosophers, since the *Critique* can be better understood against this background. Chapter Three will be an outline of Sartre's political philosophy insofar as it proposes to give a theoretical account of the phenomenon of fundamental change. Chapter Four will discuss Sartre's method and Chapter Five his uses of certain basic 'abstractions'. Totalization, a concept as essential to Sartre's account as is the concept of rules to Hart's, will be the theme of the sixth chapter, and this will lead to a discussion of 'the oath', Sartre's name for the phenomenon which underlies all institutionalized groups, in Chapter Seven. Here again, as in the corresponding chapter on "Acceptance" in the first section, the problem of institutional and moral obligation will be raised. And this will lead to a final chapter, the eighth, in which Sartre's relative neglect of the institution of LAW will be examined, clarified, and criticized.

2

MANDARINS

Les Mandarins is the title of a novel by Sartre's colleague, Simone de Beauvoir.[1] The novel itself, which I do not intend to summarize here, is something of a *roman à clé*. It deals with a group of Parisian intellectuals and their families during the period beginning with the liberation of France from German occupation. These intellectuals share many opinions and preoccupations, most notably their interest in engaging in political activity, such as partisan journalism, in support of a Marxist-oriented (but, in the case of the majority of the characters, a non-Communist) French Left Wing. Most of them are former participants in the wartime resistance movement. The name that is applied to them collectively by the title of the book is not intended mainly to be abusive. But they are a group apart, breathing an atmosphere and holding to certain presuppositions that are not common to most of their fellow-citizens.

The individuals described in the novel are the fictional counterparts of a number of the leading figures associated in one way or other with French neo-Marxism, against the background of which the *raison d'être* of the *Critique de la raison dialectique* can best be understood. I shall sketch very briefly some of the leading events, mostly in the form of books and articles, in the short history of this movement, with special reference to the development of theories concerning fundamental change.[2] I make no pretense at completeness. In the case of Kelsen and

[1] Paris, Librairie Gallimard, 1954.

[2] At least four other easily accessible accounts of some aspects of these developments deserve mention here. None, it need hardly be added, approaches the historical task with the same purposes as mine in this chapter. George Lichtheim's *Marxism in Modern France* (New York & London, Columbia University Press, 1966) covers a very wide range of topics and of names. However, as Lichtheim himself admits at the end (p. 193), "It has not been possible in the preceding pages to tackle philosophical subjects properly so called." Michel-Antoine Burnier's *Les Existentialistes et la politique* (Paris, Librairie Gallimard, 1966) is a clear, quite simple account, written by someone who is not a professional philosopher, but who is very much interested in his subject and who takes a somewhat more sympathetic

some of his followers mentioned in the first chapter of the previous section, I noted in passing the importance of the collapse of the German Empire in influencing their efforts to wrestle with the problem of fundamental change as posed in Kelsenian legal theory; but even in their case, as in the cases of the Scandinavian theorists and of Hart (though some specifically British concerns were evident in the latter's analysis of 'The Pathology'), theory could generally be dealt with on grounds independent of historical associations. In the case of the mandarins, this independence cannot be maintained, since outside historical events will be seen time and again to have important influences on theories. But this is consonant with a Marxist orientation: if there is any single theme that is central to Marx's view of the relation of history to philosophy, the necessity of such influences is that theme.

Much of the history of French neo-Marxism has been played out in the pages of a single periodical, *Les Temps Modernes*, of which Sartre has been editor, either singly or with others, since its inception in late 1945. The 'presentation' of the revue, written by Sartre for the first number, expresses its founders' sense of political commitment, and pledges that this commitment will be made non-politically, that is, not from within any political party.[3] This pledge has been maintained – though not without, at times, the severest strains, caused generally by Sartre's intense desire to adhere to most of what he regards as the objectives of the Communist Party, while still remaining outside it and always reserving the right to criticize. With regard to theory, Sartre in the same first article states the following very general policy, the importance of which for the *Critique* we shall have to examine and clarify later: "Thus we revert, against the spirit of analysis, to a synthetic conception of reality, the principle of which is that a whole, whatever it may be, is different in nature from the sum of its parts."[4]

Among the original directors of the journal, Sartre was perhaps the best-known, though his notoriety was not entirely of a favorable sort. Many of the POPULAR notions of existentialism, of course, were incom-

---

tone than most towards Sartre. *Contemporary French Political Thought*, by Roy Pierce (London, Oxford University Press, 1966), contains a full but by no means penetrating chapter on Sartre's Marxism (pp. 148-184). Finally, the first full-length treatment (mainly exegetic) of the *Critique* to have appeared in English, Wilfrid Desan's *The Marxism of Jean-Paul Sartre* (Garden City, Doubleday & Co., 1965), contains a first chapter (pp. 1-24) that in some ways parallels the present one, while diverging considerably in other respects.

[3] Sartre, "Présentation", *Temps Modernes* 1 (Oct. 1, 1945), p. 8.

[4] *Ibid.*, p. 13.

patible with regarding its leading French proponent as a serious political thinker; but even among philosophers there was a widespread belief that the basic doctrines of *L'être et le néant*, which was in print before the end of the War, were radically a-social. Wilfrid Desan well expressed this sentiment when, commenting some years later on Sartre's discussion of the ' "us"-form' which is said to be 'very humiliating... an alienation and an impotency',[5] he noted that "such theories betray clearly the extreme individualist and explain the inevitable clash between Existentialism and Marxism'.[6]

The most distinguished philosopher among French Communist Party members, Henri Lefebvre, contributed to this clash with the publication, in 1946, of a scathing attack on the existentialist movement. Lefebvre charged Sartre with irrationalism, with lack of philosophical rigor, and even with dishonesty, for which reason "M. Sartre does not yet merit the title of philosopher."[7] The final charge was based on Lefebvre's contention that, while Sartre's theory pretended that the object could be attained by consciousness alone, without the intermediary of 'the concept, of objective reason', this pretention was exploded in Sartre's own work. For Sartre's ontological primitives, the *En-soi* and the *Pour-soi*, especially the former, according to Lefebvre, are essentially CONCEPTUAL devices for coming to grips with reality.[8] The germ of truth in this polemic, reinterpreted and reapplied to Sartre's later theories, will concern us in later chapters of this section.

Coming closer to our own central concept of fundamental change, Lefebvre's declaration of war against existentialism charged that the existentialist conception of CHOICE, oscillating as it did between the void ('le néant') and wholehearted commitment, led to impotency in practical action: "The existentialist philosopher, imagining himself to be 'choosing', is simply opting against the transformative action of the world."[9] Existentialism, in other words, because of the total character of the

[5] Sartre, *L' être et le néant*, p. 490.

[6] Wilfrid Desan, *The Tragic Finale* (revised ed.) (New York, Harper Torchbooks, 1960), p. 92. Norberto Bobbio was even less sympathetic: "Certainly the existentialist is never a revolutionary. He is, if anything, a rebel. The revolutionary fights one form of society in order to create a better; the rebel fights every possible form of society ... He does not regard himself as part of a community; indeed, all social obligations are vexatious to him." (Ch. on "The Decadentism of Sartre") *The Philosophy of Decadentism – A Study in Existentialism* (tr. by D. Moore) (Oxford, Basil Blackwell, 1948), p. 59.

[7] Henri Lefebvre, *L' Existentialisme* (Paris, Editions du Sagittaire, 1946), p. 65.

[8] *Ibid.*, pp. 64-65.

[9] *Ibid.*, p. 94.

opposition that it posited as existing between consciousness and the world, could not but be hostile to the concept of fundamental change in society, at least in any sense in which that concept might resemble Marxian theories of 'revolution'. The last sentence in Lefebvre's book may be seen, in retrospect, as a challenge that Sartre's entire *Critique de la raison dialectique* is intended to meet: "Dialectical reason, and it alone, can consider the human being in all his aspects, and resolve his contradictions, without losing anything of his reality." [10] Sartre may be said to have met this challenge, in the final analysis, by agreeing with it.[11]

Sartre did not reply directly to Lefebvre's vituperative attack, but a long article first written at about the same time as *L'Existentialisme* was published shows Sartre's tremendous concern with revolution, or one kind of fundamental change, and the question of how to give a theoretical account of it. In "Matérialisme et Révolution", Sartre admits that the two concepts (materialism and revolution) have always been connected, but prefers to think of materialism as a myth rather than as a philosophy. But materialism, he thinks, denies man's freedom,[12] whereas the revolutionary act is the free act *par excellence*.[13] The task of the philosopher, therefore, is to come to a TRUE understanding of society that will have the same transformative effects as the myth of materialism has had in the past.[14] It is obvious that Sartre is here aware that his earlier ontology and his later social philosophy have not yet been brought together to provide a coherent account of any type of fundamental change in society; he seems to be encouraging himself to further reflection when he says, for example, that "it is these new notions of 'situation' and of 'being-in-the-world', for the elaboration of which the revolutionary, by his entire pattern of behavior, is expressing a demand".[15] In 1946, then, Sartre was groping for a political philosophy that would meet objections of the sort raised by Lefebvre.[16]

[10] *Ibid.*, p. 256.
[11] "I used to think that total indetermination was the real basis of choice. But from the point of view of the group . . . the contrary is true." *Critique de la raison dialectique*, p. 491.
[12] Sartre, *Situations* III ("Matérialisme et Révolution", ch. reprinted from *Temps Modernes*, 1946) (Paris, Librairie Gallimard, 1949), p. 174.
[13] *Ibid.*, p. 216.
[14] *Ibid.*, p. 175.
[15] *Ibid.*, p. 221.
[16] A mediocre book with the misleading title, *Marxism and Existentialism* (Garden City, Doubleday & Co., 1965), written by Walter Odajnyk, consists almost entirely of an analysis of this early essay. Its discussion of the *Critique*, which relies almost entirely on Desan's *The Marxism of Jean-Paul Sartre*, is confined to the final 32 pages of text.

A few years later, interestingly enough, Sartre was raising very similar objections against his friend and fellow existentialist, Albert Camus. In 1951 Camus published his much-heralded essay on fundamental change, *L'Homme Révolté* (The *Rebel*). In it, he makes a basic distinction between revolt ('la révolte) and revolution ('la révolution'): the former notion originates in the individual's experience of the absurdity of human existence – a theme that plays a leading role throughout Camus' writings –, whereas the notion of revolution is political. Later in the book, however, Camus says that "in fact, revolution is only the logical successor to metaphysical revolt".[17] Revolution is apparently, like Sisyphus, doomed to failure ("Historical revolution is obliged always to operate in the hope, unceasingly disappointed, of existing some day"[18]), and so is revolt – at least to the extent to which it confines itself to the level of historical (group) activity alone.[19] Camus' conclusions are somewhat difficult to capture, but he eventually takes refuge in a sort of individualistic aestheticism: all great art, according to him, is the expression of a full-fledged and highly desirable form of individual "revolt",[20] and he suggests that it may be possible to bring about a renaissance of human virtue "far from the formal principles and degraded values of history".[21] He sees the concept of revolt as being worthwhile if it is thought of as relative, a 'mediation', a movement within limits, rather than as an absolute.[22]

Although I fully agree with Camus' LAST-mentioned conclusion about the concept of revolt, *L'Homme Révolté* is not, in my opinion as in Sartre's, a highly successful attempt at dealing with the philosophical issues that it raises. It is always difficult to trade satisfactorily in paradox, though as a novelist Camus has sometimes done this very well. But when, for example, Camus proclaims that "revolution destroys at once both men and principles. But, for the same reasons, one can say that there has not yet been a revolution in history. There can only be one such, which would be the definitive revolution",[23] and then goes on to talk about the failures both of revolutionary theorists, such as Hegel and Marx, and of modern historical 'revolutions', the reader senses

17 Albert Camus, *L' Homme Révolté* (Paris, Librairie Gallimard, 1951), p. 135.
18 *Ibid.*, p. 308.
19 "In the purely historical universe that they have chosen, both revolt and revolution issue in the same dilemma: either the police or madness." *Ibid.*, p. 306.
20 *Ibid.*, p. 335.
21 *Ibid.*, p. 342.
22 *Ibid.*, p. 356.
23 *Ibid.*, p. 136.

contradiction rather than paradox. Camus has defined revolution as an absolute, a limiting concept, incapable of empirical realization, and now expresses moral indignation at the failures of self-proclaimed historical revolutions to coincide with that concept. Lefebvre's previous denomination of Camus as 'the "purest" existentialist',[24] in Lefebvre's pejorative use of that term, is here vindicated by Camus' treatment of important aspects of the concept of fundamental change in society.

Sartre himself followed this line of criticism, among others, in a celebrated public exchange of letters with Camus which appeared in *Temps Modernes* in 1952. The occasion for it was a highly critical review of *L'Homme Révolté*, written by Francis Jeanson, one of Sartre's younger associates on the staff of the magazine.[25] Camus replied with a letter to the editor, Sartre, in which he treated the review as something of a personal insult and as symptomatic of a certain degeneracy in contemporary attitudes, notably those of *Les Temps Modernes*, towards political issues.[26] Sartre's answering letter appears in the same issue. In it, Sartre refers to his past admiration for Camus' person,[27] for his earlier writings, and for his moral concern, but points out that circumstances have changed since the period of the Resistance: "Today, it is different. It is no longer a question of *defending the status quo*, but of changing it: that is what you will accept only if you have the most formal guarantees."[28] Camus' philosophy of the absurd, according to Sartre, has now led him to refuse to participate in the process of history: "'Has history a meaning?' you ask, 'has it an end?' For me, it is the *question* that is meaningless: for History, outside of man who makes it, is only an abstract concept."[29] Finally, Sartre chides Camus for having allowed his own moral sensibility to degenerate: "Your ethics changed first into moralism, today it is nothing more than literature, tomorrow it will perhaps be immorality."[30] The polemic is excessively acerbic, but the issues are among the most important both in the brief history of French neo-

[24] Lefebvre, *L' Existentialisme*, p. 219.

[25] "[Camus'] effort, in sum, seeks to reduce the concept 'revolution' to the concept 'divinization of man'." Francis Jeanson, "Albert Camus ou l'Ame Révoltée", *Temps Modernes* 79 (May 1952), p. 2077.

[26] "The truth is that your collaborator would like us to revolt against everything, except against the Communist Party and State." Albert Camus, "Lettre au Directeur des *Temps Modernes*", *Temps Modernes* 82 (Aug. 1952), p. 331.

[27] Sartre begins: "My dear Camus, Our friendship was not easy, but I shall miss it." "Réponse à Albert Camus", *Temps Modernes* 82 (Aug. 1952), p. 334.

[28] *Ibid.*, p. 352.

[29] *Ibid.*

[30] *Ibid.*, p. 353.

Marxism and in understanding the concept of fundamental change in society.[31]

Camus, himself a member of the French Communist Party for a year in 1934, had already broken with Sartre's closest collaborator in the early years of *Les Temps Modernes*, Maurice Merleau-Ponty, over an ethical issue. In 1947, the author of *La Phénoménologie de la Perception* published his "Essai sur le Problème Communiste", entitled *Humanisme et Terreur*. This was Merleau-Ponty's most sympathetic appraisal of both Marxism and the Communist Party; in it, he tried better to understand some of the more disturbing events in the recent history of that Party, such as the Moscow Purge Trials of the 1930's, in terms of "the stern Marxist rule which insists that a man be defined, not by his intentions, but by what he does, and an action not by its subjective meaning, but by its objective meaning".[32] He emphasized the importance of a sense of 'historical responsibility' in a philosophy of history such as that of Marx, and pointed out that ethical concepts, such as the notion of justice, are never, historically, entirely separable from political objectives and from the sort of compromising of principles that politics entails: "We do not have the choice between purity and violence, but between different sorts of violence."[33] As Sartre tells it in the biographical sketch that he wrote on the occasion of Merleau-Ponty's death, *Humanisme et Terreur* caused a scandal at the time of its appearance: many, including Camus, thought it a justification of the concentration camps and other excesses of the Stalinist regime in the Soviet Union. Camus made this accusation in person to Merleau-Ponty, who did not reply to him; the two were never reconciled.[34] Camus' charge was of course false, but he had at least been correct in pointing to the ethical questions raised by Merleau-Ponty's book.[35] In this respect, as Sartre relates, *Humanisme et Terreur* had a profound effect on Sartre himself:

[31] For a treatment of this dispute that is somewhat more sympathetic to Camus, cf. Emmett Parker, *Albert Camus: The Artist in the Arena* (Madison-Milwaukee-London, University of Wisconsin Press, 1966), pp. 136-142.

[32] Maurice Merleau-Ponty, *Humanisme et Terreur* (Paris, Librairie Gallimard, 1947), p. 9.

[33] *Ibid.*, p. 117.

[34] Sartre, "Merleau-Ponty Vivant", *Temps Modernes* 184-185 (Oct., 1961, special edition), p. 323.

[35] A joint editorial written by Sartre and Merleau-Ponty at the time of the publication of certain detailed disclosures concerning Soviet labor camps illustrates how far both of them were from being blanket defenders of Stalin's policies. It also alludes to the problem of ethics in neo-Marxist theory: "That means that we ... have the same values as a communist. A communist, it will be said, has no values. He has only fidelities. We reply that he indeed does what he can to arrive at that

In a word, it was Merleau who converted me: at the bottom of my heart, I was a relic of anarchism, I posed an abyss between the vague phantasms of collectivities and the precise ethics of my private life. . . . He revealed to me that I was making history just as M. Jourdain was making prose.[36]

Again, Sartre is acknowledging the insufficiency of his earlier philosophy.

While Sartre's dispute with Camus was occupying the public's attention, however, a conflict of opinion far more serious for the development of French neo-Marxism was building up between Sartre and Merleau-Ponty. The outbreak of the Korean War apparently convinced Merleau-Ponty of the bad faith of the Communist Party and of the impossibility of making any common cause with it in the future. At the same time, domestic political events in France were increasing Sartre's sympathy for the Communist Party. The two men continued to try to work together on *Les Temps Modernes* for several months in late 1952, when Sartre was writing the first two of three articles entitled "Les Communistes et la Paix" (the leading theme of which was that the Communists favored peace), but their political disagreements led to personal ones:

Underneath our intellectual divergences of 1941, so calmly accepted when Husserl alone was in dispute, we were soon astounded to discover conflicts that had their origin in our infancies, . . . our organisms. . . . In the one, a mad activism, covering up his aberrations; in the other, emotional withdrawals, an extreme quietism.[37]

The actual break, together with Merleau-Ponty's resignation from the magazine that he had helped to establish, occurred over a trivial question of editing. The two men resumed their personal friendship three years later, in 1956. Meanwhile, however, Merleau-Ponty had written a noteworthy book, *Les Aventures de la dialectique*, which includes a long chapter on "Sartre et l'Ultra-Bolshevisme". Here are summarized many of the most important charges against Sartre that the *Critique de la raison dialectique* may be regarded as an attempt to meet. To document his criticisms, Merleau-Ponty relied chiefly on Sartre's series "Les Communistes et la Paix", which, as Simone de Beauvoir rightly points out in her rebuttal of *Les Aventures*, was an occasional article and not

---

point, but that, thank God, no one can live without breathing. He has values *despite himself*." "Les Jours de Notre Vie", *Temps Modernes* 51 (Jan. 1950), p. 1161.

36 Sartre, "Merleau-Ponty Vivant", p. 324.

37 *Ibid.*, p. 325.

intended to present a whole philosophy of history.[38] But, obviously, Merleau-Ponty was relying as well on his great personal familiarity with Sartre's thought. The charge of 'ultra-Bolshevism' seems to rest on new elaborations of the old accusation that Sartre's view of human action is so radical as to be inapplicable to the real world: "The question is whether, as Sartre says, there are only *men* and *things*, or whether there is also that intermediate world that we call history, symbolism, truth to be forged."[39] Sartre's ideal, according to Merleau-Ponty, would be a Party whose decisions were pure action, ungoverned by the nuances of historical reality. This is 'ultra-Bolshevism', an atomistic, opportunistic view of political action in which the spontaneous decisions of the Party "translate *as a matter of principle* the movement of history"[40] and in which theory is discarded: "The conception of communism that Sartre proposes is a denunciation of dialectic and of philosophy of history, and substitutes for them a philosophy of absolute creation in the unknown."[41] There would be, then, nothing but ABSOLUTE changes according to Sartre's philosophy, and any sort of fundamental change in society, in any of the more ordinary senses of that expression, would be excluded: "At times, to read Sartre, one would think that he has assigned himself the task of proving that revolution is impossible."[42] Thus, as is seen, Merleau-Ponty believes that Sartre has given up the possibility of providing a theoretical account of social change: Sartre's analyses of facts are clear, but he has no theory.[43] As for Merleau-Ponty himself, he admits to having changed his views since the writing of *Humanisme et Terreur*. He still believes that the dialectical way of viewing history is correct (though he never provides any very explicit definition of what he understands this to be), and he says that "what is moribund is not the dialectic, but the pretense of terminating it in an end of history or in a permanent revolution".[44] He goes on to deny that any revolutionary change in society can be permanent and to insist on the inevitable degeneration of revolutionary movements when they become institutionalized regimes.[45] Finally, expressing the hope that a new liberalism may arise

[38] de Beauvoir, "Merleau-Ponty et le Pseudo-Sartrisme", *Temps Modernes* 114-115 (June-July 1955), p. 2072.
[39] Merleau-Ponty, *Les Aventures de la dialectique* (Paris, Librairie Gallimard, 1955), p. 269.
[40] *Ibid.*, p. 175.
[41] *Ibid.*, p. 138.
[42] *Ibid.*, p. 225.
[43] *Ibid.*, p. 144.
[44] *Ibid.*, p. 276.
[45] *Ibid.*, p. 279.

which would render both Communism and contemporary capitalism outmoded, Merleau-Ponty concludes by renouncing his claim in *Humanisme et Terreur* "that Marxism 'remains true as a negation'": his Marxism of that period, he says, was based on morality rather than on any philosophy of history, and was 'Kant in disguise'.[46]

Simone de Beauvoir's reply was the only answer to *Les Aventures* from the Sartrean camp; Sartre himself never publicly attacked his former co-editor. Merleau-Ponty's remark about Kant[47] gave his critic an opening wedge, which she used to set the tone of her article:

> When, in the light of the Korean War, Merleau-Ponty discovered that he had up to that time confused Marx with Kant, he realized that he must renounce the Hegelian idea of the end of history and concluded to the necessity of destroying the Marxist dialectic.[48]

Mlle. de Beauvoir goes on to deny categorically most of Merleau-Ponty's charges, including the basic one that Sartre's philosophy is unable to cope with social reality (the 'intermediate world between men and things') and that he therefore must hold as an ideal an atomistic, *ex nihilo* creation of history by an ideal Party. As for Merleau-Ponty's renunciation of Marxism, Mlle. de Beauvoir attributes this to his having misunderstood Marxism on at least two counts: first, in having thought of it as being primarily an economic system, and secondly (as an allusion in her opening sentence also points out), in having thought that Marxism entailed the belief that history would somehow come to an end after some "definitive" fundamental change: "For him, communism becomes the utopia that it is for Aron and for all the bourgeois thinkers."[49] Most emphatically of all, perhaps, she rejects Merleau-Ponty's charge that Sartre regards the notion of dialectic as an illusion: "No text of Sartre's", she says, "authorizes these assertions. Sartre has

[46] *Ibid.*, p. 312.

[47] What makes this reference especially ironic is the fact that Kant's name has been highly suspect for many 'orthodox' Marxists ever since Eduard Bernstein invoked it in defense of his rather thoroughgoing 'revisionism' in 1899. Cf. "Kant vs. Cant" in Bernstein's *Evolutionary Socialism* (tr. by E. C. Harvey) (New York, Schocken Books, 1961), pp. 200-224.

[48] de Beauvoir, "Merleau-Ponty et le Pseudo-Sartrisme", p. 2072.

[49] *Ibid.*, p. 2119. Raymond Aron's *L'Opium des Intellectuels* (Paris, Calmann-Lévy, 1955), published in the same year as *Les Aventures de la dialectique*, is an attack on the entire French neo-Marxist movement, notably on Sartre, Merleau-Ponty, and Camus, and on its 'myths'. Aron, a noted political commentator and sociologist, helped to establish *Les Temps Modernes* but resigned from its board soon thereafter.

dismissed as inane the teleological optimism which is usually concealed behind dialectics; not dialectic itself." [50]

The lasting philosophical value of Merleau-Ponty's attack on Sartre is, I believe, fairly slight. Sartre had not, at the time at which *Les Aventures de la dialectique* was written, published any systematic work in social philosophy, and the fact that it was an article concerned with current affairs, "Les Communistes et la Paix", that Merleau-Ponty was chiefly attacking undoubtedly testifies to the latter's tremendous preoccupation with the somber events of the moment. Such a preoccupation, however, renders more difficult the attainment of philosophic objectivity. One may or may not sympathize with Merleau-Ponty's concern over the political direction that *Les Temps Modernes* was at least temporarily taking, but that matters little to us here. The relatively few important original (as opposed to purely critical) claims made by Merleau-Ponty (such as the announcement that communism and capitalism are equally moribund today) are not argued in sufficient detail, and the central notion of 'dialectic' is never explained. *Les Aventures* is in fact a series of essays, the first of which is on Max Weber, the second and third on Lukacs (to whom I shall return later), the fourth on Trotsky, and the fifth and longest on Sartre. But Merleau-Ponty did succeed in indicating rather clearly some of the principal objections that Sartre would be forced to try to meet in his *Critique*: the charge that Sartre was basically unsympathetic to dialectic, the alleged inability of Sartre's radically individualistic philosophy to deal with social phenomena, and the claim that fundamental change in a Sartrean perspective must mean some impossible ideal of absolute revolution. Finally, despite the unfortunate reference to Kant, *Les Aventures* contained very little of substance about another important problem that has previously been mentioned in this chapter, namely that of the relation of ethics to neo-Marxist theory.

Les Aventures de la dialectique was soon subjected to a violent attack from another quarter: the French Communist Party, which devoted a special mass meeting to speeches denouncing the book. A letter from Lukacs was read, in which the latter renounced the use made by Merleau-Ponty of his own early writings. Roger Garaudy, the leading orthodox theoretician in the French Party, found in Merleau-Ponty's

[50] de Beauvoir, "Merleau-Ponty et le Pseudo-Sartrisme", p. 2092. Sartre later claimed that Merleau-Ponty himself more or less repudiated the term 'dialectic' around 1955. This is not very important for our purposes. ("Merleau-Ponty Vivant", p. 318)

emphasis on 'choice' the roots of an ARBITRARY philosophy of history.[51] What seemed to bother Garaudy and several other speakers most of all was Merleau-Ponty's refusal to admit a 'dialectics of nature' (Engels' phrase), i.e., to admit that inanimate things as well as men in society develop dialectically. This criticism, however, did not very much concern Henri Lefebvre, who seemed, by comparison with his comrades, almost hesitant in his attack on Merleau-Ponty for being ambiguous and somewhat aesthetic in his approach to history.[52] Lefebvre could not know at that time that he was soon to sever his own ties of thirty years' standing with the Party. At about the same period, a very short article written by Sartre called attention to the dearth of intellectuals within the Party's ranks and specifically mentioned Lefebvre as an interesting writer who seemed to be under some mysterious sort of constraint.[53]

Later in the same year, 1956, an abortive rebellion took place in Budapest, Hungary, and Russian tanks were the chief instruments used for quelling it; Sartre, along with many others, felt himself constrained to give up his former hopes of seeing the formation of a new alliance between Communist and non-Communist Marxist parties, and announced that "we return to the opposition".[54] *Les Temps Modernes* thus suddenly reversed the political direction that Merleau-Ponty had found so deplorable.

The events in Hungary, though their repercussions in France were numerous, were not themselves the immediate occasion for Lefebvre's departure from the Communist Party ranks. An article by Lefebvre, originally written for the same special issue of a Polish journal as Sartre's "Question de Méthode", was reprinted in *Temps Modernes* in mid-1957; it shows both Lefebvre's optimism for the future and his extreme dissatisfaction with contemporary Communist thought.[55] An elaboration of these ideas was published under the title, *Problèmes actuels du marxisme*.[56] It was for this book that, in 1958, Henri Lefebvre was finally expelled from the Party, which thereby lost its most

[51] R. Garaudy, G. Cogniot, *et al.*, *Mésaventures de l'Anti-Marxisme* (Paris, Editions Sociales, 1956), p. 11.

[52] *Ibid.*, p. 103.

[53] Sartre, "Le Réformisme et les fétiches", *Temps Modernes* 122 (Feb. 1956), p. 1160.

[54] Sartre, "Le Fantôme de Staline", *Temps Modernes* 129-130-131 (Nov.-Dec. 1956, Jan. 1957), p. 696.

[55] Lefebvre, "Le Marxisme et la Pensée Française", *Temps Modernes* 137-138 (July-Aug. 1957), pp. 104-137.

[56] Lefebvre, *Problèmes actuels du marxisme* (Paris, Presses Universitaires de France, 1958)

competent philosopher. But soon thereafter, the reading public gained a most extraordinary new book by Lefebvre, *La Somme et le reste*, without mention of which no account of the history of French neo-Marxism and of its leading philosophical issues would be complete.

What is most immediately attractive about *La Somme* is its autobiographical aspect. Lefebvre's private life, his political activities, and his life as a philosopher were all very closely interwoven, and the following passage best describes the impasse into which he had been led in all three regards:

> Thus it was, then, that a philosopher saw his philosophic ambitions constantly diminish, uniting in his 'career' the themes of the goatskin and of lost illusions. He started from the idea that philosophy was going to change the world, or at least make a decisive contribution to that change, by achieving in the relative life of men the ancient absolutes, justice, truth, freedom. He became a simple functionary in a political action further and further removed from justice, from truth, from freedom, an action that he agreed to by telling himself that it would come back to them after some rather labyrinthine detours (which he continues to hope). He surveys the dissolution of his hopes, as he notes that the technician can act on things and on men better than can the philosopher, and the politician better than the technician. . . . He has come to think that the highest hope that a man of thought can permit himself is to act on language, to modify some terms, to introduce one or several words into the vocabulary that serves as a grillwork for minds.[57]

But, as the passage further shows, Lefebvre also has some original ideas about philosophy and philosophic method, which his removal from the restraint of Party discipline has permitted him more fully to express. *La Somme et le reste* is a melange of autobiography, literary and philosophic essay, sociology, and even some poetry; but, curiously enough, this does not testify to any lack of mental rigor on Lefebvre's part. He regards Marx's *The German Ideology* as announcing (whether rightly or wrongly) the end of philosophy, and one of his strongest criticisms of Sartre is that the latter fails to put the philosophic enterprise itself into question.[58] Lefebvre himself proposes a new approach to philosophy, which he calls 'programmatic', and which he opposes to both the systematic and 'problematic' (sceptical) alternatives of the past.[59] He is convinced that philosophy can provide no conclusive demonstrations: "If philosophic discourse is a second-level discourse (a rigorous discourse about ordinary language), it must propose to prove itself without

[57] Lefebvre, *La Somme et le reste* (Paris, La Nef de Paris Editions, 1959), p. 577.
[58] *Ibid.*, p. 81. Cf. also Lefebvre's *Introduction à la Modernité* (Paris, Les Editions de Minuit, 1962), p. 247.
[59] *La Somme et le reste*, p. 717.

ever arriving at that point."[60] 'Programmatic philosophy' would bear considerable resemblance to sociology, but would be more concerned than the latter with the domain of possibilities. Philosophy, according to Lefebvre, must entertain even the most extreme hypotheses, or limiting cases, even that of the disappearance of philosophy itself.[61] It is in this light, he thinks, that the extreme form of freedom examined by Sartre in *L'être et le néant* finds its justification.[62]

How would the concept of fundamental change in society be treated in this new way of philosophizing? The idea of it has obviously fascinated Lefebvre most of his life, and he joined the Communist Party largely with a view to helping to bring such a change about. But, well versed as he was in the Marxist classics,[63] he apparently never followed the lead of most latter-day Communist Party leaders in thinking of fundamental change primarily in terms of the POLITICAL overtones which the word 'revolution' usually evokes today. In his own defense, he says: "Basically, I don't like politics... It was only towards 1934 that the spirit of the Party changed, and that, instead of calling ourselves revolutionary, we called ourselves political."[64] The key to understanding Lefebvre's view of the concept of fundamental change in society is to be found in the following passage, in which he states the principal thesis of an earlier work of his, one accepted, though with no enthusiasm, by his political superiors, and one in which he still takes pride. Its title was *Critique de la vie quotidienne*:[65]

> In effect, this book implies the idea that there is no antinomy-like contradiction between reform and revolution; it contains the idea that only changes in daily life make a substantial difference, that beside them the overthrows of political superstructures remain superficial.... Political changes, those which modify the government and the economic structure (the relations of production), have human interest only inasmuch as they change daily life.[66]

60 *Ibid.*, p. 111.

61 One of Lefebvre's most recent works, *Métaphilosophie* (Paris, Les Editions de Minuit, 1965), is a more extended development of this theme. In it, Lefebvre is more severe than in *La Somme et le reste* concerning the entire traditional conception of philosophy (as systematic and totalizing). *Métaphilosophie* also contains some more detailed criticisms of Sartre's *Critique*, notably on pp. 77-88.

62 *La Somme et le reste*, p. 723.

63 "According to Marx and Lenin, the only true, profound historical discontinuity, the *revolutionary discontinuity*, is that which separates the State from the end of the State, politics from the end of politics, power over men from the administration of things in the name of men." Stalin, he says, revised this doctrine. *Ibid.*, p. 228.

64 *Ibid.*, pp. 159-160.

65 Lefebvre, *Critique de la vie quotidienne* (Paris, Editions Bernard Grasset, 1947).

66 *La Somme et le reste*, p. 612.

There are echoes, in these views of Lefebvre's, both of the early, more utopian Marx of the *1844 Manuscripts* and of an apolitical attitude toward society that may well have characterized the remote world to which Lefebvre has devoted much of his non-philosophical research, his native Basque country of the medieval and pre-medieval epochs. What is interesting, in any case, is that Lefebvre is one French neo-Marxist (Sartre will hopefully be found to be another) who has tried to get beneath the contemporary shibboleth of 'revolution' and to explore what the concept of fundamental change in society might really mean.

Is it merely Lefebvre's anti-systematic bias in philosophy, or some form of irrationalism, that has led him to deny that there is an antinomy between reform and revolution? By no means. Lefebvre is no irrationalist: since his youth, he has retained a strong interest in logic[67] and mathematics, and he is to be taken seriously when he praises Sartre highly for the *rigor*[68] of his thought or when he speaks of the conflict between 'rationalism', which in certain forms he deplores, and 'reason'.[69] The fact is that Lefebvre most resembles Hart (and many of the other British philosophers mentioned in the first section of this study) in his extreme concern with PROBLEMS OF LANGUAGE. At the close of the passage that I quoted earlier Lefebvre indicates that the modification of language, perhaps only of a few words, is the best hope that he now sees for a philosopher to effect any changes in society. This may profitably be compared with Wisdom's encouragement of analysts to discover 'unconventional' patterns in phenomena. It will be recalled that even in *L'Existentialisme*, a book which Lefebvre now recants in large measure because of its unwarrantably polemical and politically subservient character,[70] Lefebvre had called attention to the importance of CONCEPTS, which he claimed that Sartre had entirely neglected while over-emphasizing consciousness. Once again, in *La Somme et le reste*, he calls attention to the logical point that it is the concept, language, rather than pure consciousness, which serves as our criterion of truth.[71] And, while he is now quite willing to praise Sartre for having modified

[67] His *Logique Formelle et Logique Dialectique* earned him criticism from the Communist Party for its strong insistence on the thesis, rather suspect among the leadership at the time, that dialectics did not supersede formal logic. *Ibid.*, p. 47.

[68] *Ibid.*, p. 512.

[69] *Ibid.*, p. 582. He goes on to study briefly the potential conflicts within other pairs of words, such as 'nationalism against the nations', 'individualism against individuals', 'formalism against form', and 'humanism against the human'. (pp. 582-585)

[70] *Ibid.*, p. 512.

[71] *Ibid.*, p. 455.

his views and for attempting to 'rediscover' 'mediations (social practice, social groups)'[72] in *Critique de la raison dialectique*, Lefebvre remains in other ways strongly critical of Sartre, among other reasons for the latter's alleged abuse of language.[73]

For Lefebvre, then, it is only through an analysis of language, the concept, that a phenomenon can be understood. This is perhaps especially true for the concept of fundamental change and the family of related concepts, which seem to him to be playing an increasingly dominant role in the modern era.[74] 'Fundamental change in society' and 'political revolution' are by no means equivalent concepts; the latter is certainly conceivable without the former, and perhaps – Lefebvre at least hints at this – even the former without the latter. The philosopher, if he wishes to have any transformative effect whatever on society, must get beyond the stultifying trivialities of ordinary usage: [75] "Philosophy issues forth from wordgames by means of which living speech breaks through the structure of discourse. In this way alone can dialectic intervene and be manifested." [76] Dialectical reason, it would seem, may begin to function only after a re-examination of language. Language must not be abused, for it has a 'specific obscurity' of its own that must be respected; [77] but (as our chapter on 'analysis' has already led us to conclude) the philosopher MAY, indeed MUST, somehow change language, if he is to make his contribution.

La Somme et le reste appeared in 1959, one year before the publication of *Critique de la raison dialectique*. During these two years, Sartre took an active interest in the Cuban revolution of Fidel Castro, but otherwise there were no other new developments or special events in the world of the mandarins that I consider it necessary to mention here. To this statement, I make one further exception: the publication in 1960 of the first full French translation of Georg Lukacs' *Geschichte und Klassenbewußtsein*. The translation did not, however, come as a revelation to the French reading public, for Lukacs' influence on French neo-Marxism had long been felt. *Les Aventures de la dialectique* testifies to Merleau-Ponty's thoroughgoing acquaintance with this Marxist classic,

[72] *Introduction à la Modernité*, p. 90, and *Métaphilosophie*, p. 80.
[73] *Introduction à la Modernité*, p. 354.
[74] (In this era), "the differential schema (addition by infinitesimal variations) is relegated to second place. The differential schema is subordinated to the concepts of mutation, of abrupt change, of qualitative difference." *Ibid.*, pp. 179-180.
[75] *La Somme et le reste*, p. 131.
[76] *Ibid.*, p. 129.
[77] Lefebvre, *Introduction à la Modernité*, p. 352.

and there are numerous evidences of the influence of Lukacs' ideas on Sartre and Lefebvre, as well. The fact that this talented Hungarian Communist philosopher had long since repudiated his best-known work and had turned to producing studies, often of inferior quality, that would be acceptable to the new 'orthodoxy', had done nothing to diminish the respect of many French thinkers for *Geschichte und Klassenbewußtsein.*

It would be too lengthy a task, and one not in keeping with the remainder of this chapter, for me to discuss in detail the interesting treatments given by Lukacs to such questions as the concept of class, his demonstration of the methodological limitations of 'formalist systems' in philosophy, or his attempts to clarify the notion of 'dialectic'. It is from Lukacs, among others, that Lefebvre inherited both his concern with emphasizing the pre-Marxist, 'bourgeois' origins of Marxist thought, and his insistence that a purely POLITICAL revolution is not equivalent to a fundamental change in society.[78] But Lukacs does deal with one phenomenon of which very little mention is to be found in the works of the French writers discussed in this chapter, and perhaps it is Lukacs' treatment of it, written in the spirit of some of Marx' own statements on the subject, that is partly responsible for its later neglect. The phenomenon in question is LAW.[79] Lukacs wrote his classic between 1919 and 1922, and he was familiar at the time with the works of Kelsen. Indeed, he refers to Kelsen and makes brief criticisms of the insufficiencies brought about by the latter's methodology,[80] and of the dangers of trying to make individual sciences (such as *Rechtswissenschaft*) too autonomous,[81] along lines very similar to those that I have taken in the first section of this book. But it is especially in later chapters of *Geschichte und Klassenbewußtsein,* notably in an essay entitled "Legality

[78] "It is precisely because proletarian thought has as its practical goal the *fundamental* overthrow of the whole of society that it seizes upon bourgeois society and all its intellectual, artistic, etc., productions as its methodological *starting-point.*" . . . "A [purely] political revolution merely consecrates a socio-economic state which has already been imposed, at least partially, in economic reality." Georg Lukacs, *Histoire et Conscience de Classe* (tr. by K. Axelos and J. Bois) (Paris, Les Editions de Minuit, 1960), pp. 204 and 295.

[79] There is considerable evidence that some *other* French writers, though still not, in general, those of the mandarin circle, are beginning to take a great interest in the relationship between Marxism and law. Cf. Volume 12 of the *Archives de Philosophie du Droit* (1967), which is devoted to "Marx et le Droit Moderne", and esp. the article, "À propos de la théorie marxiste du droit" (pp. 145-162), by Nicos Poulantzas, an admirer (p. 150) of the controversial anti-humanist Marxist, Louis Althusser.

[80] *Ibid.*, pp. 138-139.

[81] *Ibid.*, p. 265.

and Illegality", that Lukacs' views on law are made very clear. His argument is that, although the romantic longing (found in some new communist parties) to indulge in illegality for its own sake is childish and absurd, law as a phenomenon merits no more special respect or attention than does the philosophy of law, of ethics, or of metaphysics. All such distinctions, and even the distinction between 'law' and violence, according to Lukacs, are purely social and historical.[82] In "Legality and Illegality", he concludes:

> The proletariat of central and western Europe still has a difficult road ahead of it. In order to arrive, by struggling, at the consciousness of its historical vocation and of the legitimacy of its domination, it must first learn to grasp the purely tactical character of legality and of illegality, in short, to get rid as well of the cretinism of legality as of the romanticism of illegality.[83]

Such an attitude has noteworthy implications for the future.

Although Camus and Merleau-Ponty are both dead now, the history of the mandarins is not yet at an end, nor has this chapter been an attempt at a definitive tracing of that history even up to the time of publication of the first volume of Sartre's *Critique*. Since then, among other things, both Sartre and Simone de Beauvoir have published much additional, revealing autobiographical material; new intellectual currents, notably that of structuralism, have gained sufficient favor in France to challenge the general humanist philosophical approach to man represented by Sartre and the other mandarins in all phases of their thought; and, in the political arena, the American war against Vietnam, the French student uprising of May 1968 (during which the names of both Sartre and Lefebvre received prominent attention), and the Russian invasion of Czechoslovakia (which had a significance probably even greater than that of the Budapest events for the future of Marxism) have all taken place. But the present chapter has served its purpose if it has illuminated some of the background against which *Critique de la raison dialectique* may be rendered more comprehensible. Events in world history and in the history of the Communist Party, personal quarrels among the mandarins, and of course, most importantly, differences in philosophic theory have all played a part. Among these last, I wish especially to recall the following problems: the nature of dialectics as a philosophical method and its relationship to language; the charge that Sartre's philosophy was atomistic and excessively indi-

82 *Ibid.*, p. 277.
83 *Ibid.*, p. 308.

vidualistic and that his view of consciousness did not permit him to deal with 'mediations' such as language (concepts) and social groups; the role of ethics as well as that of law in neo-Marxist thought; and, finally, the meaning of 'fundamental change in society' when seen from the different perspectives of social revolution, of political revolution, and of individual, 'metaphysical' revolt. We may now turn to our résumé of Sartre's theoretical account of fundamental change.

3

SARTRE

The chapter on "Hart", in which I recounted Hart's analysis of the concept of fundamental change in law, was brief and unelaborated. I simply summarized the main points of the short section in *The Concept of Law* on "The Pathology of a Legal System". Hart's analysis of fundamental change, at least at first sight, might have seemed to stand on its own, to be fairly intelligible without one's needing to have recourse to the rest of Hart's book or analysis. Later on, of course, I showed that this appearance was somewhat misleading.

In order to give even initial intelligibility to Sartre's theoretical account of the phenomenon of fundamental change in society, it might be suspected that more reference to the rest of the theory would be required than in the case of Hart. This suspicion is correct. As Sartre constantly insists, "The fundamental intelligibility of dialectical Reason – if the latter is going to exist – is that of a totalization." [1] The difficulty of summarizing any part of Sartre's account, without summarizing all that has preceded that part, seems extreme. In addition, Sartre's neologisms – the abuse of language to which Lefebvre objected – often require special explanation.[2]

Furthermore, I now have the additional obligation of attempting to begin to indicate, at least in some general way, the relationship and possible points of contact between Hart's account and the present one. This is by no means easy. First of all, Sartre is approaching the concept of fundamental change from a quite different perspective, a perspective

[1] *Critique de la raison dialectique*, p. 137. (At this point, he is criticizing the view of Engels that there is a plurality of basic 'laws' of dialectic.)

[2] I shall not attempt, in most cases, to point out possible precedents for the more difficult Sartrean terminology: Hegel is obviously the main inspiration for his use of certain terms (dialectic, mediation, reciprocity), Marx for others (PRAXIS, scarcity, class), recent sociology (regressive-progressive method, totality, group) and Sartre's own existentialism (project, inertness) for still others, and even Kant for at least one – for the notion of a 'critique'.

of a broad social philosophy, in which the whole field of law recedes, at least for the moment, into almost total obscurity. Moreover, the whole idea of 'fundamental change IN SOCIETY' is considerably more difficult to conceptualize (more complex, more elusive) than was that of 'fundamental change in law' – and yet, we know that the problems raised by Kelsen's and others' initially plausible conceptualizations of the latter eventually turned out to be formidable enough! Sartre's way of coping with this difficulty is, as we are about to see, to give an account that begins on a very high level of abstraction and that remains sufficiently abstract throughout his treatment of fundamental change so as to stand in stark contrast to Hart's relatively concrete analysis of 'the pathology of a legal system'. But this does not mean, as we shall see, that the effort to establish points of contact and contrast between the two is utterly hopeless. To begin with, we shall want to consider more closely the very differences in method which serve to make a fruitful comparison so difficult.

Sartre's single "Question de Méthode" is, "Do we have today the means of constructing a structural and historical anthropology?" [3] His tentative answer is affirmative, and the first volume of his *Critique* is meant to be a STRUCTURAL anthropology, a "Prolegomenon to any future anthropology".[4] (He uses the term 'anthropology', of course, in the broad sense, strange to English-speaking persons, of 'science of human activities'.) Here, contrary to the ordinary 'progressive' method of certain contemporary Marxist writers [5] (in many of whom this method has degenerated into the malicious practice of imposing their already-formed preconceptions on every new experience [6]), Sartre proposes to proceed at first REGRESSIVELY, that is, to begin at the most abstract and FORMAL level of human (dialectical) experience, the individual in his abstract PRAXIS,

> ... in order to rediscover, across stronger and stronger conditionings, the totality of his practical relations with others, through this the structures of diverse practical multiplicities, and, across the contradictions and struggles of the latter, the absolute, concrete reality: historical man.[7]

[3] *Ibid.*, p. 9.
[4] *Ibid.*, p. 153.
[5] *Ibid.*, p. 86.
[6] *Ibid.*, p. 34. He gives numerous examples of this, including Lukacs' treatment of the existentialist movement (p. 34) and the official Communist Party explanations of the uprising in Budapest (p. 81).
[7] *Ibid.*, p. 143.

The treatment of history awaits the second volume of the *Critique*, however; the first volume deals with individuals, social structures, and their 'contradictions and struggles'. The two major types of structures, for Sartre, are the SERIES ('la série') and the GROUP ('le groupe'). The phenomenon of fundamental change in society as dealt with by Sartre is best located in the movement from the series to the group; fundamental change is also to be found in the reverse movement from group to series. Thus it would be quite misleading simply to compare a Sartrean fundamental change with, let us say, the transition (leaving out all considerations of any interim period) from one Kelsenian legal order or Hartean legal system to another: groups and series are two different ideal TYPES of structures. But when Hart, in his section on 'the pathology of a legal system', points to the possibility of a 'healthy' legal system's 'breaking down' (in the face of anarchy, banditry, etc.), then he is referring to possible concrete instances of what might be regarded as a fundamental change from a group back to a series within the framework of the Sartrean account.

The question arises immediately as to how Sartre proposes to prove the validity of his schema, and he deals with this question at great length. Briefly, he acknowledges that dialectics as a METHOD must be established *a priori*,[8] since any amount of induction from empirical facts must still be finite and thus insufficient. But his is a 'critical' as opposed to a 'dogmatic' dialectic:

> If it is said that this dialectical Reason can only be *criticized* (in the sense in which Kant took this term) by dialectical Reason itself, we shall reply that this is true but that it is necessary, precisely, to let it be founded and developed as a free critique of itself and simultaneously as a movement of History and of knowledge.[9]

He strongly affirms that there is an absolute necessity about his schema, given the structure of 'certain regions of materiality' (and notably the fact that human history has thus far taken place in a regime of SCARCITY, which is not a LOGICAL necessity but is the 'fundamental relation of *our*

[8] *Ibid.*, p. 118. His meaning here is very elusive. What is claimed to be *a priori* is no law or category, but only a heuristic methodology (p. 153). As Sartre says in the course of criticizing contemporary 'orthodox' Marxist writers in "Question de Méthode": "There is *resistance*, on the part of History already experienced, to *a priori* schematism" (p. 81).
[9] *Ibid.*, p. 120.

History' [10]), and yet that the dialectic is only a RESULTANT of human actions within these 'regions'.[11] As for the philosopher, the 'critic' himself, he must take an INTERNAL, rather than an external, contemplative point of view, on the 'totalization', or dialectical movement, that he is investigating.[12]

From the formal, non-historical perspective that Sartre is adopting in this book, it is obvious that all the movements, including that from series to group, are REVERSIBLE: there is no necessary temporal priority of one to the other.[13] His account is similar to Hart's in this respect, except that Hart had not considered it necessary even to make such a point. The reason why Sartre, on the other hand, feels the need to do so is quite evident: Sartre must anticipate the historically-oriented conclusions of his second volume, and he must leave the way open for a Marxist vision of the future according to which this 'reversibility' would not continue forever.

It is simply for convenience' sake, Sartre says, that he begins with abstract, individual PRAXIS – Nowell-Smith's 'desert island case'. *Praxis* is defined (much later in the book) as "organizing project going beyond material conditions towards an objective, and imprinting itself through labor in inorganic matter as a reworking of the practical field and a reunification of the means with a view to attaining the end".[14] Time and again, Sartre will repeat that "*The whole historical dialectic rests on individual* praxis".[15] PRAXIS is characterized, above all, by FREEDOM. Sartre's approach thus clearly represents the alternative to the Wittgensteinian-Hartean view of human activity as primarily rule-governed, and it exemplifies, as we shall see in detail later on, both the strengths and the weaknesses of this alternative approach.

At its most abstract, PRAXIS originates in NEED: the individual experiences need, and so he begins to work on inert matter in order to alter the material condition of being in need. Matter, for Sartre, is radically non-dialectical. This primitive experience is the basis of all that is to follow. Sartre next discusses the relations of reciprocity between and

[10] *Ibid.*, p. 202. This is precisely the point that Hart made, of course, in outlining his 'minimum content of natural law', except that Hart did not give the fact of scarcity, the fourth in his list, an especially privileged status among his 'five salient truisms'.

[11] *Ibid.*, p. 132.

[12] *Ibid.*, p. 140.

[13] *Ibid.*, p. 567.

[14] *Ibid.*, p. 687.

[15] *Ibid.*, p. 165.

among individuals. In a reciprocal relation, Sartre holds, one always sees the other person as a means to an end (the realization of a 'project'), whether that relation be of a friendly or of a hostile sort.[16] The basis of hostility is the material condition of scarcity, and as long as there is scarcity in this world there will be 'an inert structure of inhumanity in everyone', even though there is no such thing as an unalterable human nature (one of Sartre's oldest themes).[17] Now he begins to develop the notion of the SERIES, as he shows how it is possible for the 'indissoluble couple', man and inert matter, to change roles, and for the producer to become his product (the Marxist concept of ALIENATION) by the operation of human PRAXIS alone. Throughout the *Critique*, Sartre provides numerous illustrations from different periods of history; in this case, the very familiar modern notion that men, both workers and owners, can and do become slaves to their machines provides an obvious example for him to use. The situation in which we find individuals, in principle free, applying their labor to inert matter, altering it, and yet at the same time so greatly determined by their present material conditions that they make no attempts to change or 'go beyond' the latter, is what Sartre calls the 'practico-inert field' ('le champs pratico-inerte'); he terms the individuals' PRAXIS in these circumstances a 'passive activity'.

Seriality is the most commonplace, banal form of social structure, according to Sartre, and for that very reason it must be studied. Sociologists have tended to neglect it, and Marxist writers, while they acknowledge its existence, tend to underrate its importance as a 'material resistance of aggregates and of masses to the action of groups',[18] including the Marxists' own groups. Individuals experience the serial 'collectives' of which they are a part as being EXTERNAL to themselves, as being 'inert', and as rendering their own PRAXIS at least partially inert; among the examples that Sartre studies here are the radio audience listening to a political broadcast[19] and the more complex illustration, from economics, of the free market.[20] We shall also want to keep in

[16] *Ibid.*, p. 189.
[17] *Ibid.*, p. 207.
[18] *Ibid.*, p. 319.
[19] *Ibid.*, pp. 320-325.
[20] *Ibid.*, pp. 328-338. A class, too, when all its members regard their membership in it as an inevitable, unalterable destiny, as their 'Being', is nothing but a collective (p. 353). An actual class, for Sartre, is never so simple as this, however. It may be a very complex mixture of series and groups of various kinds, as he shows in the last part of his volume. Thus he claims to have avoided the usual objections to

mind, however, certain basic similarities between Sartre's notion of a 'series' and Hart's portrayal of an 'unhealthy' legal system which is not 'accepted' by most of its subjects. Sartre seems to regard it as highly unlikely, if not absurd, that ANY modern legal system might be 'healthy' in the sense of abetting the free 'totalizing projects' of any group at all, even of the group of officials of that system; but we shall want later to ask ourselves whether he has demonstrated the logical impossibility of the existence of a Hartean legal system which was 'actively accepted' by the majority of its subjects, or whether his attitude is merely the result of a prejudice or of some limited empirical observations.

The following sentence can best be taken as Sartre's introduction to the treatment of fundamental change:

> It is [the] passage from Being to organization that we must consider at present: we have grasped the dialectical intelligibility of individual *praxis* and of the passive activity of the collective; we must grasp and pinpoint that of collective *praxis*.[21]

It would be easier to describe the formation of the group, remarks Sartre, if one had a 'transcendental and idealist' conception of dialectic: in that case, one could speak of the group as a hyperorganism, with powers of its own, analogous to individual organisms. But Sartre unequivocally rejects (even more strongly than does Hart) organicist social theory. For Sartre, individual human PRAXIS always remains the active, constitutive element; group PRAXIS, at its best, can never be more than a CONSTITUTED form of activity.[22]

It must first be noted that the coming into existence of this new kind of reality, the organized group, is *a priori* not necessary but only logically possible.[23]

> There is no means of deciding, outside of an appreciation of their concrete situation and of their own history within the web of totalizing History, whether such-and-such particular individuals or aggregates will get out of their abstract condition as practico-inert beings.[24]

Material conditions limit and determine individual PRAXIS and its 'totalizing project' of fundamental change; such a change, when it does

---

Marxist concepts of class, such as the contention that there are 'borderline cases' of intermediate classes, by his denial that a class is ever a 'total and synthetic form' of social structure (p. 356).

21 *Ibid.*, p. 358.

22 *Ibid.*, p. 377.

23 *Ibid.*, p. 381.

24 *Ibid.*, p. 369.

occur, is not a negation of the role of matter in human history, but only of matter's 'adversity coefficient'.[25] Thus it is that Sartre can unhesitatingly agree to the 'obvious' point that, for human beings in a world of scarcity and need, the origin of the 'bouleversement qui déchire le collectif par l'éclair d'une *praxis* commune' is some material happening occurring within existing structures – famine, an economic crisis, transformations in technology, etc.[26]

The phenomenon with which Sartre now finds himself confronted is that of the GROUP IN FUSION.[27] He illustrates his treatment of it with interspersed references to one of its truly classic historical manifestations, the revolutionary PRAXIS of the residents of the geographically isolated Faubourg Saint Antoine which resulted in the capture of the Bastille. A 'neo-positivist' account of this phenomenon, according to Sartre, would be of the following sort: an individual, in a particular social structure, has hitherto clung to the hope that the various disorders occurring around him will not touch him; now, however, he comes to believe that the total social structure of which he is one member is in danger, and that therefore the only hope for himself, as an individual, is to take part in (to be a part of) the destructive, negative, revolutionary action of that totality.[28] But such an explanation is based on an over-simplified psychology and fails to provide an adequate understanding of the NOVELTY of group action; the dialectical account is more complex. "It is not a question either of altruism or of egoism",[29] but of a new form of social relations. The individual has undoubtedly thought of his particular social structure as a totality (e.g. 'the residents of the section', 'the clientele', etc.) on previous occasions, but this has always been "insofar as he does not think of himself as figuring in the totality".[30] Now, however, he realizes that the new danger (the external, 'material happening' mentioned in the previous paragraph) menaces his social structure insofar as it is a totality of which he is an INTEGRAL part. In this new

[25] *Ibid.*, p. 370. Final quotation marks are Sartre's.

[26] *Ibid.*, p. 384.

[27] Sartre mentions Malraux's novel about the Spanish Civil War, *L'Espoir*, in which this first movement towards the group is called 'the Apocalypse'. *Ibid.*, p. 391.

[28] *Ibid.*, p. 399.

[29] *Ibid.* Olivecrona, who, as we saw earlier, opts entirely for egoism as the motivation in all social change, could provide almost a caricature of the neo-positivist type of account that Sartre is opposing.

[30] *Ibid.*, p. 400. It must be remembered that, despite his generous use of examples, Sartre's account is a formal one. To raise the objection that some residents of the Faubourg may in fact have thought of themselves and their Faubourg in a radically different way at some previous time would be pointless.

realization, the individual plays a new role, a role of 'mediation': he sees that he and his fellows are menaced both as members of a series (distinct individuals) AND as a human totality, unified (in a rough way) by the existence of this menace. The collective of which the 'mediator' is a member thus appears at one and the same time to be both serial, impotent to act collectively, and a totality, menaced as a whole, and therefore needing to act as a whole. But this is a 'contradiction' – a contradiction not in terms of formal logic, of course, but in terms of practical action. And indeed, "the overcoming of this contradiction can only take place in action".[31] The mediator forms a new 'project', which involves going beyond the present structure, the present social state, in which he (along with the others in his situation) finds himself. But presumably, in any interesting attempt at bringing about fundamental change in society, many others will more or less simultaneously also become 'mediators', viewing their situation in a radically new light; with them, too, this 'mediation' does not remain at the stage of mere theoretical understanding, but expresses itself in action. Sartre claims that his dialectical account is superior to the 'neo-positivist' one because his account alone is able to explain the fundamentally different nature, resulting from the new reciprocal relations of mediation, of the new social structure that is being formed.

The passage from understanding to effective action is not completely abrupt. The example of the Faubourg Saint Antoine remains before our mind's eye: the residents, at the hours of crisis, descend into the streets and form small gatherings.

> These gatherings (still serial and yet already quasi-intentional[32]) are going to become groups by their internal tension and in a passive activity which is changed into common action according to rules that are rigorous and peculiar to each event.[33]

The activity is at first passive – aimless. But each individual is in the process of dissolving his status as a member of the series.[34] The moment comes when some individual takes some initiative,[35] performs some act

[31] *Ibid.*
[32] By 'quasi-intentional' Sartre means having only the vaguest, most indeterminate kind of objective in view.
[33] *Critique de la raison dialectique*, p. 400.
[34] "This transformation is not a change in what he knows or in his perception, it is a real change, in him, from inert activity to collective action." *Ibid.*, p. 401.
[35] The first example that Sartre provides of this is the individual who, part of a fleeing street mob, suddenly stops and shouts, "Let's stop!" *Ibid.*, p. 402.

of ORGANIZING the collective: "At that instant, he is *sovereign*, that is to say that he becomes, by the change of [his own] *praxis*, the organizer of the common *praxis*. Not that he wishes himself to be such: simply *he makes himself such*."[36] At this first moment of 'totalization', in the ideal case of the group in fusion, there is complete unanimity: the organizer is followed by all the members of the group, merely because he has expressed the objective which each member recognizes as his own – as the common PRAXIS.[37] It would be a misuse of words to say that this individual, who could have been anyone in the group in fusion, is being 'OBEYED': "In the limiting case, the [mediator] does not even appear: watchwords circulate."[38]

This completes my résumé of Sartre's account of the fundamental social change from the series to the group; however, as I shall note below, a reverse transformation from the group back to seriality is also conceivable and in a sense equally fundamental.[39] First, a few comments are in order concerning the nature of this new reality, the group. Serial activity was also teleological, purposive, but the objective pursued by the individual in the series was somehow external to him, an ALIENATION, because the products of his PRAXIS were not truly his own. Each individual's relationship to the GROUP, on the other hand, is an internal one: "the leader is always *myself*, there are no others", and the objective is each individual's own.[40] The group is, in fact, defined by its objective(s); "the group is not a metaphysical reality but a certain practical relationship of men to an objective and among themselves".[41] This means that, unlike an organism, a group is never really a (completed) totality, but is only considered as such with relation to its objectives. "The group can only be a totalization in process."[42] In the fusion of the group, there is NO fundamental change in the basic reality, the free PRAXIS of each individual, which created the group and sustains it. The individual's integration into the group, therefore, will never be a *fait accompli* once and for all; it will always remain a 'task to be accom-

[36] *Ibid.*, p. 401.

[37] It is perhaps in this conception of the group in fusion that Sartre comes closest to Rousseau's conception of the General Will; very little elaboration of the similarities and differences between them, however, can be attempted in this study.

[38] *Critique de la raison dialectique*, p. 409.

[39] Formally speaking, of course, it IS equally fundamental, but it may not be so in terms of a philosophy of history of which only a few hints are provided in the first volume of the *Critique*.

[40] *Ibid.*, p. 421.

[41] *Ibid.*, p. 427.

[42] *Ibid.*, p. 412.

plished', so that there is always an (in the extreme case) infinitesimal but necessarily unbridgeable gap between the PRAXIS of each person and the common group action.[43]

Sartre now points out that the group, once formed, is confronted with a new problem, that of PERMANENCE – or, as he also calls it, of BEING. The group has hitherto been only a MEANS to objectives, but now the group wishes to guard against its disintegration by giving itself a certain amount of 'inertia' ('inertie'). There is a new practical 'contradiction' involved in the fact that the group aims at being both free PRAXIS and something permanent. Out of this contradiction come future developments. The name that Sartre gives to the new, inert (and therefore non-dialectical) element, which he regards as the necessary formal basis of all future group organizations and institutions, is the OATH ('le serment').[44] It is Sartre's suggested substitute for the social contract. The oath is based on violence (which in a world of scarcity is an ever-present condition, whether in overt or in masked form), seen here in its dual aspects of FRATERNITY and TERROR. By means of the oath, a fear internal to the group is substituted for the earlier external fear (fear of an external menace) that is now receding. Anticipating possible doubts about his nomenclature, Sartre admits: "The legal name that I have given to this reality may appear premature, since the oath founds institutions at a subsequent time but is not itself institutional."[45]

The concepts that are studied next by Sartre include the following: task, function (of an individual), structure, and a new form of 'active passivity'. Gradually the group, in its struggle to maintain itself, becomes an increasingly inert and 'degraded' form of community (though the term 'degraded' is not to be taken in any ethical sense, says Sartre).[46] Once the individual is seen to be inessential, the 'function' which he previously was thought to have is transformed (e.g., by a constitution) into an INSTITUTION. The institution is the group's new inert unity, an 'active passivity' which is to be distinguished from the 'passive activity' of the 'inert' series:[47] "The model of the institutional group will be the

[43] *Ibid.*, p. 430.
[44] *Ibid.*, p. 438. Sartre's term is a peculiar one; it was undoubtedly suggested to him by the historic Tennis Court Oath, which constituted a first step towards the formation of a new institution, the National Assembly, during the French Revolution. As we see once again, the image of that Revolution was never far from Sartre's mind during the writing of the *Critique*.
[45] *Ibid.*, p. 456.
[46] *Ibid.*, p. 574.
[47] *Ibid.*, p. 580.

forged tool."[48] Individual liberty is now almost entirely hidden, reduced to necessities in the form of obligations.

It is only at the point at which Sartre begins to discuss 'institutions' that he arrives, on his abstract level of discourse, at a type of social structure that is sufficiently developed to bear some resemblance to legal systems as we know them. He has almost nothing to say about the institution of law as such, since, at this abstract level, he is not yet concerned with particular forms of institutions; for example, he claims to have shown that the LOGICAL basis of organization is not essentially different whether we are dealing with democratically-formed institutions or those produced 'from above', however great the political, ideological, and ethical differences between these forms may be.[49] But what is most likely in Sartre's account to raise eyebrows among those who have carefully considered the concept of law is the dim view that Sartre appears to take of institutions in general.

It must always be remembered that Sartre is not describing any actual or necessary historical development of groups, since every step in the dialectic, considered from the formal point of view with which we are now dealing, is reversible; as he says in beginning a discussion of institutional sovereignty (which, he holds, has its basis in the real sovereignty, seen in the group in fusion, of each individual): "These remarks concern in no way the historical origin of sovereignty but only logical and dialectical relations which are perfectly abstract but which every historical interpretation will have to contain within itself as its intelligibility."[50] Sartre turns now to a consideration of SOCIETIES, which he defines as human multiplicities, materially united in some way by a territory, and consisting of both groups and series and an "internal and fundamental relationship of society – . . . *that of groups to series*".[51]

The most obvious example of a society, he says, is that which is unified by the sovereign institutional group, the State, ruling over, and imposing new and modified institutions on, collectives. The institutionalized group, as it becomes more complex (creating sub-groups, etc.) and more 'inert', has an increasing number of possibilities open to it. One of the most obvious is that it may simply dissolve, its members returning to the serial form of existence (or, of course, becoming mem-

[48] *Ibid.*, p. 585.
[49] *Ibid.*, p. 518.
[50] *Ibid.*, p. 608.
[51] *Ibid.*

bers of new groups); in that case we have, once again, a fundamental change.

At this point,[52] according to Sartre, we have at last come to the stage in dialectical experience at which the formal *milieu* in which concrete history takes place can be seen. The remainder of his *Critique* is not of any great importance for my summary: its principal contribution is to provide a very detailed examination of the concept of class, although there are other interesting discussions of method, of colonialism, of scarcity, of struggle, of partial or total failure[53] and the alleged limitations that this places on the intelligibility of the dialectic, and of Engels' 'economism' and the differences between PRAXIS and mere process. Near the beginning of this final part of the *Critique*, Sartre voices a suspicion that many who have followed his account of fundamental change from the series to the group and back again may have: "Is there not a perpetual double movement of regrouping and of petrification?" He answers: "It makes little difference to us: the essential thing was to establish the intelligibility of these possibles: that we have done."[54] In concluding this first volume of the *Critique*, he says:

> Up to now, we have attempted to get back to the elementary and formal structures and – in the same motion – we have ascertained the dialectical bases of a structural anthropology. Now, we must let these structures live freely, opposing one another and being composed with one another.... In replying to the ultimate question posed by the regressive experience, we shall discover the profound meaning of History and of dialectical rationality.[55]

Fortunately, however, Sartre has not deemed it necessary to elaborate his philosophy of history BEFORE giving us his theoretical account of the phenomenon of fundamental change in society. For, as a result of reflecting on certain aspects of this abstract, formal account, we shall be

[52] *Ibid.*, p. 637.

[53] Sartre wishes to distinguish sharply between the failure (in attaining an objective) brought about by the individual's own shortcomings ("*praxis*, by definition, brings with it ignorance and error as its fundamental structures") and that brought about by the free action of another, hostile individual. *Ibid.*, p. 749.

[54] *Ibid.*, p. 643. Probably the single most serious misrepresentation in Desan's generally accurate exegesis of the *Critique* is his transformation of this question, raised by Sartre, into a positive declaration: "All of history is shown to be a 'perpetual double movement of regrouping and petrification'." (*The Marxism of Jean-Paul Sartre*, p. 215.) To insist on the difference here is not mere pedantry, for it seems to me that Sartre's only chance for developing, in his projected second volume, a philosophy of HISTORY that would be somehow compatible with Marxism depends on his allowing for the possibility that the 'double movement of regrouping and petrification' might some day END.

[55] *Ibid.*, p. 755.

able by ourselves to reach some conclusions concerning the underlying Marxist theme that, at some future time in history, a truly DEFINITIVE fundamental change – definitive in ways still to be specified – might take place, by comparison with which the fundamental changes treated by Hart and even by Sartre, throughout the account that I have just given, would appear as relatively insignificant. And such conclusions will, among other things, enable us to reassess the importance of methodological differences, and to reappraise the value of Hart's analysis of rules, of acceptance, and of the law itself, in explaining and justifying fundamental change in law and society.

Meanwhile, certain obvious points of contrast between Hart's analyses and the Sartrean account that I have just summarized should be kept in mind. First of all, whereas Hart espouses the 'analytic' method, Sartre clearly rejects it in favor of a method presumably capable of yielding a more systematic theory. Secondly, Hart's analysis retains a 'commonsense' tone throughout; Sartre's explanation is given on a rather high level of abstraction, which permits of at least some momentary doubt as to exactly which elements in his supposedly general account best apply to the sorts of instances of fundamental change with which Hart is dealing. Thirdly, there is a vast difference in the ways in which Hart and Sartre conceive of the human social activity that brings about fundamental changes: the single concept which, more than any other, holds the key to understanding Sartre's view of such activity is that of 'totalization', not at all that of 'rules'. Fourthly, though there are most certainly many value-laden terms (e.g., Hart's 'unhealthy legal system' and Sartre's 'alienation') connected with both treatments, Sartre's approach to ethics (insofar as he treats of this subject) is quite alien to Hart's. And finally, as I noted at the beginning of this chapter, Sartre's perspective of social philosophy is such as to pose problems quite different from those of Hart's legal perspective. The Sartrean side of these contrasts is now to be examined in some detail, and we shall begin, quite naturally, with the methodological question.

4

DIALECTICS

What 'label' shall we attach to Sartre's philosophical method in the *Critique*? The book's title itself provides the answer, which I have already suggested: the DIALECTICAL method. To attempt, however, adequately to define this method in a phrase or a few sentences would be an impossible undertaking;[1] we shall see why this is so as we proceed. Nevertheless, it is necessary to begin somewhere in characterizing the dialectical method; perhaps we shall do best by recalling the statement of principle, quoted in Chapter Two of this section, that appeared in the "Presentation" of the first issue of *Les Temps Modernes*. "We revert", it was said there, "against the spirit of analysis, to a synthetic conception of reality." The dialectical method is the method of synthesis, and it is in being such that it first attempts to distinguish itself from Sartre's *bête noire*, analytic reason, which was, supposedly, the avowed method of H. L. A. Hart.

What the notion of 'synthesis' most obviously implies, as the statement of principle goes on to indicate, is wholeness: dialectical reason is the comprehension of a whole. The reader of the *Critique* is constantly reminded of this claim to universality by Sartre's repeated use of the word 'totalization', to an examination of which we shall return later. But what IS the whole that Sartre's dialectical method is intended to comprehend? The answer to this question is to be found in the formulation of the 'question de méthode': the *Critique* is to be a 'structural and historical anthropology'. The whole to be comprehended, therefore, is nothing less than all of human social activity.

Considered in its undifferentiated entirety, however, the whole of human social activity would be an almost completely meaningless notion. Specific forms of this activity must somehow be separately

[1] J. N. Findlay notes similar difficulties in his chapter on "The Dialectical Method" in Hegel. Cf. *Hegel: A Re-Examination* (London, George Allen & Unwin Ltd.; New York, The Macmillan Company, 1958), pp. 58 ff.

examined without at the same time the dialectician's having to abandon his comprehensive vision of the whole. The 755 pages of the first volume of Sartre's *Critique* may be seen, as I have already pointed out, as a painstaking effort by the author to restore recognition to the 'mediations' – i.e., the varieties of societal institutions – which his earlier philosophy had appeared incapable of accounting for. But surely the examination of specific forms of human activity is not the peculiar province of the dialectician: the analytic method might be useless for the achievement of a genuinely SYNTHETIC comprehension, but is there any difference between analysis and dialectics when it is merely a question of describing a PART of the whole?

Sartre's answer to this challenge is that analysis is indeed incapable of achieving a synthesis, but that, furthermore, 'analytic (or positivistic) Reason' is, at its best, merely a part of the dialectic:

> Thus analytic Reason ... is only ... a certain practical moment of dialectical Reason. ... We shall see later – if our experiment succeeds – that dialectical Reason sustains, guides, and constantly reinvents positivist Reason as its own external relation with the externality of nature.[2]

The dialectical method is characterized by INTERNALITY, that is, by a rejection of empirical description (which is the act of an external, analytic observer) as the primary means of understanding either the whole or any of its parts:

> No one can *discover* the dialectic if he keeps to the standpoint of analytic Reason, which means, among other things, that no one can discover the dialectic if he remains *external* to the object considered. ... The dialectic is discovered only by an observer interiorly located.[3]

Sartre's entire account of the fundamental change from the series to the group may be seen as the account of an INTERNALIZATION: the individuals who act as "mediators" in the transformation comprehend their own situation and the status of their collective in a new, different way, and the formation of the group is nothing but the activity that results from the individual members' abandonment of their previous, merely external way of regarding that collective. The philosopher, such as

[2] *Critique de la raison dialectique*, p. 148. As Claude Lévi-Strauss notes, at the very beginning of his defense of HIS type of analytic reason against Sartre, Sartre sometimes seems to hesitate between the view that dialectical and analytic reason CAN be complementary to one another, and the conception of the latter as mere error, in contrast to the truth of dialectics. – *La Pensée Sauvage*, pp. 324-325.

[3] *Critique de la raison dialectique*, p. 133.

Sartre, who is not a member of the social ENSEMBLE of which he is giving a theoretical account, must nevertheless, by means of the dialectical method, be able to comprehend that ENSEMBLE 'in interiority'.[4] But suppose that it were granted that the dialectician is better qualified than the analyst to account for 'parts' of the 'whole' of social activity from a point of view internal to each part; might it not still be argued that, for many purposes (for example, in attempting to arrive at a clear, dispassionate understanding of what has TRULY happened, as distinguished from what the participants may think has happened, in a fundamental change from a series to a group), the viewpoint of the external observer is more important than that of the person who comprehends a phenomenon in its internality, and that the method of analysis is at least as good as, if not better than, dialectics for such purposes?

Sartre, for one, would reject this suggestion on the grounds that every externally observable phenomenon of social life is, in reality, a product of human PRAXIS, and that it is only the dialectical method that can comprehend PRAXIS as the agent throughout all historical changes. PRAXIS plays a role in Sartre's philosophy somewhat comparable to that played by SPIRIT in Hegel's thought: it is through its comprehension of human PRAXIS that, Sartre claims, his dialectical method is able to account for progress, transformation, development. For, though PRAXIS is governed by no determinate law or laws,[5] it can at least be generally characterized as always capable of forming new 'projects' and of acting to bring about such projects. In short, the dialectical method alone is PROGRESSIVE; analysis, according to the dialectician, can never be so. The analyst can only describe distinct phenomena, and, if he is at all able to deal with such a phenomenon as that of change, he can make no real sense of it. In making this point, Georg Lukacs speaks of 'formalist systems' instead of Sartre's 'analytic Reason'; Lukacs explains the

[4] For one SOCIOLOGIST's extended discussion of the methodological need for such interiorized comprehension, cf. Severyn T. Bruyn, *The Human Perspective in Sociology* (Englewood Cliffs, Prentice-Hall, 1966). Bruyn discusses the possibility of borrowing phenomenological, though not dialectical, techniques from philosophy.

[5] It is in connection with this contention that Sartre most explicitly condemns his predecessor in Marxist thought, Friedrich Engels. Engels had the temerity to reduce the essential 'most general laws of natural history and of social history' to three specific notions (the transformation of quantity into quality and the reverse, the interpenetration of opposites, and the negation of the negation). Even if there existed a very high inductive evidence for the probable truth of these 'laws', Sartre points out, this would lead us practically nowhere in accounting for social phenomena: any such laws would be contingent and external to men – irrational, transcendental caprices about which nothing more could be said. *Ibid.*, pp. 127-128.

triumph (in the history of philosophy) of the dialectical method over formalism in the following way: "This rigid and unreal image of a perpetual motion is replaced by a meaning as soon as the rigidity is resolved into a process of which man is the motive force." [6] Sartre prefers not to call dialectical progress a PROCESS,[7] but otherwise he would find himself in agreement with Lukacs' remark. The dialectical method offers the opportunity of discovering a direction in changes among phenomena; could analysis ever do this? But suppose, once more, that we were to accept the dialectician's claim to methodological superiority, this time with respect to the notion of directed movement, or progress; still it might well be said in Sartre's case that this alleged superiority is empty and valueless. For the Sartrean dialectic, at least as it is developed in the first volume of the *Critique*, makes no claim to discern a single necessary direction of progress in every phenomenon to which it is applied: [8] every step in his dialectic is, as I noted in the preceding chapter, REVERSIBLE. The dialectician may be better equipped than the analyst to convey a sense of progress; but, given Sartre's reversible dialectic, is this anything more than a formal advantage?

A mere formal advantage is never enough to satisfy a good dialectician; Sartre makes a further claim about the advantages of dialectics over analysis as a means of comprehending sociological and historical progression that is truly extraordinary. In cases of fundamental social change, he says, 'analytic' explanations are totally unsatisfactory:

In other words, if dialectical Reason exists, it must be defined as the absolute intelligibility of an irreducible novelty *insofar as* that novelty is irreducible. This is the opposite of the positivist and analytic method which seeks to illuminate new facts by referring them back to old facts. And, in a certain sense, the tradition of positivism is so rooted in us, even today, that the demand for intelligibility here may appear paradoxical. The new seems, *qua new*, to escape the intellect . . .[9]

[6] Lukacs, *Histoire et Conscience de Classe*, p. 225.

[7] He believes that Engels and many others – some economists, sociologists, *et al.* – have reduced history to a mere external process, a product of inert forces, instead of insisting sufficiently on human PRAXIS as the agent. Cf. *Critique de la raison dialectique*, pp. 667 ff.

[8] Findlay's principal criticism of Hegel's method seems to be that Hegel is making some such claim as this: "... Hegel's main mistake, both in what he SAYS about his Dialectic and in what he tries to do with it, lies in his assumption that it has *a kind of deductive necessity*, different from, but akin to, that of a mathematical system, whereby we shall find ourselves forced along a *single* line of reasoning . . .", *op. cit.*, p. 81.

[9] *Critique de la raison dialectique*, p. 147.

The above passage is an especially interesting one for our purposes. It states with a certain clarity one of Sartre's principal claims concerning the advantages of the dialectical method in philosophy over what he has been calling 'analysis'. The method of dialectics, says Sartre, can deal better with NOVELTY. Fundamental changes in societies are often novelties; indeed, they are ALWAYS such if one accepts the hypothesis that the movement of history is non-circular. IF the meaning of the above passage can be satisfactorily explained, and IF the contention that it contains can be sufficiently well defended, then the analytic philosopher will have no further reply to make to the claim of the dialectician to be able more adequately to deal with fundamental change.

The dialectical method, we have seen, is characterized by synthesis, internality, progression, and novelty. It is on the basis of these significant characteristics, among others, that Sartre opposes his own method to that of analysis and defends the superiority of the former. But we need not simply accept Sartre's word for it: we have the advantage of having examined in some detail the treatment of one kind of fundamental change, that in legal systems, given by a philosopher who is generally regarded as being in the analytic 'camp'. If it be granted that Hart is an analyst, are Sartre's claims to methodological superiority vindicated? I suggest that they are not, and I further suggest that 'analysis' in Sartre's pejorative sense is best epitomized by a certain interpretation of the characteristics, listed at the beginning of Chapter Two of the first section of this study, of Hans Kelsen's methodology.

Four of the five characteristics of Kelsen's General Theory to which I called attention, it will be recalled, were: (1) the distinctness of its subject-matter from that of all other 'sciences', (2) its empirical and descriptive cast, (3) its exclusion of 'ideals' and 'ideologies' from its scope, and (4) its rigor, system, and unity. (The fifth, its applicability to all instances of truly legal orders, may be dismissed as irrelevant for present purposes.) The divergences of Hart from all four of these Kelsenian ideals of scientific method became clear in the course of our discussion of Hart's account of fundamental change in law.

In my concluding chapter on Hart, I pointed to his almost casual comment that *The Concept of Law* could also be regarded as an essay in descriptive sociology, as one further proof of his abandonment of the Kelsenian ideal of scientific autonomy in favor of some more unified view of social philosophy which might very well be called 'synthetic' by the dialectician. Indeed, this fact served as a justification for our beginning the study of Sartre's account of fundamental change in society.

Later, I mentioned that Lukacs had severely criticized Kelsen's 'bourgeois' tendency to consider every science as in principle autonomous. Sartre's synthetic, dialectical method, with its emphasis on the interrelationships among all the phenomena of a social field, is foreign to Kelsen's approach, but not to Hart's, on this point. It may be argued, on the other hand (and I shall return to this later), that Sartre's treatment of society is so 'synthetic', so opposed to the atomization of disciplines which a positivist like Kelsen seeks to promote, that a treatment of a particular institution such as law becomes very difficult within the framework of his dialectical method. But at least Sartre cannot theoretically object to such a treatment. Kelsen, however, has taken a firm theoretical stand on the issue of complete distinctness of subject-matters in the social sciences. It is Kelsen's variety of 'positivism' or 'analysis', not Hart's, which on this point is inconsistent with Sartre's dialectical method.

The second of Kelsen's methodological demands, that a science be strictly empirical and descriptive, is another characteristic of the 'analytic Reason' which Sartre opposes. Kelsen, we saw, made the paradoxical claim that his 'normative science' was descriptive, rather than prescriptive, because it DESCRIBED norms. I pointed out immediately that there was considerable empirical evidence, especially from international law, to cast doubt on this claim. But even if there were no such contrary evidence, the question would remain as to whether the purely 'descriptive' approach to legal norms constitutes an adequate explanation of legal phenomena. Sartre, the dialectician, holds very clearly that it does not – but so, once again, does H. L. A. Hart. Hart's insistence on the internal aspect of rules may be seen as the key to his departure from Kelsen on this matter.[10] I have already explored the implications of this aspect of Hart's theory, and it obviously bears some striking resemblances to the second feature of the dialectical method that I have singled out, namely internality. Hart places comparatively greater stress than does Sartre on the THEORETICAL value (i.e., the value for the legal philosopher) of the internal aspect of rules, but its use in explaining 'acceptance', especially as applied to Hart's account of fundamental change in law, shows that 'internality' may indeed be a characteristic

[10] In Chapter Eight of the first section I quoted Kelsen to the effect that "Normative jurisprudence describes law from an external point of view although its statements are ought-statements." (*General Theory of Law and State*, p. 164.) Later modifications (or clarifications) in Kelsen's theory, which have brought him somewhat closer to Hart, Wedberg, *et al.* on this question, are not at issue here.

of more than merely theoretical importance for a supposedly non-dialectical philosophy like Hart's.

The methodological exclusion of 'ideals' and 'ideologies' from Kelsen's form of analysis is an ideal that perhaps no one would ever think of attributing to Sartre, for whom the individual's 'project', his forming of an objective to be attained, is so essential to the claim that the dialectical method alone can be PROGRESSIVE and thus can adequately explain fundamental change in society. It must be asked once again, however, whether Kelsen's procedure is endemic to analytic philosophy in general, or only to Kelsen's philosophy. Hart, though his analysis of the concept of law insofar as it concerns the functioning of legal systems in normal times does not (and, for his purposes there, need not) make much reference to 'ideals', certainly has no methodological prejudices (such as Kelsen's sharp dichotomy between thought and will and his notion of the limited range of the former) against examining the role of ideals in legal and other social phenomena.[11] In addition, in the chapter on "Acceptance", I showed the unquestionable importance of 'ideals', taken in the broad sense of 'values', in Hart's own account of fundamental change in law. Hart thus leaves room for considerations of progress, transformation, and development to an extent to which Kelsen, despite his discussions of 'Nomodynamics', cannot. If Kelsen's method is to be regarded as typifying the sort of 'analysis' by comparison with which Sartre claims his dialectical method to be superior, then once again, with regard to the third characteristic listed, *Hart's* analytic method is seen to cast doubt on that claim.

Sartre faces a further, rather peculiar problem with respect to the alleged progressiveness of dialectics as a philosophical method. The simple fact is that the final chapter of Sartre's introductory "Question de Méthode" bears the singularly unhelpful title, "La Méthode Progessive-Régressive", of the meaning of which Sartre provides the following singularly unhelpful explanation:

> The Marxist method is progressive because it is the outcome, in Marx, of long analyses; today, synthetic progression is dangerous: lazy Marxists use it in order to constitute *a priori* the real. . . . Our method is heuristic, it teaches us something new because it is regressive and progressive at the same time.[12]

[11] "It cannot seriously be disputed that the development of law, at all times and places, has in fact been profoundly influenced . . . by the conventional morality and ideals of particular social groups." *The Concept of Law*, p. 181.

[12] *Critique de la raison dialectique*, p. 86.

The regressive aspect of Sartre's method seems to consist in the discovery of the abstract, formal structures and elements which underlie society, whereas its progressive aspect concerns the use of these discoveries in making intelligible the movement of history. And Sartre seems to be saying that the first volume of the *Critique*, the one with which we are dealing, is the REGRESSIVE experience![13] A further source of potential confusion is to be found in Sartre's seeming equation of the 'regressive method' with 'analysis'. The excerpt quoted above suggests such an equation, as does the phrase, 'an analytic and regressive moment',[14] employed by Sartre several pages later. It might almost seem at this point as if Sartre were saying that the method of the first volume of the *Critique de la raison dialectique* fails, in at least one important respect, to be dialectical at all. However, if Sartre is to be taken at his word, even the 'regressive experience' of the first volume is not without its 'progressive' aspect. This is made clear from the structure of the book as a whole: Sartre begins with his discussion of abstract PRAXIS and moves in an order of increasing complexity and decreasing abstractness until, near the end, he says that he has reached the stage at which his account of the formal '*milieu*' (complex combinations of interrelated groups and series, of which social classes are a good example) of concrete history has been completed. Thus Sartre probably avoids the paradox of having written a book about dialectics that might be subject to the dialectician's censure of non-dialectical methods of philosophy for their alleged lack of progressiveness, but it can at least be said that Sartre's procedure renders less obvious the dialectician's claim to superiority over the analyst on this point.

The final characteristic of Kelsen's General Theory which marks it as being representative of a method antithetic to Sartre's own is Kelsen's version of philosophical rigor, system, and unity. Of course, Sartre also strives, sometimes very painfully, after rigor,[15] and his passionate

[13] This fact alone would give it a certain distinction, since the Communist Party, which retains the loyalties of many Marxist writers, has long been chary of sociology in general and especially of any sociological study of itself. (Lefebvre, whose own interest in sociology is strong, points this out very clearly. As he explains, some orthodox Marxists consider sociology slightly 'reformist', since it presupposes that no Revolution will immediately alter all social 'superstructures' from top to bottom. Cf. *La Somme et le reste*, pp. 544-545.) The first volume of Sartre's *Critique* is intended both to be a philosophical prolegomenon to the study of sociology and to be applicable to Communist Party 'groups', in their various forms, as much as to any other groups.

[14] *Critique de la raison dialectique*, p. 89.

[15] Lefebvre prefaces his criticism of Sartre's recent work with the following words

quest for unity will be the object of some further investigation in our discussion of 'Totalization'; as for system, it may at once be admitted without argument that Sartre is systematic in at least the loose sense in which we found Hart's method to be systematic. But the normative system of laws portrayed by Kelsen is patterned, as we have already noted on several occasions, after a 'hypothetico-deductive' formal, systematic model, with the *Grundnorm* serving as the 'source of validity' of all the other norms of the system. It was this methodological ideal, we further noted, which gave rise to the peculiar problems within Kelsen's system in connection with the concept of fundamental change in law; as Lukacs puts it, referring to Kelsen: "This conception of law transforms the birth and the disappearance of law into something juridically . . . incomprehensible." [16]

Sartre, as we have seen, maintains that the method of dialectics alone can account for novelty. This is why, he would hold, the problems that fundamental change in legal orders created for Kelsen would not arise in a dialectical treatment. This may be true, but we have observed how Hart, using his method of linguistic analysis, also avoids at least this sort of problem in his account of fundamental change. On the other hand, it is highly unlikely that Hart would go so far as to attempt to rival Sartre's claim to be able to deal with "an irreducible novelty *insofar as* that novelty is irreducible". Hart makes much of his contention that *The Concept of Law* constitutes 'a fresh start' in legal theory and opens up 'new questions'; [17] his extended metaphor, central to the account of fundamental change, of 'The Pathology of a Legal System' is preceded, as we noted, by an appeal to "take off the spectacles constituted by [misleading] terminology". [18] But the fresh look that Hart takes 'at the facts' is in this particular instance based on an analogy with what can by no means be regarded as a novelty, namely the human life-cycle. Wisdom's suggestion that the philosopher should discover unconventional patterns in phenomena seems more clearly in the spirit of Sartre's claim to be able to deal with novelty, but what Sartre is claiming is that the facts themselves, and not merely our ways of looking at them, may be fundamentally new.

---

of praise: "For a philosopher-writer of world-wide reputation and importance to revise his positions is a philosophic event, and it is a sign of a singular rigor of mind and vigor." *La Somme et le reste*, p. 517.

[16] Lukacs, *Histoire et Conscience de Classe*, pp. 138-139.

[17] These phrases are taken from the index of *The Concept of Law*.

[18] *The Concept of Law*, p. 109.

But before we can declare that there is a definitive parting of the ways between Hart's method of analysis and Sartre's method of dialectic on this issue, we must try to become more certain about what Sartre's claim entails. Does the expression 'absolute novelty' mean anything at all, and (on the hypothesis that it does) if a fundamental change in society were to bring about any such state of affairs, would this not immediately contradict Sartre's claim that the *Critique* is a 'Prolegomenon to any future anthropology'? Has he not said that there is no historical necessity about the order of structures investigated in the *Critique*? Sartre is, of course, aware of these objections, and I shall return later to the problems that they raise. But it is important, at this point, to show the difficulty of upholding an extreme interpretation of the claim that the dialectical method alone is capable of showing the intelligibility of an 'irreducible novelty', and the consequent difficulty of satisfactorily distinguishing this method from Hart's 'analysis' even on this issue. Once again, it was only Kelsen's method, not Hart's, that appeared to be somewhat susceptible to the criticisms on the basis of which Sartre could make some reasonable claim in favor of the superiority of the dialectical method.

What remains, then, of Sartre's methodological claim? I have shown that some of his most telling anti-analytic shafts would be misguided if they were aimed at Hart. I can only conclude rather tentatively and vaguely, as I did in my corresponding chapter on the method of analysis, by suggesting that dialectics must, nevertheless, have some 'hard core of meaning' which distinguishes it, as a method, from other philosophical methods. In the remainder of this chapter, however, I am going to cast even greater doubt on this suggestion. For I am going to show briefly why three characteristics commonly attributed to the method of dialectics, at least in its Marxist forms, are not readily attributable to Sartre's position. These are: (1) the tendency of the dialectic somehow to dissolve individuals into collectives, or groups; (2) the thesis that the course of history is determined; (3) the attempt to render the dialectical method plausible by recourse to mythical conceptions of society.[19]

The first characterization is the reverse of the charge, mentioned

[19] Aron's *L'Opium des Intellectuels* is divided into three principal parts which, taken in reverse order, constitute detailed (though qualified) expressions of these charges. The first part is entitled "Mythes Politiques" (including the 'myth of the Revolution'), the second "Le Sens de l'Histoire", and the third, which terminates with the suggestion that the intellectuals are attempting to overcome their own sense of alienation by surrendering their personal integrity to a substitute for religion, "L'Aliénation des Intellectuels".

several times in Chapter Two of this section, that EXISTENTIALISM was too radically individualistic to be able to deal with social groups. Camus' *L'Homme Révolté* furnishes some evidence to support the latter charge, and may itself be regarded as a strong expression of distrust towards dialectically-inclined philosophers, from Hegel on, because of their alleged disregard of individuals in favor of groups. Sartre, in his attempt to reconcile Marxism with existentialism, finds himself in the unenviable position of being attacked simultaneously both for excessive, atomistic individualism and for the anti-individualism that supposedly constitutes the more usual dialectical sin. Thus Merleau-Ponty, in addition to the criticisms noted in Chapter Two, also says that Sartre sees everything in history in terms of a single, monotonous combat, where men are only types,[20] and Camus' "Lettre au Directeur des *Temps Modernes*" contains many suggestions of the same sort.

In fact, even in *Critique de la raison dialectique*, Sartre remains more open to the accusation of excessive individualism, levelled, as it has been, in a fairly simplistic way by Schaff and more seriously by Lefebvre,[21] than he is to the accusation of excessive collectivism. Individual PRAXIS is the sole active element throughout Sartre's account; group PRAXIS, beginning with the group in fusion in the phenomenon of fundamental change, is always 'constituted', never 'constitutive'. Sartre's insistence that totalizations will never become full-fledged 'totalities', his admission, noted in the preceding chapter, that there must always remain some gap between the PRAXIS of each person and the common group action, and his persistent expressions of opposition to organicism all testify to the individualistic basis of his dialectical account.

With respect to the second issue, that of freedom and determinism in history, Sartre is again likely to be the object less of the epithet of 'determinism', frequently hurled at philosophers of dialectics, than of its dialectical opposite. In the *Critique*, Sartre upholds a long-standing dialectical tradition in claiming to reconcile freedom and necessity,[22] but his previous credentials as a libertarian, together with his continued

[20] Merleau-Ponty, *Les Aventures de la dialectique*, p. 198.

[21] Schaff, *op. cit.*, pp. 400 ff.; Lefebvre, *La Somme et le reste* (commenting on published fragments from the *Critique*), pp. 517-519. Lefebvre argues that, if free individual consciousness is made the basis of everything (in human society), then either everything or nothing constitutes an alienation of that individual consciousness, and the concept of alienation may then become unusable.

[22] The heading of one section of the book reads, "Of the Group. The Equivalence of Freedom as Necessity and of Necessity as Freedom. Limits and Extent of Every Realist Dialectic." *Critique de la raison dialectique*, p. 381.

equation of individual PRAXIS with freedom in the *Critique*, render him particularly immune to the charge of reducing history to the inevitable interplay of certain basically non-human forces. Indeed, it is the latter charge that Sartre himself, as we have seen, makes against Engels.

The third characteristic often attributed to dialectics as a method and as the source of philosophical systems is by far the most interesting for our purposes. Like the other two, it is a very broad generality, difficult either to 'prove' or to 'disprove' with any conclusiveness. But the claim that the dialectic method depends on myths for its plausibility is at least more easily debatable in terms of specific examples. 'The end of history' is often regarded as the greatest Marxist myth,[23] but Aron's list also includes several others, such as 'the myth of the proletariat' and 'the myth of the Revolution'. Recently, Lefebvre has defended the heuristic value of a myth which has something in common both with that of the end of history and with that of the Revolution, namely 'the myth of the New Life'.[24] And, of course, any dialectician who wished to make some use of myths would find abundant justification in the writings of his great predecessor, Plato. But Sartre himself avoids using myths, at least as a conscious device. He shares the usual Marxist contempt for 'mystifications' (such as the organic conception of society, which he frequently attacks), and claims that dialectical experience furnishes us with the TRUTH of social and historical reality. Does there, then, fall NO shadow between Sartre's account and the realities, such as that of fundamental change in society, that it elucidates? This is the next problem to be examined.

[23] Camus is only one of a long line of critics who have pointed to this as the summit of Marx's errors, without concerning themselves too much with analyzing the relevant texts. Camus expresses shock that the *Temps Modernes* review of *L'Homme Révolté* did not even discuss this aspect of his criticism. ("Lettre au Directeur des *Temps Modernes*, p. 330.)

[24] Lefebvre, *Introduction à la Modernité*, p. 75.

5

ABSTRACTION

Fundamental change in law and society can be no exception to the principle that the explanation of any phenomenon, if it is to be an explanation at all, must be given in terms of something other than the original phenomenon itself. Thus, to indulge in a metaphor, some 'shadow' MUST fall between fundamental change and Sartre's account of it.[1] The name of Sartre's 'shadow', i.e., his principal explanatory device, is, as we shall see, 'abstraction'. When it is used, the risk of turning it into myth is always great; but, even if we assume that mythology can be avoided, the method still has its intrinsic limitations.

Hart's principal device was analogy. In the chapter on "Analogy", I showed the dependence of Hart's account of fundamental change in law

[1] In one of the few extended treatments of the *Critique* yet published in any language, that of Klaus Hartmann, something like this theoretical inevitability to which I am pointing serves as the basis of his principal criticism of the entire Sartrean enterprise. Hartmann sees deception (*'transzendentale Täuschung'*) as probably unavoidable in any social philosophy which attempts to transcend all historical and temporal particularities and yet simultaneously to account for and include them. Cf. *Sartres Sozialphilosophie: Eine Untersuchung zur 'Critique de la raison dialectique I'* (Berlin, Walter de Gruyter & Co., 1966), esp. pp. 184-193. (Hartmann's book, like Desan's, is primarily exegetical, but it contains much more analysis and criticism than the latter.) There is, for Hartmann, a necessary 'conflict of the thesis of particularity with the transcendental foundation' (p. 190 – tr. mine), and he wonders, in conclusion, whether ANY social philosophy can bridge the gap between sociological plurality and the demands of 'transcendental' philosophy (p. 200). Sartre, of course, constantly TRIES to do so.

Although the present chapter will indicate to how great an extent I am in agreement with Hartmann's essential point here, it is perhaps in our EXPECTATIONS that we differ most significantly. Sartre himself does not commonly use the expression, 'transcendental philosophy', to designate what he is doing in the *Critique*, and I am not greatly disappointed when a reduction in the scope of some of his theoretical claims seems to be demanded – provided that, in the meantime, Sartre has provided some genuinely new and valuable insights into the social phenomena of our times. Hartmann's ULTIMATE expectations seem to be somewhat less practically oriented than mine. But we are equally concerned, I think, about the importance of becoming clear concerning the nature and validity of the theory itself.

on his extended metaphor taken from physiology; I also mentioned some other analogies of importance to Hart, and showed the influence of models on both Aristotle and Kelsen. Sartre, however, places all such methods outside the dialectical pale, as the following excerpt from his criticism of Engels makes clear: "The error of Engels, in the text that we have cited, is to have thought that he could elicit his dialectical laws of Nature through non-dialectical procedures: comparisons, analogies, abstraction, induction." [2] Much later in the book, Sartre says: "Indeed, it must be realized that the way in which dialectical transformations of the masses are spoken of is always metaphorical." [3] Taken by itself, this sentence seems to suggest that Sartre's own account of fundamental change, the passage from the series to the group, (even though it is not given in terms of 'the masses') may likewise be merely 'metaphorical'. But what Sartre intends to criticize here, as is indicated by the text that follows, is the theory that there is some single most typical revolutionary 'gestalt' [4] (e.g., a certain mixture of dissident students, workers, and soldiers) which can serve as the paradigm for every fundamental social change. To attempt to treat of fundamental change at this level of analysis is to use metaphor, he says: [5] the metaphor may be perfectly correct as far as it goes, but it does not furnish a true account. Sartre, on the other hand, claims that his account of fundamental change is, as a part of his entire theory of social structure, true.

How can one judge whether an explanation of a social phenomenon such as that of fundamental change is a true one or not? This very question (which did not seem naturally to arise very often in the course of considering Hart's account of "The Pathology") will, in the final analysis, prove to have been stated in an excessively simple way. For the moment, however, a tentative first answer may be ventured: the theoretical account should be applied to various known instances of the phenomenon, in order to ascertain whether it elucidates or distorts the facts. We may accept Sartre's argument that he cannot be expected to establish his method inductively, since any such induction would have to be infinite, but we may then expect some inductive CONFIRMATION. Sartre furnishes such confirmation in abundance, by supplying numerous

[2] *Critique de la raison dialectique*, p. 130.

[3] *Ibid.*, p. 518.

[4] Sartre uses this term, now made popular by a certain school in psychology, in its usual sense of 'configuration'.

[5] The extensive metaphorical use made of such terms as 'the masses' or 'the elites' in contemporary sociological and political discourse seems to lend further credence to Sartre's point here.

examples at various stages of his account. Nor does he, at least ostensibly, restrict the range from which his examples are chosen. He says that he will begin by assuming a knowledge of contemporary culture and past history, and so will feel free to use any examples whatever: "Nous ferons feu de tout bois." [6] This procedure would be inadmissible in a methodical reconstruction of History, he adds, but it is perfectly legitimate in the present formal study. We may welcome this, since the wider the range of examples used, the higher is the degree of confirmation of the account. Sartre's range is quite wide indeed – from the queue waiting for a bus at St. Germain-des-Prés to the complex marital customs of primitive tribes investigated by Lévy-Strauss, from the phenomenon of racism in colonial countries to the effects of the Spanish imports of American gold during the Sixteenth Century. Brief notice should be given to his use of the one central example in his account of fundamental change from the series to the group, namely the events in the Faubourg Saint Antoine that led to the fall of the Bastille.

It would be difficult to find fault with Sartre's choice of this example, for it is one of the truly classic episodes in the history of revolutions, and Sartre can claim a detailed familiarity with it. Some sort of organization seems to have developed among the previously unorganized residents of the area during a relatively brief period of time, and this development, which took place because of a widespread fear of an external menace (it was rumored that royal troops were going to be ordered to seal off the area and massacre the inhabitants) SHARPLY altered the form of their social structure. During several days in 1789, at least, something like Sartre's 'group in fusion' was to be found in the Faubourg Saint Antoine. Sartre's account of fundamental change, therefore, is certainly applicable to the example that he himself uses to illustrate that account; the more interesting question, however, is whether it is equally applicable to very different kinds of instances of fundamental change in law and society. In other words, has Sartre simply given us the outline of one more revolutionary *gestalt*, or is his account more universal?

Two kinds of fundamental change in law that Hart singled out as being somewhat atypical but necessary to consider were occupation of a territory by an enemy from without, and the onslaught of anarchy or banditry 'without political pretensions to govern'. Can Sartre's account handle THESE cases, for example? There seems to me to be no doubt that

[6] *Critique de la raison dialectique*, p. 145.

it can. The first kind (of which Sartre had a first-hand experience in occupied Paris) may be seen as the disintegration of various sub-groups of the pre-occupation government, together, perhaps, with the formation of new groups of collaborators, which would have very different objectives (or 'projects') from those of pre-occupation national groups. The 'enemy from without' itself is an efficient conglomeration of institutionalized groups (the army, the bureaucracy, etc.) which achieve their own objectives in the usual way, characteristic of a world in which there is scarcity, by the oppression of other individuals, the reduction of them to inert serial collectives, and the attempt to prevent the formation among the latter of any resistance groups. This is just the beginning of the sort of analysis that Sartre would give in terms of his account. The cases of anarchy and banditry are now seen to be simpler than that of enemy occupation: a sheer lapse into anarchy would be a paradigm case of Sartre's account of the disintegration of the group back into the series, while the domination of a region by a group of lawless bandits would be explicable as a negative form of governing by the bandits, who, as an organized group, may believe that their own objectives can best be achieved if the inhabitants of the region are kept without any institutions.

If in one way or another, then, Sartre's account could be shown to be applicable to all the empirical instances of fundamental change in society that might be suggested, would we then be completely satisfied with it? Would we regard it as being flawless? Let us assume that I have correctly indicated, in however elementary and sketchy a way, how Sartre would begin to apply his account to the peculiar kinds of examples of fundamental change in law suggested by Hart: does there not still remain in us some feeling of dissatisfaction with that account? What may be disturbing to us here, I suggest, is that, while Sartre may appear to be saying nothing false, he may appear not to be saying enough. Amid Sartre's talk of individual and common PRAXIS, inert series, groups, and various kinds of transformations between them, many a reader may long for an explanation of fundamental change in terms, however easily refutable, of certain admixtures of soldiers, workers, and students, motivated by five or six typical revolutionary considerations. But Sartre has provided an account of fundamental change on a quite different level. The accounts of the transformation from the series to the group and *vice versa* are, like all the rest of what is not simply illustrative example in the first volume of the *Critique*, ABSTRACT, formal. If Sartre's theory seems to be relatively lacking in content, that is the result of a deliberate effort on his part.

By 'abstract', Sartre says he means 'incomplete'. Thus even the human individual, while in a sense he is THE concrete thing for Sartre, is called 'abstract' when, at the beginning of the *Critique*, he is treated in isolation from his entire social and historical situation.[7] The progress of the *Critique*, as I have already pointed out, is in the direction of decreasing abstractness and thus of increasing completeness. We need not inquire deeply here into Sartre's motivations for writing the first volume of the *Critique* on such an abstract level; he explains, for example, why he thinks that some Marxist critics of his alleged 'formalism', who demand that social philosophy always take concrete society, rather than the isolated and therefore abstract individual, as its starting-point, are in fact playing into the hands of 'liberalism'.[8] But we must, if we are to decide whether or not to accept his account as valid, try to understand (1) what are the principles of Sartre's abstraction and (2) what is the status of his abstract entities.[9]

Since Sartre is not primarily interested in theory of knowledge, he gives no explanation in the *Critique* of the processes of abstraction that lead him to begin where he does. In any case, 'abstraction' here would probably have a different sense from the 'abstraction' anathematized as a non-dialectical procedure in the passage cited at the beginning of the present chapter. At one point, Sartre speaks of a process of 'abstraction and universalization' in which, from a single episode, one might try to obtain a general law of dialectic, but which in fact would yield only 'schemas constantly valid *for that episode*';[10] this is not the sort of abstraction, or 'extrapolation', in which Sartre himself would claim to have engaged. How, then, did Sartre decide to begin his account of dialectical experience where he did, at the point that he judged to be the most 'abstract' possible for social philosophy? If pressed on this matter, he would have to say, ultimately, that he had INTUITED his

[7] *Ibid.*, p. 143.

[8] "That reply which claims to refuse our 'formalism' contains the complete and formal acceptance of the *liberal* position; the individualistic bourgeoisie asks that it be granted one thing and one thing alone: the relation among individuals is passively undergone by each one of them and externally conditioned by other forces (as many of them as you please)." *Ibid.*, p. 179.

[9] For a treatment of the latter question which emphasizes *pour-soi* and *en-soi* more than PRAXIS and inert matter, cf. my "Jean-Paul Sartre: Man, Freedom, and *Praxis*" in George A. Schrader, ed., *Existential Philosophers: Kierkegaard to Merleau-Ponty* (New York, McGraw-Hill, 1967), esp. pp. 273-274.

[10] *Critique de la raison dialectique*, p. 141.

starting-point, which means that all his own previous experience had led him to consider this starting-point as the most abstract and therefore the most fundamental for an explanation of human society and history. He would deny that there was anything arbitrary about this intuition, and would point to its usefulness in constructing his account as further evidence for its validity. In the introduction to his earlier work, he says that "the entirety of the preceding remarks has been directly inspired by the revelatory intuition of the phenomenon." [11] On questions about the epistemology involved in reaching his ultimate starting-points, Sartre does not seem greatly to have altered his views. If someone should fail to accept Sartre's abstract starting-point on the grounds that he did not share Sartre's intuition, Sartre could only point to the value of that intuition in explaining experience,[12] with the added remark, in the *Critique*, that experience is *dialectical*. Sartre admits that the intuition is not apodictic.[13]

In the *Critique*, Sartre's two ultimate abstractions are called *praxis* and inert *matter*. In many ways, they resemble the *pour-soi* and the *en-soi*, respectively, of *L'être et le néant*,[14] but this historical point does not concern us here. *Praxis* and matter have the advantage of having been terms frequently used by Marx, and they can be placed immediately in dialectical opposition to one another. The human being is both matter and *praxis*; the body experiences NEED, and through need *praxis* arises as a project of the human organism attempting to preserve itself.[15] At present, according to Sartre, it is necessary to raise the question as to why there are any organisms at all, rather than just inorganic matter, although some day such questions MAY become scientific; what is important is that, if there are organisms, they can only be understood by the dialectical method.[16]

[11] Sartre, *L'être et le néant*, pp. 15-16.

[12] Desan (*The Tragic Finale*, p. 138) expresses the opinion that the starting-point of *L'être et le néant* can only be something like a POSTULATE.

[13] "The full understanding of the act and the object is characterized as the temporal development of a practical intuition, but not as the grasping of a necessity." *Critique de la raison dialectique*, p. 177.

[14] Sartre himself points to the resemblance in a footnote. *Ibid.*, p. 286. Cf. also my "Jean-Paul Sartre: Man, Freedom, and *Praxis*", section entitled "Sartre's Evolution and the Issue of Unity", pp. 294-307.

[15] *Critique de la raison dialectique*, p. 166.

[16] *Ibid.*, p. 175. Does this imply that ANIMAL organisms, too, must be regarded as 'dialectical'? Sartre does not deal with this question. When he writes, "There are only men and real relations among men (for Merleau-Ponty I add: things, too, and animals, etc.)" (*Ibid.*, p. 55), it is a good semi-private joke (Merleau-Ponty's phenomenology, because of its stress on the role of the body in perception and thought

These opening gambits in Sartre's account are not, of course, entirely original with him: what is of most interest to us is the role played by his basic abstract concepts, *praxis* and matter, in his account of fundamental change. For it is the movement from the passive, matter-like inertness characteristic of human beings in serial collectives, to the active structures of group *praxis*, which constitutes the heart of that account for Sartre. Now, although Sartre has scrupulously avoided the use of MINOR metaphors and analogies in working out his account, and although as far as we could determine earlier in this chapter, that account is applicable to a wide range of examples in addition to those that he mentions, it must nevertheless be admitted that his basic abstractions of *praxis* and inert matter give the initial appearance of being employed at least metaphorically, if not mythically, and of having very little direct applicability to actual instances of fundamental change as we have observed them. Such charges, if true, would cast serious doubt on the validity of the Sartrean enterprise.

What precisely is the STATUS of these two abstractions? Perhaps, despite what I said to the contrary at the end of the previous chapter, they will turn out to be MYTHS. '*Praxis*', after all, while it is a term made familiar by Marx, sounds strange both to French- and to English-speaking persons, and the intended referent of this word is certainly not immediately evident. Sartre himself feels obliged to italicize the word '*praxis*' in its hundreds of occurrences throughout the *Critique*, and its use by Merleau-Ponty once drew the censure of the 'official' Marxism represented by Garaudy, who considered it a deliberate mystification which should have been replaced by the word 'pratique', practice.[17] But the meaning of 'practice' is not nearly so precise as that which Sartre apparently intends to convey by using '*praxis*'; has Sartre not, perhaps, transformed this Marxian term into a primitive concept of some mythical, or at least totally undemonstrable, ontology?[18] The

---

in general, is incompatible with certain interpretations of consciousness, *pour-soi*, and now *praxis* in Sartre's writings), but the fact remains that animal activity poses some serious problems for Sartre's philosophy.

[17] Garaudy, Cogniot, *et al.*, *op. cit.*, p. 66.

[18] George Lichtheim, for one, thinks so. In his review of the *Critique*, he says: "As matters stand, Sartre's philosophy of history presents itself as a speculative system which transforms the concepts of Marxian analysis – history, *praxis*, class conflict – into ontological notions, and then sets up a dialectic between them." ("Sartre, Marxism, and History", *History and Theory* III, 2 (1963), p. 243.) But Lichtheim leaves it vague throughout his otherwise stimulating article as to exactly what the terms 'ontology' and 'ontological notion', which appear to have unfavorable connotations for him, are supposed to mean. Sartre would certainly want to

same might be asked about the use to which Sartre puts the concept of 'matter'. It will be recalled, from Chapter Two of this section, that Sartre once spoke of materialism as a myth: "Materialism is uncontestably *the only myth* which meets revolutionary requirements."[19] The philosopher, he said at the time, must construct a PHILOSOPHY having the same effect. Yet the first sentence of the main body of the *Critique* reads: "All that we have established in *Questions of Method* flows from our agreement in principle with historical materialism."[20] Furthermore, the meaning that Sartre gives to the word 'matter' is, once again, most unlike any ordinary sense of that word: "Where then is *matter*, that is, Being totally free of meaning, to be found? The answer is simple: it is presented *nowhere* in human experience."[21] Such passages DO make it sound suspiciously like a mythical entity.

However, it is certain that Sartre does not consider himself guilty of foisting a mythical explanation on his readers. Rather, he will admit that his own position vis-à-vis materialism has shifted over the years,[22] and he will continue to insist that PRAXIS and matter are REAL in some interesting way. By accepting historical materialism, Sartre has in fact given a general answer to the ontological question, "What exists?" Everything, including human beings, is material; that is why it is no contradiction – indeed, not even paradoxical – for him to say that human beings are alienated and reduced to an inert, 'material' status by their own PRAXIS in the practico-inert field and in serial activity. Later, he says the same about the result of some common PRAXIS (such as the capture of the Bastille) that has accomplished its objective: once the goal has been achieved, the 'objective reality' of the group becomes inert. At this point, Sartre finally provides a helpful explanation of the status of at least one of his basic abstractions, matter, which he here calls 'the inorganic':

It will be objected that the result is not always inert: but that is simply because one is considering the inorganic as a certain status which defines a

---

insist that 'history, *praxis*, class conflict' (the list is strange, for the concepts are so diverse) ALL have a CERTAIN reality – and, provided that some non-mythical meaning of '*praxis*' can be discovered, who would not?

[19] Sartre, *Situations* III, p. 175.

[20] *Critique de la raison dialectique*, p. 115.

[21] *Ibid.*, p. 247.

[22] "I was, at the time, further away from Marxism than I am at present. And therefore? Must one be a Marxist by birth?" Sartre, "Réponse à Pierre Naville", *Temps Modernes* 123 (Mar.-Apr. 1956), p. 1517.

certain species of materiality and not, as it must be considered, as a condition which, in definite circumstances, characterizes any type of material existents.[23]

Sartre thus claims that the inorganic, or 'matter', is a CONDITION in which any material thing, INCLUDING ESPECIALLY MAN, may at times be found.

A condition is a state, a manner of existing. For human beings, the condition that Sartre has called that of 'inert matter' or 'the inorganic' is characteristic of a passive way of life, which is the state of what he calls the 'serial' form of collective. We recall that fundamental social change for Sartre is a movement from the latter form of collective to the active structure of group PRAXIS (or else, of course, a movement in the opposite direction). '*Praxis*' may thus be taken to characterize the state which is in the sharpest contrast with that characterized by 'matter'. Sartre's two abstractions of '*praxis*' and '*matter*' are, therefore, CONTRAST TERMS referring to two ideally opposite ways of human life in society, two polar varieties of the human social condition.

But a serious problem still remains in interpreting Sartre's abstraction of '*praxis*' (if not in interpreting 'matter').[24] For PRAXIS quite obviously functions as the AGENT, the motive force, of Sartre's dialectic; a mere 'condition' or way of life, on the other hand, could never play this role. After all, the basic meaning of '*praxis*' is HUMAN ACTIVITY, or behavior, or 'practice'. Thus '*praxis*' seems to have at least two major and divergent meanings in the *Critique*; can they be reconciled? I believe that they can, at least on the level of the social collective. Their reconciliation may also lead to a better understanding of the limitations of the method of 'abstraction'.

We must refer back to a concept of which Sartre makes comparatively little use, but which is certainly the key to understanding a great deal of what he says, especially concerning the fundamental differences between his two major types of social structures, the series and the group. The concept in question is '*alienation*'. In the serial collective, according

[23] *Critique de la raison dialectique*, p. 422.

[24] There are, in fact, a number of problems involved in interpreting what Sartre means by 'matter', too; there seem to be at least two and possibly more senses in which at one time or another he uses this word. Part of his difficulty here comes from the ambiguity of his position on the question of whether or not there is such a thing as Engels' 'dialectics of nature', the existence of which he more often denies. However, the interpretation of 'matter' in Sartre is an enormously difficult question, and the nature of the method of abstraction can be more clearly illustrated, in a way that is more directly relevant to the account of fundamental change, if we now concentrate our attention on what Sartre means by '*praxis*'.

to Sartre, human PRAXIS can most assuredly be said to be the agent which produces whatever may be produced by such a society; but that agent is, by means of its own operations on material objects in a regime of scarcity, alienated and reduced to the status of 'inert matter', i.e., in more traditional Marxist language, the producer becomes the product. Fundamental change in society from the series to the group consists essentially, for Sartre, in a reorganization of the collective in such a way that PRAXIS for the first time appears, ON THE LEVEL OF THE GROUP, as genuinely free, common, and unalienated. For Sartre, genuinely human activity or PRAXIS is always, *ex hypothesi*, intrinsically free; but PRAXIS as a CONDITION, or unalienated way of life, is by no means characteristic of all social collectives; only in a GROUP may there be said to be a COMMON PRAXIS that is truly free. Thus there is an important interrelationship between the two meanings of '*praxis*' previously mentioned, but a certain amount of interpretation and further explanation is required to bring out this interrelationship.

It is largely with the aid of the abstract concepts of 'inert matter' and '*praxis*', as we have noted, that Sartre attempts to explain fundamental changes from series to groups. We may find such 'contrast terms' very helpful in comprehending differences among social structures: my earlier suggestion that Hart's concept of 'acceptance' might be further explicated in terms of 'degrees' of acceptance ranging from an active, episodic to a passive, dispositional type was of a somewhat similar nature, and indeed I shall want in my conclusion to explore the similarities and differences between the latter variety of 'activity' and 'passivity' and that by which Sartre distinguishes the group from the series. But the limitation of such concepts, once they have been interpreted or 're-interpreted' (whichever may be a more accurate description of my analysis of 'matter' and '*praxis*' in Sartre), is quite plain: it is not that they must really be MYTHICAL in any sense, but rather that they remain, when all is said and done, ABSTRACT. And what this means is that they are always capable of being interpreted in a variety of ways, and furthermore that there may always be some reasonable doubt concerning their applicability to any given concrete instance.

For it happens to be the case that the differences between activity and passivity, and consequently between the condition of freedom and the condition of alienation, between '*praxis*' and 'inert matter', and even between the 'group' and the 'series', can be conceived of (as I showed in analyzing Hartean 'acceptance') as differences IN DEGREE. This does not imply, of course, that human activity itself must necessarily pass from a relatively passive or alienated to a relatively free state only 'by degrees'. Such a change may be somewhat abrupt, and this fact is crucial if the concept of fundamental change in law and society is to make any sense at all. In his own account of fundamental change, Sartre eventually comes to the moment at which some individual makes himself 'sovereign' of the group in fusion by performing some act of organization. If the other individuals immediately follow that individual, then this moment may correctly be pointed to as the principal moment of fundamental change, even though the change would not in fact have taken place without the occurrence of many antecedent factors. Nevertheless, it remains true to say that the difference between the series and the group or between the condition of '*praxis*' and that of 'inert matter' can be conceived of as a difference in degree rather than as a *toto caelo* difference. The 'series' and the 'group', as Sartre has defined them, can never be anything more than IDEAL forms of social '*ensembles*'. This explains why it is characteristic of such abstractions to be susceptible to a wide variety of interpretations when any attempt is made to apply them to concrete instances.

And this in turn throws new light on the Sartrean claim to be giving the TRUE account of fundamental change and other social phenomena: the significance of that claim now appears to be somewhat reduced. His account may be true in the sense that we may find it to be applicable to all the examples of what it is supposed to explain, and yet we would always be justified in regarding it as somewhat unsatisfying – simply because, as abstract, it requires interpretation, i.e., it IS 'incomplete'. This is the basic limitation that necessarily follows from Sartre's reliance on the method of abstraction.

In examining the role of this method of abstraction in Sartre's account of fundamental change and of human social activity in general, I have begun to show the importance of 'alienation', as well as of a number of other related concepts, for that account. But neither the concept of 'alienation', nor the distinction between a state of activity and a state of passivity, nor the consequent distinction between the group and the series, is self-explanatory; and as for the contrast terms of '*praxis*' and 'inert matter', they were what we began by trying to explain. When a person or a society is said to be 'alienated', he or it is usually said to be so IN SOME RESPECT OR OTHER, i.e., with reference to something more than sheer abstract PRAXIS. In the case of an individual, we might call him 'alienated' if he has failed to achieve his actual or potential PURPOSES – his 'projects', to use a familiar Sartrean term. But in the case of a society, the situation is more complicated, as we have already seen in attempting to explain the meaning of 'group *praxis*'. We cannot simply say that there are NO purposes, no objectives to be achieved, in the social structure that Sartre calls 'the series', since the serial collective can and must, if it is to survive at all, also be a PRODUCTIVE form of society. What we CAN say, however, is that, in the common PRAXIS of the group, as distinguished from the series, alienation has been overcome in the sense that the communal objectives, purposes, or projects coincide with those of the individual members of that social collective.[25] Sartre designates this phenomenon of the group project by the name, 'totalization'. In order to understand the nature of Sartre's explanation of fundamental social change as it centers around his account of the group in fusion, and in order to get to the root of the differences between Sartre's and Hart's approaches to the human activity that brings about fundamental change, we must try to clarify somewhat the meaning of this Sartrean neologism.

[25] "What roughly distinguishes serial activity, which – though counter-finalized and passive – has its *teleological reason*, from group *praxis*, . . . is not the freedom of individual *praxis* (since the wave of panic, like the deliberate assault, comes about through the *praxis* of each person); it is that, in the one case, freedom manifests itself only to discover its alienation in a passive activity of impotency . . . and that, in the other case, in the group in the course of being constituted, the leader is always *myself*, there are no others, I am sovereign and I *discover in my own praxis* the watchwords which come from others." *Critique de la raison dialectique*, p. 421.

6

TOTALIZATION

"If dialectical reason exists", says Sartre, "it can only be – from the ontological point of view – totalization in course."[1] Totalization is therefore, for Sartre, the essential characteristic of human social activity. To explain more precisely exactly what 'totalization' is, however, is by no means an easy task; this concept, as Dufrenne so well puts it in his review of the *Critique*, is 'difficilement intelligible'. Dufrenne further suggests that "totalization is a substitute here for the Hegelian *aufhebung*, and has the same role as structuration in other contemporary anthropologies".[2]

We in fact faced a somewhat analogous problem in attempting to understand what Hart meant by 'rules', for the use to which Hart put the concept of 'rules' in explaining fundamental change and human social activity in general was at least a pervasive as that to which Sartre puts 'totalization' in explaining the same phenomena, and we must once again remind ourselves of the potential danger of being left with a notion which purports to explain everything and which therefore, in the last analysis, paradoxically explains nothing at all. Like Hart, Sartre avoids this paradox of explanation by pointing to something that is quite different from 'totalization': he sharply contrasts 'totalization' with 'totality'. As for the latter,

> The synthetic unity which will bring about its appearance of being a totality cannot be an act, but only the vestige of a past action. . . . Totality – contrary to what one might think – is only a regulative principle of totalization (and is, at the same time, reducible to the inert whole of its provisional creations).[3]

Unlike Hart's 'rules', however, the concept of 'totalization' is one with

[1] *Ibid.*, p. 139.

[2] Dufrenne, *op. cit.*, p. 683. Unlike 'structuration', however, 'totalization' strongly implies a conception, anathema to an anthropologist like Lévi-Strauss, of historical progression.

[3] *Critique de la raison dialectique*, p. 138.

which, initially, we are totally unfamiliar. 'Totalization' is indeed, for all practical purposes,[4] a neologism, and it may well be regarded as a particularly blatant illustration of that 'abuse of language' of which, as we have seen, Lefebvre accuses Sartre. We may begin by setting aside, for the moment at least, the great ultimate question of whether History (the use of the capital letter is significant) itself is a vast, intelligible movement of totalization. Sartre unequivocally maintains the thesis that it is (though he admits that it is undoubtedly never thought of as such by the majority of its actors),[5] but it is the second volume of the *Critique*, rather than the first, that is supposed to bear the main burden of supporting this thesis.[6] As will be seen towards the end of the present chapter, however, it is impossible entirely to separate a discussion of totalizations in Sartre from a consideration of their relevance to our understanding of history.

In attempting to arrive at a rough first approximation of what Sartre means by 'totalization', we might do well to reconsider the synonym that I suggested at the close of the preceding chapter, to wit, 'group project'. The group, unlike the series, is characterized by a common PRAXIS that is truly free and that formulates, and seeks to achieve, genuinely novel 'projects'. Furthermore, in the IDEAL form of the group, alienation has been entirely eliminated, because the communal projects completely coincide with the objectives of the individual members of the group. The activity of STRIVING TO ACHIEVE (the problem of success or failure is not an important one at this point) a certain common objective (or several objectives) by means of a total integration within a group is at least part of what Sartre's concept of 'totalization' means. Totalization, for Sartre, is always 'totalization in course', since totalization is (human) ACTIVITY. But there is a serious problem as to how any given totalization is to be defined, since it is absolutely essential to

[4] Georges Gurvitch rather gleefully points out that Sartre is NOT the first to have employed the word, 'totalization': Proudhon used it in his *La Création de l'ordre*, though Sartre appears to have been unaware of this fact. Gurvitch, *Dialectique et sociologie* (Paris, Flammarion, 1962), pp. 100 and 173 ... The term is also found in the writings of Sartre's contemporary, Teilhard de Chardin. Cf., for example, his essay, "L'Humanité se meut-elle biologiquement sur elle-même?" in which he stresses "le grand phénomène de la Totalisation humaine." – *L'Avenir de l'homme* (Paris, Éditions du Seuil, 1959), pp. 317-336.

[5] For example, cf. *Critique de la raison dialectique*, p. 152.

[6] It is interesting to note that L. J. Cohen, in *The Principles of World Citizenship*, seems to have come to maintain a very similar thesis (though he would probably not approve of Sartre's language), at least concerning contemporary history, by means of very dissimilar considerations about law.

Sartre's view of human activity, or PRAXIS, that it be regarded as, in itself, thoroughly free. However, our equation of totalization with 'group project' has already suggested a first solution to this problem: any given totalization can always be defined with respect to its PURPOSE, or end, or objective. The ACHIEVEMENT of the end is therefore also the end of the totalization, at least in its original form. This is well illustrated in Sartre's treatment of fundamental change.

The transformation of a serial collective into a group in order to achieve a radically new objective is a paradigm case of a totalization. Indeed, the group itself is, at the limit, nothing but an activity, a totalization – as Sartre's account of the group in fusion, which I recounted in considerable detail in Chapter Three, shows very clearly. The group in fusion has almost no visible structure (except for the fact that all its members are to be found in a given place at a given time) and consequently no inertness or 'being'. At the crucial moment when some individual, hardly aware of what he is doing and certainly not consciously wishing to assume a role of leadership, utters some exhortation or performs some other simple act which transforms an 'inert', purposeless mob into an at least momentarily coherent group with an at least momentary objective, the degree of organization (in the USUAL sense, i.e., structure) is minimal and the degree of unification maximal. ANY ONE of the individuals involved, as Sartre explains, could have fulfilled the role of mediator, organizer, and sovereign. That is because the members of the group, in this ideal case, are unanimous in their striving to achieve the common objective (e.g., the capture of the Bastille). The group itself does not enter into their considerations except as, precisely, their common PRAXIS or activity. The group, in other words, is in no way an end in itself, but only a means: "The group can only be totalization in course, and its totality is outside of it, in its object, i.e., in the material totality which defines it and which it attempts to appropriate to itself and to transform into its instrument."[7] Sartre has no difficulty whatever in showing the extreme impermanence of the ideal form of the group in fusion – if, indeed, it has ever occurred in anything approaching its ideal form. The simplest case, he points out, is that of victory: for example, the Bastille is captured.[8] The objective is achieved, and the group, if it does not dissolve entirely, begins to move in the direction of institutionalization.

Thus far we have re-examined what Sartre himself has to say about

[7] *Critique de la raison dialectique*, p. 412.
[8] *Ibid.*, p. 422.

totalization and have seemed to find in his account of the fundamental change from the series to the group the clearest instance of 'totalization' – this strange word, which would appear peculiar even in the profession of accounting, but which is now said to be the essential characteristic of human rationality and activity in society. No better instance of totalization than the case of the group in fusion is capable of occurring in actual human experience. But conceptually, in an experiment of thought, perhaps it is possible to find a 'purer' form of totalization than any provided by empirical reality. Our initial encouragement in this enterprise comes from the fact that Sartre himself, as we have already noted, acknowledges that totalization in society is always, not unlike Camus' Sisyphus or his Rebel, doomed to a certain degree of failure: since individual PRAXIS remains the agent even in group action, the gap between individual and common PRAXIS can never completely be closed.[9] Individual PRAXIS is irreducible, and this is one reason why we shall never find a truly 'pure' totalization in human experience. There is a further reason: the factor of time (and also of space, although technology has succeeded in reducing the importance of the latter). Sartre made his account of fundamental change much simpler than it would otherwise have been by assuming a simultaneous change from serial to group activity in all the individuals concerned, and indeed this would be the ideal case. But in fact, a perfect synchronism is never to be found in the actual fusion of any group or in the attainment by a group of the objective that it is the group's 'project' to achieve. As Sartre remarks about his entire first volume: "We have remained on the level of synchronic totalization, and we have not taken account of the diachronic dimension of practical temporalization." [10] We may therefore feel fully justified in going further than Sartre by performing (with appropriate apologies to him) a thought experiment to learn just what a truly 'pure' or perfect totalization, one such as human activity can never carry out, would be.

Sartre himself has provided us with a clue for discovering this limiting case by his footnote reference to Malraux's term for the first stages of the phenomenon of the group in fusion. Malraux had called it 'l'Apocalypse'. This is fitting. The book of Scripture which bears the same name

[9] Compare with Rousseau: "De plus, l'aliénation se faisant sans réserve, l'union est aussi parfaite qu'elle peut l'être, et nul associé n'a plus rien à réclamer", "Du Contrat Social", I, 7, *op. cit.*, p. 244. For Sartre, (1) the fundamental change from the series to the group is the DEFEAT, rather than the beginning, of alienation, and (2) the union, even under optimal conditions, is never perfect.

[10] *Critique de la raison dialectique*, p. 754.

is more than simply a mystical description of scenes of almost unspeakable upheaval and terror. It is also the expression of the perfect totalization. In 'the new Heaven and the new Earth' which it depicts as the end of the period of upheaval, there will be a perfect accord between God and His people: no gap will exist between individual and common PRAXIS.[11] The God of the Apocalypse furnishes the element that Sartre's dialectical History, 'une totalisation sans totalisateur',[12] does not have. But what is most interesting about the new Heaven and the new Earth, of course, is that it would seem to be a completed totality. All objectives have, by definition, been achieved, and there can be no more projects and hence no more Sartrean freedom. Indeed, theologians such as St. Augustine have wondered whether there would be any activity in this totalized totality.[13]

Furthermore, the 'gap' caused by problems of TIME also disappears in the pure totalization depicted by the Christian Scriptures. The Book of the Apocalypse itself details incidents that take certain lengths of time, but the reader knows that these figures are meant to be only allegorical. As the book closes, the notion that the Apocalypse is imminent and that it will in fact occur in an instant is stressed increasingly.[14] And this is not surprising, since it was to become a commonplace of medieval theology and philosophy that time for God was only an 'eternal Now' – an instant, albeit an 'immense' one.

Thus the Christian eschatology appears to be the pure, ideal model for Sartre's concept of totalization. We can see that the Creation is the paradigm case of purposeful activity, or PRAXIS, and that the philosophical implications of the mystic notions contained in the Apocalypse help to indicate what a perfect totalization would be. But we note also that the entire act, from 'project' (of creation) to achievement of the objective (the fundamental change of the human race from a state of resistance and 'inert materiality' to one of 'group *praxis*' or 'mere to-

11 "Ιδοὺ ἡ σχηνὴ τοῦ Θεοῦ μετὰ τῶγ ἀνθρώπων... καὶ αὐτοὶ λαοὶ αὐτοῦ ἔσονται, καιαὐτὸς ὁ θεος ἔσται μετ' αὐτῶν." *Apocalypse* 21, 3.

12 *Critique de la raison dialectique*, p. 754.

13 "I speak of activity, although, perhaps, I should rather say calm or repose. To tell the truth, I have no real notion of what eternal life will be like." St. Augustine, *The City of God* 22, 29 (tr. by Walsh, Zema, Monahan, and Honan) (New York, Image Books, 1958), pp. 532-533. In the following chapter, however, Augustine commits himself to the view that this state will be one of great freedom – indeed, of freedom from sin.

14 The words ἔρχομαι ταχύ 'I come quickly', are repeated seven times. Elsewhere in the Scriptures, it is repeatedly emphasized that "one day with the Lord is as a thousand years".

tality' [15]) is the work of an instant from the point of view of the Totalizer, God.[16] Several conclusions concerning totalization are suggested by this.

First of all, it is obvious that instantaneous totalization is impossible for man: human activity always takes time. We noted, in discussing Sartre's account of the group in fusion, that a single moment can sometimes be pointed to in which a change that is abrupt rather than gradual takes place in the PRAXIS of the individuals who are forming the new group; this fact is essential to an understanding of the phenomenon of fundamental change. But it would be very 'abstract', in the most pejorative sense of that word, to suppose that even in such cases the change would be intelligible or meaningful without the TEMPORAL events leading up to it and following it – the antecedent condition of seriality, the 'project', the achievement of the objective, and the aftermath of the latter.

Secondly, the ideal form of totalization is in fact formless, totally lacking in structure or rules or what contemporary French philosophy often calls 'mediations'. This was already seen in the case of the group in fusion, in which I pointed out that the degree of organization was minimal and that the group was sheerly a means for attaining the objective, its only structure at this point being the temporal and spatial contiguity of its members. The lack of structure becomes even more clear in the case of the Christian eschatology: God is bound by no rules, as Descartes points out in a particularly striking way.[17] In the paradigm case of totalization, 'mediations' of all kinds are done away with, and perfect unity results. Rules would only be hindrances to such a consummation.

Now, if Hart, taken together with Wittgenstein, Winch, and others, has demonstrated anything, it is the impossibility of conceiving of any behavior that could be called genuinely human which would not take

[15] The two opposites, group PRAXIS and mere totality, in fact meet in 'the new Heaven and the new Earth'. Christian eternal life seems at once to be pure activity and absolute completeness. But is this any more paradoxical than Sartre's *desideratum* of 'group *praxis* forever'? ("The worker will only liberate himself from his destiny if the human multiplicity transforms itself wholly for all time into group *praxis*." *Critique de la raison dialectique*, p. 351.) We shall have to see.

[16] "ἐγὼ τὸ ἄλφα και τὸ ὦ, ὁ πρῶτος και ὁ ἔσχατος, ἡ ἀρχὴ και τὸ τέλος". *Apocalypse* 22, 13.

[17] "To one who pays attention to God's immensity, it is clear that nothing at all can exist which does not depend on him. This is true not only of everything that subsists, but of all order, of every law, and of every reason of truth and goodness." (*Reply to Objections* VI, 8.) *The Philosophical Works of Descartes*, Vol. II (tr. by E. Haldane and G. Ross) (New York, Dover Publications, 1955), p. 250.

place in accordance with some rule or set of rules. During Sartre's 'Apocalypse', there MIGHT occur a moment in which rules ceased to govern the actions of the individuals involved; but then their behavior could only be characterized as madness, and this would entail the immediate dissolution of the 'project', hence of PRAXIS, hence of dialectical reason itself. (It would also entail, interestingly enough, an extreme form of 'alienation': it is no accident that, in French, the word for 'madmen' is 'les aliénés'.) If an actual 'group', in the Sartrean sense, could ever be nothing but pure 'totalization', governed by no rules, then it would be literally impossible for anyone to give an account of a fundamental change to or from that group. Thus the ideal of completely formless totalization, like that of instantaneous totalization, is impossible for man. This fact raises one further consideration, however: is such an ideal even DESIRABLE? This question has been introduced in such a way as to make inevitable, aside from all the standard problems about what 'desirable' means, a universally negative answer. Only the isolated individual in the moment before he goes mad would regard as desirable the self-contradictory madness of totalization carried to its extreme, that is, a totalization without rules. Even the less extreme, humanly possible totalization of the group in fusion is unlikely to engender great pleasure of more than a momentary kind in many of its participants. Sartre himself admits this; concerning the larger totalization that took place throughout France as a result, partly, of the local totalization in the Faubourg Saint Antoine, he says:

> This Apocalypse terrified them; in order to avoid it, the members of the Constituent Assembly would willingly have made themselves the accomplices of the aristocracy, if only that had been possible. But it is France as Apocalypse that they discern in the capture of the Bastille.[18]

With these considerations, we have begun what might be called the 'retreat from totalization' – that is, the discovery of some of the problems involved in attempting to explain human social activity and fundamental social change principally in terms of totalizations, and especially of the difficulty in conceiving of a fundamental change that could be regarded as the DEFINITIVE one.

Before I mention some of the implications of this retreat, I wish to recall the justification given by Lefebvre (in connection with the extreme concept of freedom advanced in *L'être et le néant*) for Sartre's rather frequent practice of developing a concept to a point approaching its

[18] *Critique de la raison dialectique*, pp. 410-411.

limits, as he has done with 'totalization' in the account of the 'Apocalypse', the account that I have just now tried to continue and, in a sense, to complete. The philosopher must advance even extreme hypotheses, says Lefebvre, "an exercise that is inevitable and valuable to the precise extent to which the consequences of the hypothesis have determined its limits".[19] Sartre's discussion of totalizations might therefore be regarded as being not only on account of fundamental change and other societal phenomena (an account that brilliantly emphasizes certain aspects, notably those of PURPOSE or OBJECTIVE and FREEDOM, of which Hart's analysis, for one, is rather neglectful), but also a conceptual analysis. 'Totalization', like 'freedom', is a particularly interesting concept because of its very wide range of meanings and applications – in short, because its limiting cases, as we have seen, are so very extreme. If, on the other hand, Sartre intends to use the concept of 'totalization' and related concepts as a means of breaking away entirely from the restraints imposed upon consciousness by language, as he sometimes seems to intimate,[20] then he is attempting the impossible – as Hart would certainly want to contend, and as Lefebvre has also seen very well. For although philosophy, as Lefebvre says, can and must 'break through' the stultifying trivialities of ordinary discourse, still philosophy must recognize that it is 'the concept', rather than pure consciousness, which serves, logically, as our criterion of truth. To underestimate the necessity of basing one's philosophy on linguistic concepts, therefore, would be to run exactly the same risks in the area of consciousness as the surrender of all 'structure' would cause one to run with respect to 'totalization' in social philosophy: the completely anti-conceptual philosophy of pure consciousness is self-contradictory (for, since we could neither say nor think anything about it, it would cease to be a philosophy) and could issue only in madness. Such considerations lead to a retreat from a philosophy of 'pure', immediate consciousness similar to the retreat from any philosophical position that would regard extreme totalization as either a real possibility or an ideal for man.

What follows from the latter retreat? The most important consequence, it seems to me, is that 'human nature' must be said in some basic way to be unalterable, contrary to what numerous philosophers of fundamental change, from Rousseau to Sartre, have apparently at-

[19] Lefebvre, *La Somme et le reste*, p. 723.

[20] He says at one point in the *Critique*, for example, that one of the 'fundamental characteristics' of a '*personal project*' is that "it cannot in any case be defined by concepts" (p. 105).

tempted to contend. This conclusion may at first seem such as to give support to ultra-conservative thought, but it need not be interpreted in this way at all. All that has thus far been demonstrated with respect to 'human nature' in our analysis of the concept of totalization is that human beings cannot (and ought not try to) act without using rules. Whether any particular KINDS of rules are always required has not yet been specified. And to this minimal claim concerning the permanence of 'human nature', even Sartre might ultimately find little difficulty in subscribing.

Human behavior would continue to be rule-governed even in a world in which there was no scarcity – a conceivable, logically possible world which Sartre (like Hart in his discussion of 'The Minimum Content of Natural Law') briefly mentions several times as an intriguing hypothesis, but which he seems also to envision as a possible future state of affairs in our own world, after the occurrence of some DEFINITIVE fundamental change, the time of 'group *praxis* forever'. Sartre says that in a hypothetical world without scarcity "one can perfectly well conceive of a dialectical *praxis* and even of labor", but that "what would disappear is our character as men, that is, since this character is historical, the peculiar uniqueness of our History".[21] Later in the *Critique*, Sartre returns to this hypothesis and says that it is inconceivable how intelligent beings in a world in which there has NEVER been scarcity could, if initially scattered, become unified.[22] But a more careful consideration of the concept of RULES, which I have shown to be essential to human 'totalizations', would have led Sartre to realize that, even in the logically possible 'world without scarcity', the fundamentally social nature of language and of other societal institutions WOULD bring about the 'resserrement' that was mistakenly said by him to be inconceivable in such a world. Sartre might reply that such a world would not even have a History in our sense (as noted above), and that therefore it might lack even the phenomenon of 'totalization' for which I have said that rules are essential. But it could then be answered that, on Sartre's own premises, without totalization there would be no PRAXIS, no dialectic at all. Once more, the pushing of an hypothesis to its extreme formulation would lead to the defeat of the philosophic enterprise. Any CONCEIVABLE intelligent beings living in a world without scarcity would have to have the characteristics both of engaging in 'totalizing activity' and of sharing man's rule-governed nature.

[21] *Ibid.*, p. 201.
[22] *Ibid.*, p. 352.

Let us follow just a little further the consequences of our 'retreat from totalization'. I refer back to my conclusions in the preceding chapter concerning the status of Sartre's basic abstractions of PRAXIS and inert matter. They were seen to be best understood as 'contrast terms' referring to different states or conditions of human activity, ranging from the highly 'active' and unalienated to the relatively 'passive' and alienated. We know, of course, that contrast terms cease to be of value when the referent of one of the terms is eliminated. This fact, coupled with our new observations concerning the unalterable nature (as long as the notion of dialectical reason itself continues to have any sense) of human activity considered as both 'totalizing' and rule-governed, suggests that the complete elimination of INERTNESS from human activity is no more conceivable than the elimination of its opposite, PRAXIS. (For, as we have seen, the pure PRAXIS of the extreme forms of totalization is, for human beings, madness.) But the contrast between matter and PRAXIS was a basic element in Sartre's account of fundamental change from the series to the group and the reverse. The implication is obvious: while these considerations taken together do NOT imply that certain TYPES of fundamental changes (such as the atomization of modern nation-states into 'series' of small city-states) need ever again occur in our history,[23] they DO establish an extremely high probability that the general phenomenon of fundamental change in society (both from the series to the group and from the group to the series) will at no time permanently cease to occur, as well as the CERTAINTY that a new occurrence of this phenomenon will always remain at least a logical possibility. They further suggest, in accordance with a previously-mentioned comment by Lefebvre,[24] that the eschatological notion of 'the New Life' on earth can only be a myth, though it is sometimes a fruitful one.

Such a conclusion, modest as it may seem, casts grave doubt on Sartre's occasional hints about a possible future state of affairs in which scarcity will have been overcome and 'group *praxis*' will prevail forever – presumably as the consequence of some '*really* fundamental' change. We are led to ponder, on the other hand, his thus far unanswered question, "Is there not a perpetual double movement of regrouping and petrification?"[25] But this is the central question with which Sartre is to

[23] I shall return to this general problem in Chapter Eight of the present section.

[24] Lefebvre, *Introduction à la Modernité*, p. 75.

[25] *Critique de la raison dialectique*, p. 643. The following passage is another very interesting statement of the same general question: "The real problem – which we do not have to study here – concerns less the past ... than the future: to what extent will a socialist society abolish atomism *in all its forms*? To what extent will

deal in his philosophy of history, and a final judgment concerning his views on these problems will of course be possible only when he himself has thoroughly developed them. However, our analysis of 'totalization' (it will be recalled from the beginning of this chapter that history, for Sartre, is one vast totalization) has at least indicated certain directions that Sartre's solution to his problem cannot take. Marx, who is quite obviously Sartre's inspiration for the view that, in the course of history, some fundamental change in society might conceivably be the DEFINITIVE and FINAL fundamental change, did not maintain (some of his critics to the contrary notwithstanding) that the Revolution that was to put an end to alienations would be the END of history, in the sense of a *terminus*; rather, he thought of it as being, in many only vaguely specified ways, a beginning.[26] If the phenomenon of history itself is to continue, then so must many of the other phenomena that we have seen to be essential to 'totalizations'. At present, it seems best to leave our analysis of 'totalization' within a Sartrean perspective in this unfinished state.

Our 'retreat from extreme totalization as a real possibility or an ideal' has its counterpart in the actual retreat from totalization in Sartre's account in the second half of the *Critique* (beginning about p. 433). In order to ensure permanence in the group, i.e., to guard against the occurrence of a new fundamental change from the group back to the series, an inert, structural element must be introduced into the group. As I have already noted in Chapter Three, Sartre calls this element, the necessary formal basis of all group organizations and institutions, 'the oath'.

---

collective objects, symbols of our alienation, be dissolved in a true intersubjective community in which the only real relations will be those of men with one another . . . ? Must the disappearance of the capitalist forms of alienation be identified with the elimination of *all* forms of alienation?" *Ibid.* (footnote), p. 349.

[26] "Communism therefore as the complete return of man to himself as a *social* (i.e., human) being – a return become conscious, and accomplished within the entire wealth of previous development. This communism . . . is the *genuine* resolution of the conflict between man and nature and between man and man." Marx, *Economic and Philosophic Manuscripts of 1844* (tr. by Institute of Marxism-Leninism) (Moscow, Foreign Languages Publishing House, 1961), p. 102. Marx goes on from here to argue that even PERCEPTION will somehow be different in this "next stage of historical development in the process of human emancipation and recovery". (*Ibid.*, p. 114.)

7

CONJURATION

The procedure of the oath, then, consists in freely representing the future dispersion of the group as an inert impossibility (as permanent negation of certain possibilities in the midst of the field of possibles) and, conversely, in making the future group appear to the present community as the limit of all possible development.[1]

The oath may of course take many historical forms, of which the Tennis Court Oath is merely the most obvious and explicit example.[2] In a secondary sense, of which the examples are far more numerous, Sartre admits that there is an element of the oath in everyone's birth into a given group or groups; that is why his erstwhile way of speaking, as if "total indetermination were the true basis of choice," was misleading. In fact, important and irreversible choices are made for the individual before he is at all capable of choosing for himself; "but it is also true that [this decision] can mark him only to the extent to which he will have freely interiorized it." [3]

The parallels between Sartre's concept of the oath and Hart's concept of acceptance are obvious. Acceptance, at least by officials of the legal system (who, in the typical modern state, would constitute some form of institutionalized group for Sartre), is for Hart a necessary condition for the avoidance of fundamental change in law. I showed the range of possible degrees of acceptance, from the relatively active to the relatively passive. For Sartre, the phenomenon of 'the oath', which has the status of a logically necessary presupposition for all PERMANENT social structure, exists in many possible forms, the paradigm of which is the sworn, conscious pledge to guard against the defection of others and, by means of one's fellow oath-takers, to limit one's own liberty.[4]

[1] *Critique de la raison dialectique*, p. 440.

[2] *Ibid.*, p. 439.

[3] *Ibid.*, pp. 491-492.

[4] *Ibid.*, p. 442. In other forms, of course, Sartre's 'oath' need not be an explicit or fully conscious pledge.

Sartre's oath already represents a first step towards passivity, since the group in fusion, as we saw, had no structure, permanence, or 'Being', and consequently did not yet require even the pre-juridical formula of the oath as a basis for its existence. 'The oath' for Sartre, like 'acceptance' for Hart, is what accounts for the permanence of a given system or structure – a legal system in the case of Hart, a social structure of any one of a vast variety of forms (of which legal systems are one type, as we shall see) for Sartre.

Our analysis of 'acceptance' in Hart, however, led us to note important connections between law and morality, considerations without which a Hartean analysis of fundamental change in law would have been impossible or at least highly implausible. For it was by reference to systems of moral rules that the decision no longer to accept a given legal system could be made and justified. But in Sartre, on the other hand, there is no clear preliminary distinction between social aims (in the sense of the objectives of a group) and moral values corresponding to the distinction between law and morals in Hart. There may, it is true, be disaffected individuals in Sartre's present-day social world who belong to no group whatever, or at least to no group of any widespread (historical) significance; it is also true that Sartre insists on the gap between individual and group PRAXIS, which may account for the eventual desire of some individuals to leave the groups of which they are members, though they are bound by 'the oath' not to do so. Nevertheless, precisely because of the binding character of the oath, it is initially difficult to see how Sartre can provide a theoretical account of and justification for the dissolution of a group once formed, other than its defeat by an alien group. In forming the group, the members have 'projected' the group's objectives as their supreme value(s), and the distinction at this point between social and moral values would appear to make no sense for Sartre. In their conjuration, these same individuals have limited their own liberties by pledging continued adherence to the group, so that their future obligations (moral, social, or legal – the difference does not exist at this level) are to be determined by the group's structure. How does Sartre's account allow for the possibility of future fundamental changes in (or from) this group, other than by means of outside force from other groups? If a potential difficulty in Hart's analysis of fundamental change seemed to be his initial determination to insist upon the complete separation of law and morality, does not Sartre run into the opposite difficulty by completely identifying social with moral values?

It is here that the central dialectical notion of (practical) "contradiction" comes, at least for the moment, to Sartre's rescue. Hart, it will be recalled, had allowed for the possibility, potentially generative of fundamental change in law, of regarding "a particular rule of law as valid and at the same time [accepting], as morally binding, a moral rule forbidding the behaviour required by the legal rule".[5] Sartre goes much further by seeing in the very notion of the oath an implicit dialectical 'contradiction':

> In the first moment, the group . . . requires a contradictory status, since it wishes both permanence . . . and free totalizing *praxis* or, if one prefers, since it wishes totalization, in its very freedom, to profit from the ontological condition of inert synthesis.[6]

Totalization in its paradigm form, as we saw in the preceding chapter, is sheer activity, devoid of structure; only the ideal group in fusion at an ideal moment comes close to exemplifying perfect totalization. It was quickly seen why the extreme form of totalization not only was not possible but also would, if possible, have been undesirable. The oath was the first step in the 'retreat from totalization'. But now we may also begin to call into question the desirability of 'the sworn group', the group that has begun to assure its own permanence by means of the oath. And indeed it is essential to Sartre's scheme that the desirability of the sworn group be called into question, for otherwise no further changes, and certainly no further fundamental changes such as the dissolution of a particular group, would be possible.

A closer examination of the consequences of 'the oath' in Sartre's account strengthens our conviction that the oath brings about states of affairs intrinsically no more desirable than those brought about by extreme forms of totalization. First of all, because of the binding character of the oath and its complementary aspects of 'fraternity' and 'terror' (i.e., there is a specially close relationship among the members of the group, but there are also special sanctions against defection),[7] the oath is a reaffirmation of violence in this world of material scarcity:

[5] *The Concept of Law*, p. 246. It will further be recalled that this was one of his explicitly stated points of difference with Kelsen.

[6] *Critique de la raison dialectique*, pp. 437-438.

[7] As is the case with the oath itself, so the 'fraternity-terror' atmosphere reaffirmed by the oath may occur in a wide variety of forms, depending on historical circumstances, the nature of the group (as defined by its objectives), etc. The words used here by Sartre, as it so often occurs in philosophy, are deceptively rhetorical and exciting ways of making a basically valid point concerning 'acceptance' (to revert to Hart's language) and obligation.

Thus the intelligibility of the oath comes from the fact that it is a rediscovery and affirmation of violence as the diffuse structure of the group in fusion and that it reflexively transforms this structure into a stable structure of common relationships.[8]

The pure desire for violence is inhuman,[9] as Sartre acknowledges, and yet the oath constitutes a reassertion of violence.[10] Furthermore, the oath leads to institutionalization and to its concomitant 'alienations' of individuals. Seen in a certain light, as Sartre points out, all rights and duties appear to be alienations, though they are seen not to be so in another sense, when one refers back to the original objectives of the oath that created these rights and duties.[11] Although the formation of institutions is a later stage in Sartre's account, it is the insufficiencies and 'contradictions' of the group as constituted by the original oath which lead to the increased emphasis on 'function' and 'office' (rather than the individual) that is characteristic of the institutionalized group. Sartre speaks of the institutionalized group as a 'degraded form of community', although, as I mentioned earlier, he insists that " 'to degrade', here, of course implies no reference to any value system whatever, be it even the ethical affirmation that freedom is the basis of values".[12] It is encouraging to be assured that Sartre does not wish to call all institutions morally deplorable *per se* – this would indeed be a sorry conclusion for social philosophy to come to –, but the momentum of his dialectic sometimes seems to tend toward such a conclusion. And we are half persuaded to agree with this conclusion when Sartre comments on the 'degraded' form of institution known as bureaucracy,[13] about the evils of which he can write so very convincingly. The oath,

8 *Critique de la raison dialectique*, p. 449.

9 A good case can be made, though it is not essential to the present study, to the effect that CONFLICT is now no longer so fundamental to Sartre's view of all intersubjective relationships as it was in *L'être et le néant*. In the *Critique*, the existence of violence is said to depend on the CONTINGENT fact that ours is a world of scarcity. "Ja, gebrochen wird damit in letzter Konsequenz auch das Monopol des Kampf- und Konfliktmodells." – Michael Theunissen, *Der Andere* (Berlin, Walter de Gruyter & Co., 1965), p. 233.

10 It is in commenting on this point that De Waelhens, in his review of the *Critique*, gives up on Sartre: "Let us not insist on it. If the totalization of an era really has no other basis of intelligibility – if we admit that this is one – than a dialectic (or a non-dialectic) of this sort, it is best to give up all hope concerning the history that this dialectic will produce". *Op. cit.*, p. 96.

11 *Critique de la raison dialectique*, p. 534.

12 *Ibid.*, p. 574. Would Hart characterize the legal system of a Sartrean 'institutionalized group' as 'healthy' or 'unhealthy'? This question will be considered in Chapter Eight.

13 *Ibid.*, esp. pp. 624-631.

considered in itself, may not be essentially evil, but does it not seem always to promote the tendency towards various sorts of alienation, which are evil?

The upshot of this is that the original question, concerning whether Sartre's relativistic identification of moral values with group values does not prevent him from theoretically accounting for fundamental changes in groups, must now be revised. Sartre can ACCOUNT FOR such changes. For it can be seen how the group, for Sartre, can generate internally its own destruction, beginning with the moment of 'the oath' and continuing on through stages in which members play increasingly passive roles. But an important puzzle still remains: how can Sartre now escape complete moral relativism, i.e., how can he ever JUSTIFY CERTAIN fundamental changes except in the Pickwickian sense in which he could be said to 'justify' ALL fundamental changes? How, in the first place, is it theoretically possible for us to make the GENERAL value judgment, on the basis on his account, that any instance of the extreme forms of group totalization would be undesirable or, at the other end of the spectrum, that the various alienations that constitute bureaucracy in an institutionalized group are undesirable? How is it, likewise, that Sartre can find the other form of social collective, the SERIES, to be somehow evil because of the alienation of individuals that it entails? [14]

Thus far, we have had occasion to review almost exclusively the DANGERS present in both extremes of group organization (i.e., both in the group in fusion, in its moment of fullest totalization, and in the 'active passivity' of the institutionalized group) as well as the obvious drawbacks of the 'passive activity' of the series. What all of this might lead to is the conclusion that Sartre's is a social philosophy of moral relativism combined with a radical pessimism. A remark such as the following lends weight to such a conclusion:

> There is a sort of internal void, of unbridgeable and indeterminate distance, of *malaise* in every community large and small; this *malaise* brings about a strengthening of the procedures of integration and increases in proportion as the group is more integrated.[15]

Dina Dreyfus refers to the theory of 'radical evil' to be found in the

[14] For an extended discussion of the problems of ethics and value in Sartre from the perspective of an attempted reconciliation between Sartre's earlier and later writings, cf. my "Jean-Paul Sartre: Man, Freedom, and *Praxis*", pp. 307-320. For what is perhaps the best discussion of the same problems in the earlier writings alone, cf. Francis Jeanson's recently-reprinted *Le Problème moral et la pensée de Sartre* (Paris, Éditions du Seuil, 1965).

[15] *Ibid.*, p. 568.

Critique.[16] Is Sartre's only way of 'justifying' fundamental changes in society to be, ultimately, a judgment that damnation will come in one way or the other?

No, Sartre appears to hold that some POSITIVE value judgments, too, can be made from a standpoint external to a particular group. For example, in his series on "Les Communistes et la paix", he affirmed his adherence to many of the values upheld by the Communist Party,[17] while defending his continued refusal to be a member of that group. He apparently believes that some fundamental social changes can be characterized as good and others as bad, and it would be completely inaccurate to say that, in Sartre's view, all changes from the series to the group are good and all those from the group to the series are bad. What, then, is the basis of positive values for Sartre? Is it FREEDOM? Of course; but when we have said that we have not yet said enough. The free PRAXIS of the individual is the basis of Sartre's dialectic and is also the agent in all alienations of freedom. Almost anyone, however, can conscientiously defend the abstract thesis that freedom is the basic value. The minimum that is required in addition is to provide some general clue as to which forms or expressions of human freedom have greater value. It is with this further requirement that Simone de Beau-

[16] "Jean-Paul Sartre et le Mal Radical: De *L'être et le néant* à la *Critique de la raison dialectique*", *Mercure de France* 341 (Jan. 1961), pp. 154-167. Dreyfus' excellent article examines particularly the role played by material scarcity in the theory of the *Critique.*

[17] The objection that "a communist has no values" was, it will be recalled, rejected by Sartre in his joint editorial (with Merleau-Ponty) on Stalin's labor camps, "Les Jours de Notre Vie". A further interesting, though less direct, evidence for Sartre's belief in the possibility of making value judgments outside of any well-defined group is the praise that he lavishes on Maximilien Rubel's controversial biography of Marx (*Critique de la raison dialectique*, p. 27). The controversy over Rubel centers around the following thesis, which is the key to Rubel's interpretation of Marx: "[Marx's] sociological inquiry concerning the State and Law, far from removing him from every value judgment, rests entirely, on the contrary, on a fundamental ethical premise, which is prior to all scientific investigation: the alienation of men subjected to economic, political, and spiritual oppressions, in societies based on the division of labor, private property, and the exploitation of man by man." (Maximilien Rubel, *Karl Marx: Essai de Biographie Intellectuelle* (Paris, Librairie Marcel Rivière et Cie, 1957), p. 209.) This sort of statement seems outrageous to someone like Lucien Goldmann, who has a more narrowly 'scientific' and deterministic view of sociology and of Marxism, and who complains of Rubel's 'lack of conceptual rigor' and never-defined 'ethical-sociological dualism'. (Lucien Goldmann, *Recherches dialectiques* (Paris, Librairie Gallimard, 1959), pp. 296-297.) The fact that Sartre has high praise for Rubel is important for assessing Sartre's position, among French neo-Marxists, on questions about the relationship of sociology to morality.

voir wrestled in her early attempt to outline a Sartrean, existentialist ethics that would at the same time be sympathetic to Marxism and that would, in short, justify the rising political consciousness of 'the Mandarins'.

Mlle. de Beauvoir's solution can be summarized in one word: the FUTURE; she states it in this way:

> It is in the light of the future, which is the meaning and the very substance of action, that a choice will become possible. The men of today will be sacrificed to those of tomorrow, because the present appears as the facticity that must be transcended towards freedom. No action is conceivable without this sovereign affirmation of the future. But we must still come to an agreement about what this word entails.[18]

This formulation is perhaps too simple and therefore unsatisfying, but it points to the way in which Sartre himself must ultimately try to meet the objection that an ethical justification for SOME fundamental social changes which will not at the same time justify EVERY such conceivable change is impossible in his philosophy – the objection that, in other words, beneath all the new and complicated machinery of the *Critique* and despite appearances to the contrary, Sartre's is still the irresponsible philosophy oscillating between wholehearted commitment and the void, and in fact "opting against the transformative action of the world", that Lefebvre charged existentialism with being back in 1946. Sartre's philosophy, both old and new, has always stressed the importance of the objective, or purpose, in defining any action. The group, too, is defined by its PROJECT, as we have noted repeatedly. But a 'project' refers to a proposed future state of affairs, which state of affairs is, by definition, outside of, or beyond, or transcendent to the present group. It is by reference to the future projects of groups that Sartre is able at least to avoid reducing considerations of morality entirely to descriptions of the values held by a given group at a given moment. In this sense, tenuous though it may seem to some, Sartre avoids reaching the dead end of completely identifying social values (i.e., the values of a particular social group) with moral values (i.e., values that in some way or other transcend any given social group, so that, among other things, fundamental changes in society can be justified by reference to them). In this sense, too, a comparison between the functions of morality in Sartre's and Hart's treatments of fundamental change remains possible.

[18] Simone de Beauvoir, *Pour une Morale de l'Ambiguïté* (Paris, Librairie Gallimard, 1947), p. 161.

In an interesting footnote in the *Critique*, Sartre discusses the notion of value ('in the *ethical* sense of the term', as distinguished from the economic sense) "although", as he says, "it is not our subject".[19] Values for Sartre seem necessarily to entail dialectical 'contradictions' in the same way in which the oath does: values are created by man in his free PRAXIS, but at the same time they are 'alienations' of man's freedom, since any given value places an 'inert' limitation on the projects that man forms:

Since the inertness [of value] must make *going beyond it* possible, and since its practico-inert character is the *impossibility of being gone beyond*, it is seen as the transcendent unity of all the possible 'goings beyond', that is, as the term that cannot be gone beyond – because located at infinity – towards which every action goes beyond the material conditions that occasion it.[20]

What is noteworthy about this passage is Sartre's suggestion that some ideal, ultimate state of affairs, of which the content presumably cannot be given because it is located at infinity, serves as a guide to all value judgments and serves to define every 'project', every human action. This is the BEGINNING of an ethical theory that would avoid the postulation of a separate realm of eternal values, would retain the flexibility of ethical relativism without ending all discussion of ethics, and would justify the assumption of positions on political and social issues in such a way that the approval of certain fundamental changes in society and the disapproval of others would still be theoretically possible.

Sartre's remark that it was Merleau-Ponty's *Humanisme et Terreur*, with its emphasis on the 'objective' (historical) significance of human actions, which 'converted' him from his earlier separation of social from private ethics, heralds a clearly-discernible trend in Sartre's thought.[21] Even in Simone de Beauvoir's *Pour une Morale de l'Ambiguïté*, it is difficult, if not impossible, to separate a neo-Marxist social philosophy from the ethical doctrine. Dufrenne's judicious answer, "Both yes and no", to the question that he poses[22] as to whether the *Critique de la raison dialectique* actually contains the ethical theory promised by

[19] *Critique de la raison dialectique*, p. 301.
[20] *Ibid.*, p. 302. Sartre's root word in this passage is, of course, 'dépasser', the despair of translators into English.
[21] The conclusion to the published first volume of Sartre's autobiography, *Les Mots*, in which he speaks of the extent to which he has changed, also points, though in a very literary fashion, to Sartre's sense of having undergone a theoretical conversion (Paris, Librairie Gallimard, 1964). But see my argument (in "Jean-Paul Sartre: Man, Freedom, and *Praxis*", pp. 294-307) that there still remains a greater unity than disunity between Sartre's earlier and later writings.
[22] Dufrenne, *op. cit.*, p. 678.

Sartre at the end of *L'être et le néant*,[23] is the answer that I also feel must be given: there is no longer any basic difference for Sartre between ethics and social philosophy, but much more could and must be said about value theory *per se* than is to be found in a few comments in passing in the first volume of the *Critique*.[24] The second volume of the *Critique* will undoubtedly shed much more light on problems of value, since it is to deal with concrete history, regarded as one vast totalization in which everyone (at least in modern societies) is a participant, and since it will therefore be able to treat of group 'projects' and of the FUTURE without having to remain at the level of abstraction characteristic of the entire first volume.

However, whatever Sartre in his philosophy of history may be able to contribute towards a better understanding of the precise relationship between ethics and sociology, or between social and moral values, he will continue to face a fundamental dilemma that confronts everyone who is captivated, as he is, by the 'myth of the New Life'. The philosopher who attempts to justify certain contemporary changes and to decry others by reference to a morally better future state of affairs must either (a) speak only in abstract terms about that future and refuse to provide any definite, concrete description of what it will (or would) be like, or (b) specify at least a few of the characteristics of that future state. The drawback of the first alternative is that it can provide no guide for human action: it results in the complete dissolution of Marx's attempted union of theory and practice. Yet Sartre, like Marx himself, sometimes SEEMS to speak in the spirit of the first alternative, as when he comments on Marx's 'reign of freedom' at the conclusion of the first section of "Question de Méthode":

> As soon as there will exist *for all* a margin of *real* freedom beyond the production of life, Marxism will have had its day; a philosophy of freedom will take its place. But we have no means, no intellectual tool, no concrete experience which might permit us to conceive either of that freedom or of that philosophy.[25]

[23] *L'être et le néant*, p. 722.

[24] In a passage taken from Sartre's unpublished notes that she cites in her most recent volume of autobiography, Simone de Beauvoir gives some indication of the depth of this problem concerning a Sartrean ethic: "[As regards] his ethics properly speaking, Sartre abandoned it that year [1949] because he was convinced that *' "the moral attitude" appears when the technical and social conditions make positive ways of conduct impossible. Ethics is a combination of idealist tricks to help you live through what the scarcity of resources and the lack of techniques imposes upon you.'* – *La Force des choses* (Paris, Librairie Gallimard, 1963), p. 218.

[25] *Critique de la raison dialectique*, p. 32.

And yet is it with reference to this unspecified and in principle unspecifiable future that Sartre asks us, as for example in "Les Communistes et la paix", to make certain very definite ethical and political judgments and commitments in the present? The dubious quality of such a demand, if indeed this is the essence of the demand that Sartre is making, is what has led to such violent attacks as that of Merleau-Ponty on Sartre's alleged 'ultra-Bolshevism'.

The disadvantage (for Sartre) of the second alternative, which is the one that Sartre and any neo-Marxist interested in exerting any influence over the PRAXIS of other men will in fact have to choose, is – to begin by putting it as simply as possible – that it relativizes Marxism and its values. As a matter of fact, this consequence is drawn with eminent clarity in the passage cited above: there will be a future for the understanding of which Marxism will be irrelevant, and another great epochal philosophy will succeed Marxism.[26] The Communist Party member (or other revolutionary) who promotes the formation of groups of activists committed to bringing about a fundamental change in a society may appeal to certain values in a conceivable future that he and they find highly desirable; but he must not forget that, in a more distant future, other waves are going to wash ashore. Indeed, this must be so, for we have seen that any such values, merely by virtue of being specific values (and not simply the abstract, content-less, limiting case of value in general), are 'dépassables'.

Now, what would be some examples of the ways in which Sartre or someone else with a degree of sympathy for Marx, such as Rubel, might begin to SPECIFY the values advocated by Marxism as attainable through certain sorts (the DESIRABLE sorts) of fundamental change in society? Among the broad objectives suggested at one time or another in the course of this book have been the following: the end of the reign of scarcity, the achievement of 'group *praxis* forever', and the cessation of alienations. Sartre makes much of the claim that an 'inert structure of inhumanity' will remain in everyone as long as the first objective has not been achieved. But in order to put an end to scarcity, something more than political philosophy, namely technology, is needed. In addition, a very detailed logical analysis would be needed in order to deter-

[26] Lefebvre, as I mentioned earlier, believes that Sartre is too orthodox a philosopher on this point: Marx's theory, as Lefebvre points out, purports to put philosophy itself radically into question. Lichtheim's review makes much of this particular criticism of Sartre, although Lichtheim's own view of what philosophy must be is unjustifiably narrow. (Lichtheim, review, p. 232.)

mine exactly when ALL forms of scarcity could be said to have come to an end. A whole programme might be drawn up to help implement the ending of the regime of scarcity. This phrase would no longer have the ring of a slogan, but would now appear as an attainable objective. In the process, however, what had once had the appearance of a Sartrean, neo-Marxist near-absolute would now have been, in a word, 'relativized'.

As for the complementary notions of 'group *praxis* forever' and the 'end of alienations', I have already dealt, in the chapter on totalization, with some of the senses that these phrases cannot have. Certainly, for example, the necessity that rational human behavior be rule-governed can never be dispensed with. And if that is so, we concluded, then at least the logical possibility of a fundamental change from the group back to the series (as well as the reverse) cannot ever be excluded, either. Furthermore, to return to the beginning of this present chapter, 'the oath' that is a practical necessity for assuring the permanence of a group is also the initial source of all the alienations that are possible in the course of institutionalization. Thus it would seem that alienations, in some sense or another, will never come to an end, either.[27] Perhaps it is true after all that, despite the eschatological optimism that the pages of the *Critique* occasionally seem to emit, Sartre's is still a philosophy of radical evil and will never genuinely be otherwise. Some years before the publication of the *Critique*, Sartre's colleague, Simone de Beauvoir, wrote with an almost Machiavellian realism about individual and political action and violence as follows:

> If division and violence are the definition of war, the world has always been at war, it always will be; if man waits for universal peace in order to try to found his existence in a worthwhile manner, he will wait indefinitely; there will never be any *other* future.[28]

Sartre at least seems to want to hold that violence, which is sometimes justifiable in the present, will come to an end when the regime of scarcity comes to an end in the future; but, once again, we must await

[27] This is a far cry, of course, from saying that in NO sense can alienations ever be REDUCED, even RADICALLY reduced, in the future. Sartre's treatment of 'alienation' does, indeed, at times fall under Lefebvre's stricture that to propose a theory according to which human beings cannot avoid alienation is to deprive the concept of 'alienation' of all explanatory power: "Freedom as defined (or undefined) by Jean-Paul Sartre makes the use of the concept of alienation difficult" (*La Somme et le reste*, p. 519).

[28] *Pour une Morale de l'Ambiguïté*, p. 167.

the appearance of his philosophy of history in order to determine whether he can make this thesis at all plausible.[29]

If we have cast considerable doubt on certain interpretations of Marxist and neo-Marxist claims which would envision '*the* Revolution' as bringing about a change so absolute as to put an end to all posibilities of fundamental social changes in the future, it still remains open to Marxism or to any other social philosophy advocating such changes in contemporary society to propose many less sweeping, but logically attainable, values. For example, the abolition *in perpetuum* of certain kinds of institutions might be advocated. One candidate for abolition is the institution of law. A few comments on this proposal will conclude the present section of this book.

[29] For some further reflections on the role of violence in Sartre's thought, cf. my article, "Sartre and the Phenomenology of Social Violence", in *New Essays in Phenomenology*, ed. by James M. Edie (Chicago, Quadrangle Books, 1969), pp. 290-313.

8

LAW

In the entire first volume of the *Critique*, the institution of law is hardly ever mentioned, and law is never treated as being in any way a peculiar phenomenon deserving of special attention. Why? I shall first mention Sartre's own most obvious reason, then discuss a second probable reason connected with his Marxist heritage, and conclude with a few general remarks as to how Sartre's entire social philosophy, including his account of fundamental change, might have profited from his having paid more attention to legal phenomena.

The obvious reason for Sartre's neglect of the law is that he has been writing on a more abstract plane than that on which law is located.[1] Where Hart speaks of modern legal systems, which are distinct from the pre-legal social structures of primitive societies, Sartre speaks of myriad forms of 'institutions', among which legal systems would find their place. In this sense, curiously enough, the philosophical concerns of the very historically-minded Sartre in this volume turn out to be less time-bound than are those of Hart in *The Concept of Law*. Sartre is aware of historical considerations at least in the very general sense that he believes that our history, and with it our social institutions, would have been quite different if we did not live 'in the social field of scarcity'. But, he insists, "It does not enter into my designs to study the type of groups, of collectives, and of institutions which are formed *in* this social field: it is not a question of reconstructing the moments of History or the descriptions of sociology."[2] In my chapter (in the initial section of this study) on 'sociology', I showed the necessary inadequacy of any attempt to isolate a philosophy of law from other areas of social philosophy, and indicated why Hart's treatment was more satisfactory than Kelsen's in this regard. Law is one kind of sociological phenomenon,

[1] His is simply *not* a theory of law, like that of Hegel or Fichte. Cf. Hartmann, *op. cit.*, footnote, pp. 64-65.
[2] *Ibid.*, p. 211.

though it is one about which some very special problems must be raised. Sartre, whose book is intended to be a 'prolegomenon' to sociology and history, should certainly not be expected to pay special attention to this one particular kind of sociological institution that is the law. So goes the obvious explanation.

The second reason for Sartre's neglect of the law returns us to the end of my chapter on the 'mandarins', in which I noted the contempt expressed for law by Georg Lukacs in his early essay on "Legality and Illegality". This document, written by one who was familiar with the writings of Kelsen and the idea of "Rechtswissenschaft', is a particularly straightforward illustration of the twentieth-century adaptation of a central theme in Marx and Engels: the post-Revolutionary 'withering away of the State' and of the State apparatus, notably the legal system, along with it.[3] It would be fetishistic, a mystification, to concern oneself very greatly with a philosophical study of the law or of the State when the revolutionary task of abolishing actual laws and states is at hand. This reasoning applies even to a study of fundamental changes in laws and states, since as Lukacs points out in a passage that I have already cited, a purely political revolution, as distinguished from a true social revolution, "merely consecrates a socio-economic state which has already been imposed".[4] This theme is taken up again, though with different practical implications, by Lefebvre when he insists that the only truly fundamental change is one that occurs in the structure of daily life.

Thus, Sartre's unconcern with problems of jurisprudence has some distinguished precedents among Marxist-oriented thinkers. One of his very few references to legal theory occurs in a section in which he is discussing the background of French colonialism in Algeria; as he says:

[3] "Since the State is the form in which the individuals of a ruling class assert their common interests, and in which the whole civil society of an epoch is epitomized, it follows that in the formation of all commercial institutions the State acts as intermediary, that these institutions receive a political form ... Civil law develops simultaneously with private property out of the disintegration of the natural community ... It must not be forgotten that law has just as little an independent history as religion" (Marx and Engels, *The German Ideology*, pp. 60-61). "As soon as class rule, and the individual struggle for existence based on our present anarchy in production, with the collisions and excesses arising from these, are removed, nothing more remains to be repressed, and a special repressive force, a state, is no longer necessary ... State interference in social relations becomes, in one domain after another, superfluous, and then dies out by itself; the government of persons is replaced by the administration of things and by the conduct of the processes of production." Engels, *Socialism: Utopian and Scientific*, from Mendel, ed., *Essential Works of Marxism* (New York, Bantam Books, 1961), p. 78.

[4] Lukacs, *op. cit.*, p. 295.

The liquidation of the forms of inheritance peculiar to the Moslem tribes does not stem from I don't know what idealistic interpenetration of two different juridical systems, but from the fact that businessmen encouraged by the State and supported by our armies imposed the code on the Moslems *in order to rob them better.*[5]

He is quite correct, of course. A fundamental change in law, such as occurred in this case of conquest, does not take place in a vacuum, and legalistic explanations are in fact often used by interested persons and social classes to 'mystify', to disguise more fundamental social realities that underlie the law at any given time in any given place. But the pervasiveness of legal phenomena is no less real for all that; Sartre in effect acknowledges this, as he must, when he admits that 'the oath', his name for the basis of institutions, is a legal name ('nom de droit').[6]

On yet another occasion, Sartre speaks bitingly of 'the analytic exteriority of legal relations', meaning by 'legal' in this case, as the passage shows, having reference to the so-called economic 'laws' which served nineteenth-century capitalism as a defense for systematic exploitation of workers.[7] Sartre is by no means the first to point out that these 'laws' were falsely assumed by many owners and workers alike to express certain absolute and quasi-eternal relationships, whereas in fact they constituted a plausible theoretical account only of a certain type of economic system at a certain stage in its historical development. So far, well and good; as Sartre demonstrates, these laws were 'externally' imposed (the 'imposition' being, of course, a highly complex process, the nature of which Sartre's analyses help to clarify), and yet they were falsely assumed to be 'internal' in the sense of being inescapable elements of social life, though not of any individual's making. Now, do there exist important similarities between these economic 'laws' and the laws of a given legal system? Sartre at least hints that there do, and Marx would certainly regard both as examples of 'superstructures'. And they are correct up to a point. But the fact that no institutions are absolute does not imply that all institutions are *per se* evil or deplorable. Hart's discussions of the internal and external aspects of legal systems, like Sartre's many discussions of procedures of internalization such as that of the oath, show the practical necessity for something like 'acceptance' – which need not be identified, on the other hand, with 'naive acceptance'. Thus the fact that there is a certain 'analytic exteriority'

[5] *Critique de la raison dialectique*, p. 674.
[6] *Ibid.*, p. 456.
[7] *Ibid.*, pp. 699-700.

to all legal relations should not prevent Sartre from recognizing, even in terms of his own theory, the positive values, as well as the potential internality, of legal systems.

Sartre does have a good deal that is not pure derogation [8] to say about the State, however. He defines it as "a limited group of organizers, administrators, and propagandists taking upon themselves the task of imposing *modified* institutions, in the form of serial bonds uniting serialities, on the collectives".[9] He goes on to claim that, since the majority of any country's population never constitutes anything more than a SERIAL collective, there is never a State of the whole people or even of the majority. Now, even if it is a fact that the citizenry of no country has ever approached the status of a Sartrean GROUP (if there are any historical counter-examples, they are most likely to be found during revolutionary periods), still I do not see that Sartre has established this fact as a logical impossibility. And indeed, if Sartre is correct in holding out to us the possibility of a future in which, as a result of an historical development in the direction of greater 'totalization', there may be a greater degree of group structure than there is at present in society, then of course the populations of individual countries and of the world as a whole would HAVE TO approach closer to a Sartrean GROUP status. The usual Marxist picture of the State as 'superstructure', which Sartre has – on the surface, at least – inherited, here dictates the retort that national populations will cease to be 'alienated' and (in Sartrean language) 'serial' only if and when the State apparatus, together with the rest of the 'superstructure', is abolished. But, we must ask ourselves at this point, is it not one of the results of Sartre's abstract, formal analysis of social structures and of fundamental change in them to have undercut this doctrine somewhat, by showing the extent to which the difference between the pro-State and the anti-State positions is, AT THE LIMIT, definitional? Sartre, the neo-Marxist, suggests that the State, as he has defined it in the above passage, must at some future time be abolished; a hypothetical opponent of his might agree that Sartre would be right with reference to a particular state insofar as it corresponded to the Sartrean definition, but might still go on to contend that, given Sartre's

[8] And that may in fact be somewhat heretical from the standpoint of Marxist orthodoxy. For example, on p. 612 of the *Critique* he faces up to the fact that, although the State is in an important sense the organ of the dominant class as the orthodoxy maintains, nevertheless the State also has the function of negating the class struggle and presenting itself as being impartial. Rather than merely dismissing this fact as an obvious 'mystification', Sartre considers it in some detail.

[9] *Ibid.*, pp. 608-609. (I take 'se chargent' to be better read as 'se chargeant'.)

accounts of the group in fusion and of the oath, given Sartre's admission that the chronological development that these successive accounts depict is at no point a logically NECESSARY one, and given what we know about the phenomenon of 'acceptance' of State legal systems, we can easily CONCEIVE of what we might still call a 'State' which would resemble more closely a vast, POPULAR 'group' than it would an administrative 'State' of the sort that Sartre has defined.

It is interesting to note the similarity between Sartre's definition of the State and that of contemporary 'realist' schools of political science, whose study, as A. P. d'Entrèves notes, "reduces political reality entirely to the dynamics of groups in struggle, or at least in competition, with one another." [10] In his previous chapter, d'Entrèves has discussed the sense in which the theory of the State held by the late Italian Communist, Gramsci, bears striking similarities to this reduction of the State to the sheer interplay of rival forces that has so often served, in recent years, as a defense of conservatism or even of fascism. Both Gramsci and Sartre, of course, intend the emphasis on force and violence in their theories of the State to be a propaedeutic to a vision of a radically different future state of affairs – in the case of Sartre, of a logically possible future in which 'serial' forms of human existence will have been abolished. However, it is questionable whether their accounts provide an adequate understanding of the State even as it exists in contemporary society, regardless of the future fate of present-day State institutions. D'Entrèves' own suggestion is that the State must be analyzed under at least two other aspects that are logically different from that of 'might'; the first of these, the one with which we are here concerned, is that of the State as a legal order. Kelsen and his followers are incorrect if they are taken as asserting that the State is essentially a legal order and nothing more, but their very insistence on the importance and integrity of legal philosophy provides a corrective from which Sartre's social philosophy, at least, could profit.

It is (partly) by means of the institution of law, Sartre claims, that the groups which for him constitute 'the State' impose their dominance over the collectives, the mass of citizens. But he pays little or no attention to the fact that every legal system has an internal aspect which it would be improper to dismiss as simply a 'false interiority', and to the fact that it is at least logically possible, as Hart has shown so well, for there to be a more than merely passive acceptance of a given legal system by substantial numbers of citizens.

[10] d'Entrèves, *La dottrina dello stato*, p. 97. Tr. mine.

What is this institution, the law, that Sartre seems so badly to have neglected in his social philosophy? We saw that Hart's principal attempt at a simple, concise answer, namely the union of primary and secondary rules, either was unsuccessful or else reduced to the unoriginal proposition that modern legal systems were the sets of rules that governed the peculiar institutions known as modern states. But in his elucidation of the meaning of rules and of rule-governed behavior, Hart has complemented and rendered much more intelligible Sartre's account of what the latter calls the 'active passivity' of the institution. The passivity of the individuals subject to the typical modern legal system is NOT (as Sartre must agree) SIMPLY that of the 'series'. Within such a system, it is true, the individual fulfills an impersonal function rather than, as in earlier stages of the group, having a unique task to perform. But the nature of acceptance and rule-following is such that a modern legal system CAN, to use Hart's analogy, be 'healthy'. Under optimal conditions, 'healthy' would seem a far more appropriate adjective to employ here than the (supposedly non-ethical) epithet, 'degraded', which Sartre uses to characterize the form of group exemplified for him by the modern 'State' even at its best. In other words, to follow a system of legal rules is NOT *ipso facto* to be alienated – at least in any of the more interesting senses of the concept of 'alienation'. Law is not the sort of institution that lends itself to facile definition; but it is at least clear that law is a more important, more complex, and potentially more positive factor in society than a reading of Sartre's *Critique* might lead one to believe.

Nevertheless, it is in some sense true to say that both the modern form of the State and some important features of modern legal systems might conceivably pass away at some time in the distant future. Hart has spoken of 'pre-legal societies' and has shown the ambiguities in the question of whether international law is law; if there were once pre-legal societies, then there might be POST-legal societies at some time in the future, and the development of international 'law' indicates one way (an abrupt fundamental change of a particularly fundamental sort would of course be another way) in which such societies might come into existence. The book by Hart's colleague, Cohen, gives a few indications of what a society would be like which might, by the standards of a contemporary concept of law, be called 'post-legal'. One of the values of Sartre's *Critique* lies, as I indicated in my Interlude, in the effect that it has of liberating its readers from the limitations of, for example, a perspective focused too exclusively on modern legal and societal institutions. Insofar as law, as we know it today, is simply a particular (albeit extremely important) kind of social phenomenon, then a future state of affairs in which there no longer existed any legal system is certainly conceivable. Insofar as we regard the law as a 'semi-autonomous' institution which, by definition, embodies a SPECIFIC value (or set of values), then we must admit that the law, like all other values, CAN be superseded in the future. This is the extent to which the Marxist and Sartrean disregard of legal phenomena can be justified: a fundamental social change, a great upheaval of some sort, which would abolish the institution of law AS WE KNOW IT TODAY is conceptualizable – though perhaps barely so.

But this concession is not really so great as it might at first appear. It is said that "law might be abolished", but precisely what would this mean? It could only mean, as far as I can see, that enough of the 'hard-core' characteristics usually associated with our concept of the modern legal system would have disappeared, so that it would be found convenient to designate the new system of social rules by a new term. Interesting definitional problems [11] might arise at this juncture – problems similar to that which we discovered in Hart's analysis when, in discussing the secondary 'rule of recognition', which Hart had assumed to be one of the features lacking in primitive, pre-legal societies but present in modern ones, we found some reasons for questioning the first part of this assumption. But the essential point to be noted is that the abolition of 'law' would not and could not entail the abolition of all forms of social rules. In other words, there are important features about the phenomenon of law as explained by Hart that no fundamental change in society could abolish; for it is finally only in terms of these features, the features of accepted systems of rules of behavior, and NOT SIMPLY in terms of the Sartrean extremes of inert matter and of PRAXIS in the form of totalization, that one could ever conceive of the states of affairs FROM and TO which fundamental change must always occur. No fundamental change in society is imaginable in which these features, features discerned by Hart in his analysis of 'the concept of law', would cease to characterize human social activity. With this reassertion of the value of Hart's analysis and of the importance of the matters discussed in the first section of this book, we may terminate our Sartrean phase and proceed to a conclusion.

[11] An historical illustration of such problems is provided by the difficulties of Soviet legal theorists in reconciling the continued existence of law in their country with the supposed elimination of 'bourgeois forms'. The paradoxical phrase, 'revolutionary legality', is a key to their attempt to resolve these difficulties. Interestingly enough, Hart takes Kelsen to task for the latter's contention that 'revolutionary legality' is a contradiction in terms; this would be so, says Hart, only if 'revolutionary' meant 'anarchical', which, of course, as Marxists always point out, it does not (review of Kelsen's *The Communist Theory of Law*, p. 775).

CONCLUSION

It has been said, on more than one occasion, that "Philosophy is a circular enterprise."[1] Our most recent conclusions, in the section on Sartre's theoretical account of fundamental change which has just ended, tend to reaffirm this contention. For we have seen that the obvious lacuna created by Sartre's failure to pay even a modicum of attention to legal phenomena, in his abstract 'prolegomenon to any future anthropology', has led us to look back to Hart's 'concept of law' to supply us with elements that any adequate explanation and justification of fundamental social change must include. And yet it was the limited nature of Hart's own chosen perspective, that of the philosophy of law, which had originally been the strongest single reason for our decision to adventure into some of the little-known depths of Sartre's social philosophy. Thus, as we return now to reconsider the concept of fundamental change in law and society from a point of view not limited to that of either of our two authors or their immediate colleagues, and as we reflect once more on the questions about it that were first raised in the Introduction, we should be keenly aware that the mere obtrusiveness of this phenomenon is no argument for its being easily explicable (e.g., in terms of a single definition or a single, crucial 'thesis') or readily justifiable.

Both the Sartrean and the Hartean approaches have contributed to this awareness. It was Sartre whose account of fundamental social change seemed by far the less easily recognizable, the less obviously common-sensical. He spoke with some disdain of 'metaphorical' ways of describing 'dialectical transformations of masses' – ways which pretend to discover, in certain admixtures of students, workers, and what have you, the allegedly 'typical revolutionary gestalt'. In order to furnish us with an account that would attain to the desired degree of philosophical systematization, Sartre was compelled to write about the reality of fundamental change in terms that were often highly unfamiliar to us,

[1] Weiss, *op. cit.*, p. 84.

his contemporaries, who have observed that phenomenon (at least from a distance), and who may have thought that we knew what it was. Hart, on the other hand, in analyzing fundamental change in law, tended to warn us of the dangers of systems. Revolution is only one possible kind of breakdown in a legal system, he pointed out: any definition of fundamental change in law (and here we may well recall the role of revolution in Kelsen's legal science), like any definition of the concept of law, which neglects concrete reality in order to meet the specifications of a particular system, is bound to be inadequate. Sartre is more concerned with discovering underlying realities, Hart with saving appearances. And yet both have a common opponent: the plier of easy generalizations abcut 'revolutions', the person who takes a half dozen or so instances of fundamental changes, finds some least common denominator in all of them, and proceeds to declare this to be the essence of the phenomenon in question. For both Sartre and Hart (and herein lies one of their strongest points of resemblance, as well as one of our greatest advantages in having made use of their two treatments in analyzing fundamental change in law and society) recognize the truth of Lefebvre's observation that social philosophy may well deal with many of the same issues as sociology (understood in a broad sense – 'social science'), but must distinguish itself from the latter by its concern with the limitless domain of possibilities.

In considering the concept of fundamental change, Hart and Sartre taken together have indeed explored a large number of possibilities – that much is beyond dispute. But have they really been talking about the same thing? When Hart discourses on the breakdowns of legal systems and Sartre on the transformations of groups into series, is it only their language and their levels of abstraction which differ? In the chapters on "Sartre" and on "Abstraction", I showed in some detail how certain types of cases would be dealt with by the two authors – how, for example, a sheer 'breakdown... in the face of anarchy', as Hart would describe it, would be treated by Sartre as a paradigm case of group disintegration. But this does little to allay the sort of scepticism to which I am now giving voice. I further pointed out that the difference between Sartrean groups and series was a difference between two dissimilar ideal forms of social organization, rather than a difference between two instances of the same form (such as two successive Hartean legal systems);[2] but this clarification, likewise, somehow fails to be suf-

[2] Or, to use a language which some find illuminating, it is a 'vertical' rather than a 'horizontal' difference.

ficient. Why? I am not entirely sure. Both men CLAIM to be dealing with the same phenomenon – Hart when he introduces his account of 'The Pathology of a Legal System' by pointing out that 'revolution' is only one example of such a breakdown, and Sartre when he uses events in the history of the French Revolution to exemplify the more general phenomenon of fundamental change from the series to the group. Hart's discussion of 'breakdown' stresses the negative aspect, and Sartre's account of the 'group in fusion' the positive aspect, of fundamental change; but both authors would maintain, of course, that this difference of emphasis does not indicate a blindness on the part of either of them to the complementary aspect of fundamental change about which each has had less, directly, to say. They are both talking about the same world, the same human race, and the same type of event in the social history of that race. It would be utterly illogical to maintain that, nonetheless, their subject-matters are entirely diverse. Yet the temptation to say precisely this is strong, and I have been anxious, in undertaking this study, not to gloss over the sharp differences which give rise to this temptation. Perhaps one of the sources of the temptation is the sharp divergence in the philosophical traditions from which the two authors can be said to have come.

Towards the close of my Introduction, I suggested that our respective authors might be looked at as the current heirs of two long philosophical traditions, traditions that I designated rather arbitrarily (for indeed ANY designation of diverse 'movements' as broad, as complex, and of such long duration must necessarily be rather arbitrary) as those of the 'system-builders' and of the 'sceptics'. Later, I hinted at the presence in Sartre's thought of tendencies that could be regarded as vaguely Platonic, and, in Hart's thought, of Aristotelian strains. Of course, in one sense, this is quite absurd. Plato was no mere wildly speculative thinker, in the sense of attempting to construct a system that had no reference to experience; and Aristotle is clearly more 'systematic' than 'sceptical', if these two terms are to be contrasted. Of course. And the same can be said of Sartre and of Hart – of Sartre, who is so concerned with developing a philosophy which will help to strengthen certain actual contemporary political currents, and of Hart, who reserves some of the strongest criticisms for the legal philosophers whom he calls 'rule-sceptics'. Nevertheless, my suggestion is not entirely wide of the mark, though it is not the sort of remark that either permits of or demands rigorous proof. An historian of philosophy could easily point out intriguing resemblances between (1) the primacy of the wise ruler in Plato and of the rule of law in Aristotle – and the respective emphasis on social and legal philosophy in Sartre and Hart; (2) the grounding of virtue in wisdom with Plato and in an habitual way of life with Aristotle – and the somewhat diverse, though largely reconcilable, tendencies in Sartrean and Hartean views of ethics; (3) the strong Platonic quest for the Good as contrasted with Aristotle's relatively greater interest in the means of living the practically attainable good life – and Sartrean and Hartean explanations of human activity in terms, respectively, of totalizations and of rules; (4) Plato's attempts to define ideal forms and Aristotle's more frequent use of analogy in explanation – and the methodological diversity of Sartrean abstractions and Hartrean analogies; and, finally, (5) the previously-mentioned uses of dialectics by Plato and Sartre and of analysis by Aristotle and Hart, uses which all differ greatly one from another, but which still suggest many fruitful points of contact. It is very much out of fashion at present simply to regard Aristotelianism and Platonism as being two hostile and mutually irreconcilable philosophies; I approve of this current state of affairs, and I believe that the fashion should be extended to Aristotle's and Plato's modern 'heirs', as well. It is my hope that this examination of the treatments of fundamental change in law and society by Hart and Sartre has remained faithful to the principle that differing APPROACHES to philosophic problems should be recognized for what they are, and that thoroughgoing IRRECONCILABILITIES, on the other hand, should be pointed to only if and where genuine contradictions exist.

No doubt the underlying basis of the suspicion that Sartre and Hart are in fact talking about two different things is to be found, precisely, in this vast difference in the APPROACHES or PERSPECTIVES of the two men. The very extent of this difference was, as I indicated in the "Interlude", one of my principal reasons for choosing to effect the 'fundamental change' which characterized the transition from Section One to Section Three of this book. My interest in doing so was by no means merely an aesthetic one, however, for I am in agreement with the contention that "Only an insight into the many *angular* visions as components of a wider integrated vision can constitute an approximative approach to the Truth."[3] It is to be hoped that the contrast between two such different approaches as Sartre's and Hart's to what is at least ostensibly the same phenomenon, therefore, will prove ultimately to have

[3] Desan, *The Planetary Man*, Vol. 1 (Washington, Georgetown University Press, 1961), p. 127.

been in the service of the truth itself; for it is my belief that genuine 'comprehension' requires 'comprehensiveness' of vision.

In the ordering of chapters in the two main sections, I have maintained a certain formal parallelism between the various elements that I have selected for special considerations in the two authors' treatments. Is this parallelism, which has been maintained without in any way detracting from a respect for perspectival divergences, anything more than a purely formal one? I am sure that it is, but to the further question, "How much more?" I am convinced that a single, simple answer is, from the nature of the case, impossible. All that I can do here, in concluding this examination of fundamental change in law and society with respect to problems both of its explanation and of its justification, is to hint at a few of the ways in which the Hartean and Sartrean approaches might fruitfully be compared with regard to the substantive issues first mentioned in the Introduction. Both Sartre and Hart agree that the phenomenon of fundamental change is open to philosophical explanation, at least up to a certain point, and that it can at least at times be justified. They further agree that the key to such explanation and justification is some account of human activity in society,[4] and that any such account must respect individuality and refrain from hypostatizing the social collective (i.e., that organicism is unacceptable as a social theory).[5] Beyond these basic premises, to which we also may subscribe, their points of view begin to diverge. It is therefore proper at this point to turn to some substantive issues concerning the concept of fundamental change in law and society, which I shall discuss in the reverse order to that in which they were first raised in the Introduction.

The first issue concerns the propriety or impropriety of combining 'fundamental change in law' and 'fundamental change in society' into a single concept and treating them together. Are they not 'separable and therefore distinct'? Not ultimately. For one of the principal thrusts of each section of this study has been to show why a consideration of the concept of fundamental change central to that section would be inadequate without reference to the concept central to the other. In the

[4] Not everyone would agree to this. I submit the following curious remark by M. le comte Joseph de Maistre, who speaks of "... la profonde imbécillité (il est bien permis de parler comme Platon, qui ne se fâche jamais), la profonde imbécillité, dis-je, de ces pauvres gens qui s'imaginent que les législateurs sont des hommes ..." (*Essai sur le Principe Générateur des Constitutions Politiques* (Lyon, Pélagaud et Lesne, 1838), XXI, p. 29).

[5] Neither Sartre nor Hart, in other words, could lay much of a claim to being a political conservative in the traditional sense.

language of Kelsenian legal theory, revolution is 'normative fact'. Fundamental change is, in other words, a fact of enormous importance for legal philosophy, since it is generative of legal systems; and yet it can be dealt with only 'from one side' by anyone who, like Kelsen, is determined to maintain a 'purely' jurisprudential perspective. Hart does not share Kelsen's methodological prejudice on this matter, but it remains obvious (and we have seen it demonstrated) that a work on 'the concept of law' could not be expected to place fundamental change in the broader perspective that is available to a philosophical treatment of sociological phenomena as a whole. What might at first have appeared less obvious is the dependence of social philosophy, in dealing adequately with fundamental change, on considerations that Hart regarded as most central to his analysis of the concept of LAW – considerations, most notably, about the nature of rule-governed behavior in societal institutions. But this dependence, together with the insufficiencies of Sartre's account that stem from his failure fully to recognize it, has been shown in the course of the development of Section Three of this study. Fundamental social changes always occur from and to some systems of social rules, and therefore cannot be conceived apart from the latter. An account of fundamental change in society at the present time in history MUST include more than a passing reference to the concept of fundamental change in law; but there is a certain sense in which, as we have also seen, the truth of this contention is not limited merely to the present time in history.

The limiting case of a fundamental change in law and society is an ABSOLUTE change, after which no aspect of human life (and consequently not even human life itself) would be the same as before. But this is clearly a myth ('the myth of the New Life', to use Lefebvre's term), though it may sometimes prove suggestive and helpful in liberating the intellect from habitual presuppositions and in making it aware of new possibilities. Short of the utterly impossible in fundamental change is a whole range of changes which are conceivable only with the greatest difficulty, but which, if conceivable at all, must be regarded as somehow possible. Perhaps the single most significant such change to have been suggested (HERE, as a result of reflecting on Sartre's almost total neglect of the subject) is the abolition of the institution of law.

It must again be repeated that law as we normally think of it is only one particular kind, however pre-eminent, of societal institution. As such, it has what I have called a 'semi-autonomy': it can, for certain purposes, be treated in isolation from other social phenomena, and

Kelsen's legal philosophy has met with considerable success in doing just that. Hart has shown that some of the most venerable models for conceiving of law, notably that of 'orders backed by threats', are not essential to the concept. What all of this may suggest is that the advocacy by Marxists and others of a '*really* fundamental' change which would result in the withering away of both the State and its legal institutions may, after all, be plausible. Since society is logically prior to any of its particular institutions, a society without the particular institution that we call 'law' would be conceivable.

But we have seen, in this study, that Hart's development of 'the concept of law' constitutes one of the strongest vindications of the ancient maxim, "*ubi societas, ibi jus*".[6] For Hart regards law as essentially a particular variety of systems of rules of behavior. And a number of considerations, notably our thought experiment in the chapter on Sartrean 'totalization', have helped to strengthen our conviction that non-rule-governed human social activity is indeed inconceivable. The defense of the necessity of rules as coeval with human activity has been purchased at a price for the legal theorist, however. For Hart himself admits that there were 'pre-legal', though still rule-governed, primitive societies, and so the concept of a 'post-legal' society appears less fantastic than it might have seemed before. But further disputes as to whether, given the fact that certain systems of rules would still govern such a society, it would really be correct to denominate it 'post-legal', or as to whether Hart's 'pre-legal' category is justified, would unfortunately tend to become highly arid and purely verbal: Hart's Wittgensteinian-Austinian notion of 'family resemblances' among words shows the way to escaping some of the artificial perplexities that such disputes might engender.

The net result is, I think, a justification of my procedure of treating 'fundamental change in law and society' (though without the blessing of either Hart or Sartre on this matter) as, in some sense, a single concept. The many interrelationships between the concept of fundamental change in law and that of fundamental change in society suggest the need to consider each with reference to the other in order adequately to understand the philosophical questions that they both raise. Of course, it must never be forgotten that, although a fundamental change IN LAW might assume the proportions of a total *Cäsur*, a complete break, in

[6] A recent monograph on the development of Soviet and Yugoslavian legal theory since the Russian Revolution of 1917 strongly concludes to a like vindication. Cf. Ivo Lapenna, *State and Law: Soviet and Yugoslav Theory* (New Haven, Yale University Press, 1964), p. 117 and *passim*.

terms of a certain legal philosophy's model of legal systems, nevertheless a sufficiently fundamental SOCIAL change, though the conceptual difficulties involved in defining and treating of the latter type of change are much greater than those faced by the legal theorist, will always be of more ultimate significance for the history of human activity in society.[7] This last remark further suggests that a more fully adequate account of the concept of fundamental change in law and society would have to deal, additionally, with problems in the philosophy of history. Consequently this study is impoverished to the extent to which it has failed (both for reasons of space and also because of a dearth of suitable material in the writings of the two authors principally treated[8]) to consider such problems.

But it cannot be said that a consideration of problems in the philosophy of history has been ENTIRELY neglected. For we have noted, in examining Sartre's ethical theory, that questions of JUSTIFICATION of fundamental social changes are ultimately resoluble only by means of some reference to an historically future state of affairs, subsequent to a proposed fundamental change, which is deemed better than the present state of affairs. In order for any such 'justification' to be meaningful, it must be possible to specify at least a few important features of the envisaged future state of affairs: to refuse to state any such specifications would be to fall into what Merleau-Ponty has called an 'ultra-Bolshevism' of the most extreme sort. On the other hand, the statement of these specifications serves to relativize the value of the proposed future state of affairs, because it will always be theoretically legitimate to make the value judgment that THAT state of affairs, while it would perhaps be better than the present, would not be the best possible. Thus Marxism, like any other theory that appeals to a possible future in order to obtain general approval of activity directed towards bringing about a fundamental change in the present, must face the dilemma: either resort to myth (by specifying the characteristics of the promised 'new life' in only the vaguest, least concrete terms, and by claiming this fundamental

[7] The ultimate conclusion of this view is to be found in Lefebvre's remark that "only changes in daily life make a substantial difference . . ." (*La Somme et le reste*, p. 612). I agree.

[8] Hart has very little of a systematic nature to say about history (his discussion of the differences between primitive and modern societies' systems of social rules is the most notable exception to this), and Sartre has deliberately reserved his treatment of problems in the philosophy of history for the second volume of the *Critique*. The latter, which he says is to deal with diachronic (as distinguished from synchronic) totalizations, will probably prove to be much less easily susceptible to contrast with anything that Hart has written than is the first volume.

change necessarily to be the last in history), or admit the temporally RELATIVE nature of its own enterprise. The latter course is obviously the more reasonable.

But what of fundamental change in LAW? Here, an appeal to the historical future would seem less necessary, for it is quite possible for one legal system to 'die' and be replaced by another without there occurring any very significant (i.e., 'fundamental') changes of more than a temporary sort in the structures of society and especially 'in daily life'. Moreover, a system of legal or quasi-legal rules which included sufficiently flexible 'rules of change' (Hart's term) could, by definition, survive through an indefinite number of fundamental social changes. Thus it was that, within a Hartean type of framework, a justification for the replacement of one system of legal rules by another could be found simply in an appeal to a different kind of rules, namely moral rules. (This, of course, required the assumption that human beings are in some sense FREE to change the rules by which they are governed. It also, as we saw, brought Hart's position very close to certain elements in the natural law tradition *malgré lui*.) Such an appeal apparently required no reference to history.

However, I consider this appearance to be misleading, and I am supported by some of the relevant factors in Hart's own brief excursus into natural law theory, his attempt to discover 'the minimum content of natural law'. In the first place, the basis of this 'minimum content' is Hart's 'five salient truisms' – fundamental but contingent facts about men in this world. The fourth truism that he mentions is the condition of scarcity, and he admits that law and morality would be different if this condition did not prevail: scarcity is a contingent rather than a necessary fact about human history. Sartre agrees with Hart on this point, but Sartre is the more optimistic and interested of the two philosophers with respect to the possible elimination of scarcity in the future. The second and more important remark to be made about Hart's 'minimum content', however, is that the truisms could still not be used as arguments in favor of particular legal systems and against others, were it not for the fact that Hart suggests a minimal IDEAL to be sought by men in society. The suggested ideal is 'survival'; it may seem minimal and uncontroversial enough at first, but it cannot with certainty be said to have been the DOMINANT ideal of all past legal systems, and, in any case, it decisively injects an element of value into Hart's analysis of the reasons in favor of accepting certain legal systems and not others.

Moreover, Hart's proposed ideal introduces a reference to the FUTURE into his proposed solution to problems of the justification of legal systems or, conversely, of fundamental changes in law. For the concept of 'survival' points to an allegedly desirable (though perhaps not very exciting – but that is irrelevant here) future state of affairs. Now, I do not believe that this is merely the result of an error or of an oversight on Hart's part; rather, it seems to me to support my own view that a justification of a fundamental change in law is logically just as dependent as is any justification of a fundamental social change on an attainable future state of affairs that is deemed better than the present. (Another way of arriving at the same result would be to examine in greater detail the problem of how, on the assumption that changes in legal rules are justifiable by references to systems of moral rules, fundamental changes in the latter could ever be justified.) Thus, the Hartean 'rules' approach to explanation certainly requires some further reference to the objectives towards the attainment of which rules can be made to serve as means. As for Hart himself, it happens to be the case that his *Concept of Law* is weak in its treatment of social goals, ideals, purposes, or what Sartre would call 'projects';[9] Hart does not, however, deny the relevance of these considerations to his subject, nor would he be entitled to do so.

The Sartrean type of ethic, with its strong appeal to the future, on the other hand, at times suffers from the opposite weakness of failing to exhibit sufficient respect for the role of moral and legal RULES in governing fundamental social changes and human activity in general. Sometimes, for example when he says that the 'malaise' of any community tends to increase "in proportion as the group is more integrated", Sartre seems to be suggesting that institutions and their systems of rules must *per se* constitute 'alienations' of the individuals who are members of given institutions or who follow given rules systems. Indeed, he maintains at one point that every value is, in a sense, an 'alienation'.[10] Such dubious and pessimistic claims as these are the logical outcome of attaching an extreme interpretation to that approach to human social activity that "would", as I said in my Introduction, "make much of the

[9] His short section on "Moral Ideals and Social Criticism" (*The Concept of Law*, pp. 176-180), for example, is one of the least interesting and least original sections in his book.

[10] He goes on to criticize as excessively facile, however, the traditional Marxist assignment of values to the "superstructure", which is undoubtedly one of the historical influences on his own view. As he says: "All the pretended superstructure is already contained in the infrastructure . . ." This is a considerable concession. *Critique de la raison dialectique*, pp. 302-303.

freedom of such activity and would emphasize its functions of creation and fulfillment". Sartre must be given his due, however: he certainly recognizes that the promiscuous uses of the concept of 'alienation' in the above-mentioned senses are not very helpful, and that there are legitimate and positive arguments to be given in favor of what he calls 'the oath', which is for him the logically necessary presupposition of all social institutions and systems of rules. Nevertheless, the Sartrean explanation of human activity in terms of an almost absolute freedom (and it must be remembered that Sartre's is a type of explanation which would seem, at least at first sight, to be especially well suited to account for fundamental changes just because of its emphasis on novelty and creativity) displays its one-sidedness in a particularly dramatic way when, at one point, Sartre remarks that institutions are 'degraded' forms of groups, although, as he adds, the word 'degraded' is not to be understood in an ethical sense. Hart's 'rules' approach to human activity, as we have already noted, is more satisfactory than the Sartrean type of approach for providing some general characterization, in terms of patterns of rule-governed behavior, of the earlier and later states of affairs from and to which fundamental changes take place. Moreover, in the notion of 'acceptance' of a given system of rules, the Hartean variety of explanation DOES allow SOME room for the categories of freedom, creativity, and choice or decision (in bringing about or in neglecting to bring about fundamental changes) that it was the merit of the other approach to have emphasized.

Hart himself, however, seems unaware of many of the complexities suggested by the notion of 'accepting (or refusing to accept) a legal system'. He wants (as does Sartre also, for that matter) to avoid giving an excessively intellectualist analysis which would pretend that fundamental changes in law and/or society are always the results of protracted deliberations on the part of all those who participate in bringing about such changes. Even more urgently, Hart wishes to avoid painting a similar picture of citizens who obey their legal systems in ordinary times. However, it is true that the concept of 'acceptance' suggests 'an act of choice', and therefore some way must be found of reconciling the various possible meanings of 'acceptance'. I have pointed out that 'acceptance' may be conceived of either as a highly conscious act, an episode, or as a long-range disposition, or as any degree between these two extremes. At least the relatively 'passive' variety of acceptance of a given legal system, even (in most cases) among the general citizenry, and CERTAINLY among the officials, is a necessary prerequisite for the avoidance of fundamental change in law. My analysis serves as a needed further clarification of the implications of Hartean 'acceptance', and also points to a particularly interesting area of comparison between Hart and Sartre on the question of 'activity' and 'passivity'.

The Sartrean account of fundamental social change as a 'totalization' or its opposite is excellent in that it gives greatest prominence to the transformation of a collective from a 'passive' to an 'active' state or *vice versa.* However, Sartre himself appears almost deliberately to ignore the many unhappy consequences of equating (as he seems to, when all is said and done) passivity with STRUCTURE, and activity with the absence of structure. True, he is careful to distinguish between the 'passive activity' of his 'inert', or passive, 'series', and the 'active passivity' of the institutionalized 'group' that is again becoming increasingly 'inert'. Sartre has failed, however, adequately to take account of the logical possibility of there being a widespread and ACTIVE 'acceptance' (in the Hartean sense) of a given legal system or other institution. A legal system is not *per se* an alienation, at least not in any very interesting sense of 'alienation'.

What, after all, can be considered a condition of 'alienation' in the case of a social collective (as distinguished from the case of an individual)? Presumably, an UNalienated collective would be one in which the products of the common (group) activity coincided as closely as possible with the 'projects' (or ideals, or purposes, or objectives), conscious or capable of being brought to consciousness, of the individual members of that collective. An alienated collective would be, conversely, one in which such a coincidence was not to be found. If we accept, at least tentatively, this proposed definition, we shall be in a good position to understand the somewhat complex relationship that exists between, on the one hand, the 'active' and 'passive' kinds of 'acceptance' that I have discerned as being necessarily implied by Hart's 'rules' approach to fundamental change, and, on the other hand, the Sartrean sort of 'activity' and 'passivity'.

There are, quite naturally (if we assume that the two pairs are not identical), four possibilities. First, the state or condition of a given social collective may be 'active' in the sense that there may exist a widespread, active acceptance of a given legal system or other institution, and yet 'passive' in the sense that the products of the common, 'totalizing' group activity fail to correspond with the highest possible aspirations of its members. This is the paradigm of what Sartre calls the 'active passivity of the institution'; it is this possibility that a critic like Marcuse has in mind when he condemns modern societies for being radically alienated even though, and indeed just BECAUSE, most of their members accept or even enthusiastically endorse the legal and institutional arrangements of the STATUS QUO.[11] Secondly, an active acceptance of a given legal system may be combined with the active dynamism of a relatively unalienated group; this is the possibility that Sartre's account of human activity makes it most difficult to admit, but it is certainly the democratic ideal, and I think that, in my efforts at reconciling the two basic alternative approaches to human social activity which we have seen outlined in this study, I have at least shown its conceivability. Thirdly, there is the state of affairs in which acceptance of, or even concern for, institutions or systems of rules remains relatively passive or ALMOST non-existent,[12] while the activity of 'totalization' exemplified by Sartre's account of fundamental change is in progress; such a state of affairs is usually of short duration, or at least has been so up to the present time in history, but those who advocate doing away with certain types of rules (e.g., some varieties of legal rules) feel that this third possibility may be held up as an ideal for the future which would not necessarily entail Camus' dilemma, "ou la police ou la folie".[13] Finally, there exists the possibility of a state of affairs in which there is neither an active acceptance of any institution or system of social rules nor any genuine common 'activity'; this situation, the time of breakdown both in the legal system and in social activity as a whole, borders on both total alienation and total anarchy.

The etymology of the word 'anarchy' suggests yet another way of summarizing the basic strengths and weaknesses of our two diverse approaches to an explanation and justification of the human social activity that brings about fundamental changes in law and society. 'Αρχή' can mean either 'first principle' or 'magistracy'. Fundamental change may be a change either in 'first principles' or in 'magistracies' or in both.

11 Is the society of the 'organization man' and the 'status-seekers' really radically alienated – active in its acceptance of 'the system', yet thoroughly 'passive' in Sartre's sense? This is not the place to attempt to answer such a question, but I may at least admit to being less pessimistic than Marcuse in this regard. And a number of events that have taken place since the publication of *One-Dimensional Man* have tended to shake Marcuse's pessimism, too.

12 If rule-following were ENTIRELY abandoned at such a period, as we have seen in our analysis of 'totalization', the result could only be pure madness.

13 It is this third possibility which engenders the greatest number of conceptual difficulties. We have noted some of the things that it CANNOT mean (e.g., a TOTAL absence of ALL types of rules), but exactly what it WOULD mean remains less clear. This does not authorize us to cease exploring it as a possible future ideal, however.

But a would-be explainer of changes in 'first principles', i.e., in social objectives or projects, must not overlook the fact that the attainment of objectives is inconceivable apart from the means to their attainment, and that the means of 'totalization' in SOCIAL life must always be some form of rules or institutions. Similarly, a would-be explainer of changes in 'magistracies' must acknowledge the need to explain and justify any such changes by reference to first principles, or objectives. The danger of the Sartrean 'projects' (or 'totalizations') approach is that, while it stresses the aspects of creativity and of discontinuity that are involved in any fundamental change, it tends to absolutize the account of any such change and to make it difficult to explain it in terms of any already known patterns of human behavior. The danger of the pure 'rules' approach is that, while it can explain fundamental changes in terms of known patterns, it fails to comprehend the distinctiveness of particular fundamental changes or even of particular kinds of patterns,[14] because it fails to recognize the fact that both fundamental changes and rules systems themselves must ultimately be defined by the purposes which they are directed towards accomplishing. It is the enormous merit of BOTH types of explanation to allow for a distinction between human behavioral patterns and mere natural regularities: the phenomenon of fundamental change in law and society is one of the most striking manifestations of the potentialities for free, creative activity and self-determination that characterize human behavior, and the two approaches that I have outlined both, in different ways, take account of this. Each type of approach will be stronger if it can somehow be complemented by the other.

Perhaps the source of divergent approaches to explaining the concept of fundamental change in law and society is to be found in divergent philosophical methodologies; this, at least, is the suggestion that I first made in the Introduction and that I have examined in the early parts of each of the two principal sections of this study. It was noted that the Sartrean 'totalizations' approach, which attempted to explain societal 'alienation' and the basic differences between its two paradigmatic types of collectives (as well as changes from one to the other type) primarily in terms of their relative 'activity' or 'passivity', relied most heavily on

[14] It is practically impossible, for example, to distinguish legal rules from other kinds of rules as long as one's analysis is confined to characteristics internal to the rules themselves. The failure of Hart's 'key to the science of jurisprudence', the allegedly unique combination of 'primary' and 'secondary' rules in law, illustrates this.

the contrast between two basic kinds of realities designated as '*praxis*' and 'inert matter'. In Sartre's case, we were forced to ask whether these two concepts did not, perhaps, play the role of mythical entities that ruled over the destiny of Sartre's entire dialectic; we found, however, that they could be interpreted as 'abstractions' referring, precisely, to the contrast between 'active' and 'passive' social activity and linking this up, for heuristic purposes, with the contrast between human behavior and other kinds of natural, material phenomena. The Hartean 'rules' approach, on the other hand, profited greatly from pointing to analogies, not only between different types of rules (e.g., between the rules of law and those of games), but also between rules and what are usually thought of as quite dissimilar phenomena (e.g., in the account of fundamental change, human 'pathology'). SOME such methodological devices as these two, namely 'abstraction' and 'analogy', are essential to any explanation at all, since it is self-evident that any helpful explanation must be given in terms of something other than the very phenomenon that is to be explained.

But methodological devices always distort an explanation in some way, and so, to the extent to which the dangers of distortion are overlooked, the usefulness of these devices is diminished. The principal limitation of the method of abstraction was seen to be the fact that the applicability of abstractions to any concrete instance of a phenomenon is subject to INTERPRETATION, and this fact in turn was seen to diminish the importance of Sartre's claim to be giving the TRUE account of fundamental changes and of social reality as a whole. The abstractions themselves are ideal types rather than components of concrete reality, and, insofar as they are applied to the latter, their hard-and-fast natures as ideal types must be qualified by the fact that the differences existing between contrasting phenomena are always characterizable as differences merely IN DEGREE. Thus, the actual occurrence of fundamental change in society itself is never a clear-cut transition from a perfect Sartrean 'series' to a perfect Sartrean 'group', or *vice versa*: we must cease to think of fundamental change of any sort as an ABSOLUTE (though we must continue to think of it as being relatively ABRUPT). We noted that the principal limitation of the method of analogies, on the other hand, is that it will inevitably issue in absurdity and contradiction whenever the alleged resemblances are taken too literally or 'carried too far'. Thus, Hart certainly does not want to say that a fundamental change in law is like human pathology and embryology or like a fundamental change in the rules of a game IN EVERY RESPECT: analogies are merely suggestions for augmenting understanding of a different and therefore NOVEL phenomenon. It is a further, very interesting question whether there is any necessary or even probable connection between the Sartrean method of abstraction and the explanation of human activity as 'totalizing', on the one hand, and the Hartean use of analogies and the 'rules' approach to explanation, on the other. I have made no attempt to answer this question, since I believe that, if answerable at all, it would require a full treatise on philosophic method. But the very manner in which this study has been developed probably furnishes some good reasons for giving an affirmative answer. In any case, some links have clearly been established in another direction – to wit, between the two contrasting methodological devices that we have examined and two fundamental types of philosophic method, namely dialectics and analysis.

The basic conclusion that we have reached with regard to these two types of method is that, while they may appear to be very different from one another, neither is in exclusive possession of any significant characteristic that is totally inaccessible to the other – regardless of the extravagant claims that are sometimes made on both sides. It is especially important to establish this in determining how to go about explaining fundamental change in law and society, since the claim is sometimes made, from the side of the dialectician, that only dialectics can take account of the genuine novelty that is involved in the occurrence of fundamental change, and furthermore, that only within a fully systematic social philosophy does an adequate explanation and justification of fundamental change in law and society become possible. Moreover, the ANALYST may make the counter-claim that a dialectical account of fundamental change in law and society must entail some reliance on myths, on determinism, and on collectivism. By examining our two authors' treatments of the subject, however, we have found no such claims to be necessarily true. Sartre, the dialectician, for example, repudiates the use of myths and gives an account which is, if anything, excessively libertarian (as evidenced by the difficulties noted in his account of 'totalizations') and excessively individualistic (as evidenced by the obstacles that the 'mediations' of language and of other social institutions still represent for him). The dialectical method may, indeed, be valuable for showing the artificiality of all rigid separations of related subject-matters (such as law and sociology), for explicating the internal aspects of the norms that govern human social activity, and for indicating the necessity of a dynamic FUTURE reference in all such activity, especially in the case of the phenomenon of fundamental change; but all these features are also to be found in Hart's analysis. Some proponents of the analytic method may actually try to support the dialectician's boast that only his own method is able to take account of genuine novelty, by maintaining that pure analysis is nothing but a description of concepts as they are to be found in ordinary language. But we have discovered that the latter set of claims must be abandoned, because an analyst like Hart must also employ technical language, and because the ideal of a pure description of the meanings of concepts that would effect no changes in the understanding of concepts is a chimerical ideal, even if it could be shown to be a worthwhile one. Indeed, it is theoretically possible for a philosophical analysis to bring about changes, even FUNDAMENTAL CHANGES, in the things to which concepts are applied! Consequently, the dialectical method is not alone in being able to "deal with novelty" (inasmuch as this latter claim can be made at all meaningful), and therefore not alone (Herbert Marcuse to the contrary notwithstanding) in being able to account for and to justify fundamental changes.

Finally, we return once again to the contention that it is only the 'system-builders', as distinguished from the 'sceptics', who can adequately explain and justify fundamental change in law and society. This would be unqualifiedly true only in the case of thoroughgoing sceptics, if such persons could ever exist: the whole idea of a completely unsystematic explanation is self-contradictory. The thoroughly incautious system-builder, on the other hand, would be an equally rare and undesirable species of philosopher: any account that he might give of fundamental change would be quite worthless. The dialectician and the analyst, therefore, both approach the concept of fundamental change in law and society with the same tools, though each will prefer to use certain devices more than others, and any judgment concerning the particular products of their respective labors must ultimately be an individual value judgment.

IN THE SAME WAY, the JUSTIFICATION of any given fundamental change will itself always have to be an individual value judgment, and, unfortunately from the point of view of the strongly systematic thinker, the fact remains (whether or not Kant would agree) that no *a priori* determination is possible as to the value or disvalue of such changes in general.

Thus our investigation of the concept of fundamental change in law and society comes to an end. The dialectic of alternative methodologies, methodological devices, ways of understanding human social activity, justifications, and subject-matters, however, has not ended and will not end. The same is true both of philosophy itself and of the very changes, whether relatively more or less fundamental, which are occurring and are likely to continue to occur in the actual societies and legal systems that we can observe. I have not attempted to exorcise the phenomenon, but only to explain it and to indicate the grounds of its possible justification.

When I first began concentrated work on this subject, more than six years ago, there were of course numerous instances of revolutionary activity throughout the world, but the situation in the developed, or 'metropolitan', countries – notably the countries of Europe and the United States – seemed relatively stable. When Herbert Marcuse's *One-Dimensional Man*, to which I have referred in my Introduction, was first published in January 1964 (when, by coincidence, I had the occasion to invite him to lecture to the Graduate Philosophy Club at Yale), his voice, still comparatively unknown either to the general public or to the philosophical community, seemed to be that of an eccentric, talking about matters in which general interest was at best slight. Since then, very fundamental changes have taken place, especially in the developed countries themselves. Marcuse is considered by many to be a prophet of the first order. Sartre's prestige as a theorist has diminished in many French academic circles, but his reputation as an advocate of change has become greater. And the world about which Marcuse and Sartre are speaking has become very much more familiar, as a result of the war in Vietnam and its domestic American repercussions, to citizens of that former bastion of stability and conservatism, the United States. No longer does it strike anyone as unusual, as it might have done just a few years ago, for a major philosophy department to sponsor a series of public lectures on "Revolution", as the Yale Department did in the fall of 1968.[15] No longer, therefore, is it as much of a tactical necessity as it once for a philosopher to justify his own professional concern about the subject of fundamental change.

'Fundamental change in law and society': what is it, and how can it be justified? 'Revolutions': what are they? Philosophers can say a great deal about these things, but perhaps the philosophers' greatest single service is the critical one of getting beneath the shibboleths which are almost inevitably associated with the concept of 'revolution'. Once the first part of the philosopher's critical task has been completed, he is in

[15] Cf. my report on this series, "Reflections on Reflections on Revolution", *The New Journal* (student publication, Yale University) 2, 5 (Dec. 8, 1968), pp. 13-17.

a better position, in the light of his increased understanding, to recommence a critical analysis of his own or other societies. If these societies are not utopias, and if he is indeed a philosopher, he is unlikely to be completely satisfied with present states of affairs. He may then have occasion to reflect on and to put to use, though perhaps without having to mount either on soap-boxes or on barricades, the 'formula of knowledge' proclaimed by the French proto-existentialist, Jules Lequier:

FAIRE,
non pas *devenir*, mais faire, et, en faisant, SE FAIRE.[16]

[16] Jules Lequier, *Œuvres Complètes* (ed. by J. Grenier) (Neuchâtel, Éditions de la Baconnière, 1952), p. 71.

BIBLIOGRAPHY

BOOKS CITED

Aristotle, *Metaphysics*, tr. by W. D. Ross, ed. by R. McKeon (New York, 1941).
Aron, Raymond, *L'Opium des Intellectuels* (Paris, 1955).
Augustine, Saint, *The City of God*, tr. by Walsh, Zema, Monahan, and Honan (New York, 1958).
Austin, John, *The Province of Jurisprudence Determined Etc.*, introd. by H. L. A. Hart (London, 1954).
Baier, Kurt, *The Moral Point of View: A Rational Basis of Ethics* (Ithaca, 1958).
Beling, Ernst, *Revolution und Recht* (Augsburg, 1923(?)).
Benn, S. I. and R. S. Peters, *Social Principles and the Democratic State* (London, 1959).
Bernstein, Edouard, *Evolutionary Socialism*, tr. by E. C. Harvey (New York, 1961).
Bobbio, Norberto, *Giusnaturalismo e positivismo giuridico* (Milano, 1965).
—, *The Philosophy of Decadentism – A Study in Existentialism*, tr. by D. Moore (Oxford, 1951).
Bradley, F. H., *Ethical Studies* (London, 1876).
Brinton, Crane, *The Anatomy of Revolution* (New York, 1958).
Bruyn, Severyn T., *The Human Perspective in Sociology* (Englewood Cliffs, 1966).
Burnier, Michel-Antoine, *Les Existentialistes et la politique* (Paris, 1966).
Camus, Albert, *L'Homme Révolté* (Paris, 1951).
Cattaneo, Mario, *Il concetto di rivoluzione nella scienza del diritto* (Milano-Varese, 1960).
Chapman, J. W. and J. R. Pennock, eds., *Voluntary Associations* (*Nomos* XI) (New York, 1969).
Cohen, L. Jonathan, *The Principles of World Citizenship* (Oxford, 1954).
Cohn-Bendit, Daniel *et al.*, *The French Student Revolt*, tr. by B. R. Brewster (New York, 1968).
de Beauvoir, Simone, *La Force des Choses* (Paris, 1963).
—, *Les Mandarins* (Paris, 1954).
—, *Pour une Morale de l'Ambiguïté* (Paris, 1947).
d'Entrèves, A. P., *La dottrina dello stato* (Torino, 1962).
de Maistre, Joseph, *Essai sur le Principe Générateur des Constitutions Politiques* (Lyon, 1838).
Desan, Wilfrid, *The Marxism of Jean-Paul Sartre* (Garden City, 1965).
—, *The Planetary Man*, Vol. I (Washington, 1961).
—, *The Tragic Finale*, revised ed. (New York, 1960).
Descartes, René, *Philosophical Works*, Vol. II, tr. by E. Haldane and G. Ross (New York, 1955).

Edie, James M., ed., *New Essays in Phenomenology* (Chicago, 1969).
Engels, Friedrich, *Socialism: Utopian and Scientific*, cf. Mendel, ed., *Essential Works of Marxism*, pp. 45-82.
Findlay, J. N., *Hegel: A Re-Examination* (London, New York, 1958).
Flew, Antony, ed., *Essays on Logic and Language* (New York, 1951).
Friedrich, Carl J., ed., *Revolution* (*Nomos* VIII) (New York, 1966).
Fuller, Lon, *The Morality of Law* (New Haven, 1964).
Garaudy, R., G. Cogniot *et al.*, *Mésaventures de l'Anti-Marxisme* (Paris, 1956).
Goldmann, Lucien, *Recherches dialectiques* (Paris, 1959).
Gurvitch, Georges, *Dialectique et sociologie* (Paris, 1962).
Hare, R. M., *The Language of Morals* (Oxford, 1952).
Hart, H. L. A., *The Concept of Law* (Oxford, 1961).
—, *Punishment and the Elimination of Responsibility* (London, 1962), reprinted in *Punishment and Responsibility* (New York and Oxford, 1968), pp. 158-185.
Hartmann, Klaus, *Sartres Sozialphilosophie: Eine Untersuchung zur 'Critique de la raison dialectique I'* (Berlin, 1966).
Hegel, Georg W. F., *Hegel's Philosophy of Right*, tr. by T. M. Knox (Oxford, 1942).
Hobbes, Thomas, *Leviathan*, ed. by M. Oakeshott (Oxford, 1960).
Hook, Sydney, ed., *Determinism and Freedom in the Age of Modern Science* (New York, 1958).
Hume, David, *A Treatise of Human Nature*, ed. by L. A. Selby-Bigge (Oxford, 1958).
Jeanson, Francis, *Le Problème moral et la pensée de Sartre* (Paris, 1965).
John, Saint, *Apocalypse*, in *Novum Testamentum Graece et Latine*, ed. by H. J. Vogels (Freiburg-im-Breisgau, 1955).
Kant, Immanuel, *The Metaphysical Elements of Justice*, tr. by John Ladd (Indianapolis-New York-Kansas City, 1965).
Kelsen, Hans, *The Communist Theory of Law* (London, 1955).
—, *General Theory of Law and State*, tr. by A. Wedberg (Cambridge, Mass., 1945).
—, *Reine Rechtslehre* (Wien, 1960).
Lapenna, Ivo, *State and Law: Soviet and Yugoslav Theory* (New Haven, 1964).
Lefebvre, Henri, *Critique de la vie quotidienne* (Paris, 1947).
—, *L'existentialisme* (Paris, 1946).
—, *Introduction à la Modernité* (Paris, 1962).
—, *Métaphilosophie* (Paris, 1965).
—, *Problèmes actuels du marxisme* (Paris, 1958).
—, *La Somme et le reste* (Paris, 1959).
Lequier, Jules, *Œuvres Complètes*, ed. by J. Grenier (Neuchâtel, 1952).
Lévi-Strauss, Claude, *La Pensée Sauvage* (Paris, 1962).
Lichtheim, George, *Marxism in Modern France* (New York, London, 1966).
Lukacs, Georg, *Histoire et Conscience de Classe*, tr. by K. Axelos and J. Bois (Paris, 1960).
Lundstedt, Anders Vilhelm, *Legal Thinking Revised: My Views on Law* (Stockholm, 1956).
Marcuse, Herbert, *One-Dimensional Man* (Boston, 1964).
Marx, Karl, *Economic and Philosophic Manuscripts of 1844*, tr. by Institute of Marxism-Leninism (Moscow, 1961).
— and Friedrich Engels, *The German Ideology*, ed. by R. Pascal (New York, 1947).
Melden, A. I., ed., *Essays in Moral Philosophy* (Seattle, 1958).
Mendel, Arthur P., ed., *Essential Works of Marxism* (New York, 1947).
Merleau-Ponty, Maurice, *Les Aventures de la dialectique* (Paris, 1955).

——, *Humanisme et Terreur* (Paris, 1947).
Nowell-Smith, P. H., *Ethics* (London, 1954).
Odajnyk, Walter, *Marxism and Existentialism* (Garden City, 1965).
Olivecrona, Karl, *Law as Fact* (Copenhagen, 1939).
Parker, Emmett, *Albert Camus: The Artist in the Arena* (Madison-Milwaukee-London, 1966).
Pierce, Roy, *Contemporary French Political Thought* (London, 1966).
Plato, *Republic*, tr. by B. Jowett (New York, 1937).
Ross, Alf, *On Law and Justice* (Berkeley-Los Angeles, 1959).
Rousseau, Jean-Jacques, *Du Contrat Social, Discours, Lettre à d'Alembert*, etc. (Paris, 1955).
Rubel, Maximilien, *Karl Marx: Essai de Biographie Intellectuelle* (Paris, 1957).
Ryle, Gilbert, *Philosophical Arguments*, Inaugural Lecture (Oxford, 1945).
Sartre, Jean-Paul, *Critique de la raison dialectique*, Tome I (Paris, 1960).
——, *L'être et le néant* (Paris, 1943).
——, *Les Mots* (Paris, 1964).
——, *Search for a Method*, tr. by Hazel E. Barnes (New York, 1963).
——, *Situations* III (Paris, 1949).
——, *Situations* IV (Paris, 1964).
——, *Situations* VII (Paris, 1965).
Sayre, Paul, ed., *Interpretations of Modern Legal Philosophies* (New York, 1947).
Schrader, George A., ed., *Existential Philosophers: Kierkegaard to Merleau-Ponty* (New York, 1967).
Schwarz, Theodor, *Jean-Paul Sartres 'Kritik der dialektischen Vernunft'* (Berlin, D.D.R., 1967).
Teilhard de Chardin, Pierre, *L'Avenir de l'homme* (Paris, 1959).
Theunissen, Michael, *Der Andere* (Berlin, 1965).
Toulmin, Stephen, *An Examination of the Place of Reason in Ethics* (Cambridge, 1961).
Weiss, Paul, *Modes of Being* (Carbondale, 1958).
Weldon, T. D., *The Vocabulary of Politics* (Baltimore, 1960).
Winch, Peter, *The Idea of a Social Science and its Relation to Philosophy* (London, New York, 1958).
Wisdom, John, *Philosophy and Psycho-Analysis* (New York, 1953).
Wittgenstein, Ludwig, *Philosophical Investigations*, tr. by G. E. M. Anscombe (New York, 1961).

ARTICLES CITED

Abel, Lionel, "Metaphysical Stalinism", *Dissent* 8, 2 (Spring 1961), pp. 137-152.
Ago, Roberto, "Positive Law and International Law", tr. by J. Hammond, *American Journal of International Law* 51, 4 (Oct. 1957), pp. 691-733.
Austin, J. L., "A Plea for Excuses", the Presidential Address, *Proceedings of the Aristotelian Society* NS 58 (1956/57), pp. 1-50.
Bernstein, Richard J., "Summary and Comment" on *Critique de la raison dialectique*, Tome I, *Review of Metaphysics* 15, 3 (Mar. 1962), p. 529.
Broad, C. D., "Hägerström's Account of Sense of Duty and Certain Allied Experiences", *Philosophy* 26, 97 (Apr. 1951), pp. 99-113.
Camus, Albert, "Lettre au Directeur des *Temps Modernes*", *Les Temps Modernes* 82 (Aug. 1952), pp. 317-333.
Cohen, L. Jonathan, review of *The Concept of Law*, *Mind* 71, 283 (July 1962), pp. 395-412.
Condorelli, Orazio, "Ex Facto Oritur Jus", *Rivista internazionale di filosofia del diritto* 11 (1931), pp. 585-600.

de Beauvoir, Simone, "Merleau-Ponty et le Pseudo-Sartrisme", *Les Temps Modernes* 114-115 (June-July 1955), pp. 2072-2122.

d'Entrèves, A. P., "The Case for Natural Law Re-Examined", I, *Natural Law Forum* 1 (1956), pp. 5-52.

—, " 'Un noyau de bon sens' (à propos de la théorie du droit naturel chez H. Hart)", *Revue internationale de Philosophie* 65 (1963, Fasc. 3), pp. 312-334.

De Waelhens, Alphonse, "Sartre et la raison dialectique", *Revue Philosophique de Louvain* 60 (1962), pp. 79-99.

Diederichsen, Uwe, "Topisches und systematisches Denken in der Jurisprudenz", *Neue Juristische Wochenschrift* 19 (April 21, 1966), pp. 697-705.

Dreyfus, Dina, "Jean-Paul Sartre et le Mal Radical: *De L'être et le néant à la Critique de la raison dialectique*", *Mercure de France* 341 (Jan. 1961), pp. 154-167.

Dufrenne, Mikel, review of *Critique de la raison dialectique*, Tome I, *Esprit* 19, 294 (April 1961), pp. 675-692.

Fuller, Lon, "Positivism and Fidelity to Law – A Reply to Professor Hart", *Harvard Law Review* 71, 4 (Febr. 1958), pp. 630-672.

Hart, H. L. A., "Definition and Theory in Jurisprudence", *The Law Quarterly Review* 70, 277 (Jan. 1954), pp. 37-60.

—, "Legal and Moral Obligation", cf. Melden, ed., *Essays in Moral Philosophy*, pp. 82-107.

—, "Legal Responsibility and Excuses", cf. Hook, ed., *Determinism and Freedom in the Age of Modern Science*, pp. 81-104.

—, "Positivism and the Separation of Law and Morals", *Harvard Law Review* 71, 4 (Feb. 1958), pp. 593-629.

—, "Scandinavian Realism", *The Cambridge Law Journal* (Nov. 1959), pp. 233-240.

—, review of *The Communist Theory of Law* (by Hans Kelsen), *Harvard Law Review* 69, 4 (Feb. 1956), pp. 772-778.

—, review of *Inquiries into the Nature of Law and Morals* (by Axel Hägerström), *Philosophy* 30, 115 (Oct. 1955), pp. 369-373.

Jeanson, Francis, "Albert Camus ou l'Âme Révoltée", *Les Temps Modernes* 79 (May 1952), pp. 2070-2090.

Laserson, Max, "Revolution und Recht", *Zeitschrift für öffentliches Recht* 8 (1930), pp. 553-570.

Lefebvre, Henri, "Le Marxisme et la Pensée Française", *Les Temps Modernes* 137-138 (July-Aug. 1957), pp. 104-137.

Lichtheim, George, review of *Critique de la raison dialectique*, Tome I, *History and Theory* 3, 2 (1963), pp. 222-246.

Lundstedt, Anders Vilhelm, "Law and Justice: A Criticism of the Method of Justice", cf. Sayre, ed., *Interpretations of Modern Legal Philosophies*, pp. 450-483.

Macdonald, Margaret, "The Language of Political Theory", cf. Flew, ed., *Essays on Logic and Language*, pp. 167-186.

McBride, William Leon, "The Acceptance of a Legal System", *The Monist* 49, 3 (July 1965), pp. 377-396.

—, "The Essential Role of Models and Analogies in the Philosophy of Law", *New York University Law Review* 43, 1 (March 1968), pp. 53-87.

—, "Jean-Paul Sartre: Man, Freedom, and *Praxis*". Cf. Schrader, ed., *Existential Philosophers: Kierkegaard to Merleau-Ponty*, pp. 261-329.

—, "Reflections on Reflections on Revolution", *The New Journal* (Student publication, Yale University) 2, 5 (Dec. 8, 1968), pp. 13-17.

—, "Sartre and the Phenomenology of Social Violence", in James M. Edie, ed., *New Essays in Phenomenology* (Chicago, 1969), pp. 290-313.

——, "Voluntary Association: The Basis of an Ideal Model, and the 'Democratic' Failure". Cf. Chapman and Pennock, eds., *Voluntary Associations*, pp. 202-232.

Melden, A. I., "On Promising", *Mind* 65, 257 (Jan. 1956), pp. 49-66.

Merkl, Adolf, "Das Problem der Rechtskontinuität und die Forderung des einheitlichen rechtlichen Weltbildes", *Zeitschrift für öffentliches Recht* 5 (1926), pp. 497-527.

Morris, Herbert, review of *The Concept of Law, Harvard Law Review* 75, 7 (May 1962), pp. 1452-1461.

Ofstad, Harald, "The descriptive definition of the concept 'legal norm' proposed by Hans Kelsen", *Theoria* 16 (1950), pp. 118-151 and 211-246.

Pierandrei, France, "La rivoluzione e il diritto", *Nuova rivista di diritto commerciale*, etc. 5 (1952), pp. 134-153.

Poulantzas, Nicos, "À propos de la théorie marxiste du droit", *Archives de la Philosophie du Droit* 12, "Marx et le Droit Moderne" (1967), pp. 145-162.

Rapoport, David C., "*Coup d'état*: the View of the Men Firing Pistols", cf. Friedrich, ed., *Revolution*, pp. 53-74.

Ross, Alf, review of *The Concept of Law, Yale Law Journal* 71, 6 (May 1962), pp. 1185-1190.

Sander, Fritz, "Das Faktum der Revolution und die Kontinuität der Rechtsordnung", *Zeitschrift für öffentliches Recht* 1 (1919/20), pp. 132-164.

Sartre, Jean-Paul, "Le Fantôme de Staline", *Les Temps Modernes* 129-130-131 (Nov.-Dec. 1956, Jan. 1957), pp. 577-696, reprinted in *Situations* VII, pp. 144-307.

——, "Merleau-Ponty Vivant", *Les Temps Modernes* 184-185 (Oct. 1961, special edition), pp. 304-376; reprinted under the title, "Merleau-Ponty", in *Situations* IV, pp. 189-287.

——, "Présentation", *Les Temps Modernes* 1 (Oct. 1, 1945), pp. 1-21.

——, "Le Réformisme et les fétiches", *Les Temps Modernes* 122 (Feb. 1956), pp. 1153-1164; reprinted in *Situations* VII, pp. 104-118.

——, "Réponse à Albert Camus", *Les Temps Modernes* 82 (Aug. 1952), pp. 334-353; reprinted in *Situations* IV, pp. 90-125.

——, "Réponse à Pierre Naville", *Les Temps Modernes* 123 (Mar.-Apr. 1956), pp. 1510-1525; reprinted in *Situations* VII, pp. 119-143.

—— and Maurice Merleau-Ponty, "Les Jours de Notre Vie", *Les Temps Modernes* 51 (Jan. 1950), pp. 1153-1168.

Villey, Michel, "Une définition du droit", *Archives de Philosophie du Droit* 4 (1959), pp. 47-65.

Wade, H. W. R., "The Basis of Legal Sovereignty", *The Cambridge Law Journal* (Nov. 1955), pp. 172-197.

Waismann, Friedrich, "Verifiability", cf. Flew, ed., *Essays on Logic and Language*, pp. 117-144.

Wedberg, Anders, "Some Problems in the Logical Analysis of Legal Science", *Theoria* 17 (1951), pp. 246-275.

INDEX

Bei Fragen zur Produktsicherheit wenden Sie sich bitte an:
If you have any questions regarding product safety,
please contact:

Walter de Gruyter GmbH
Genthiner Straße 13
10785 Berlin
productsafety@degruyterbrill.com